Wider World

AMERICAN EDITION

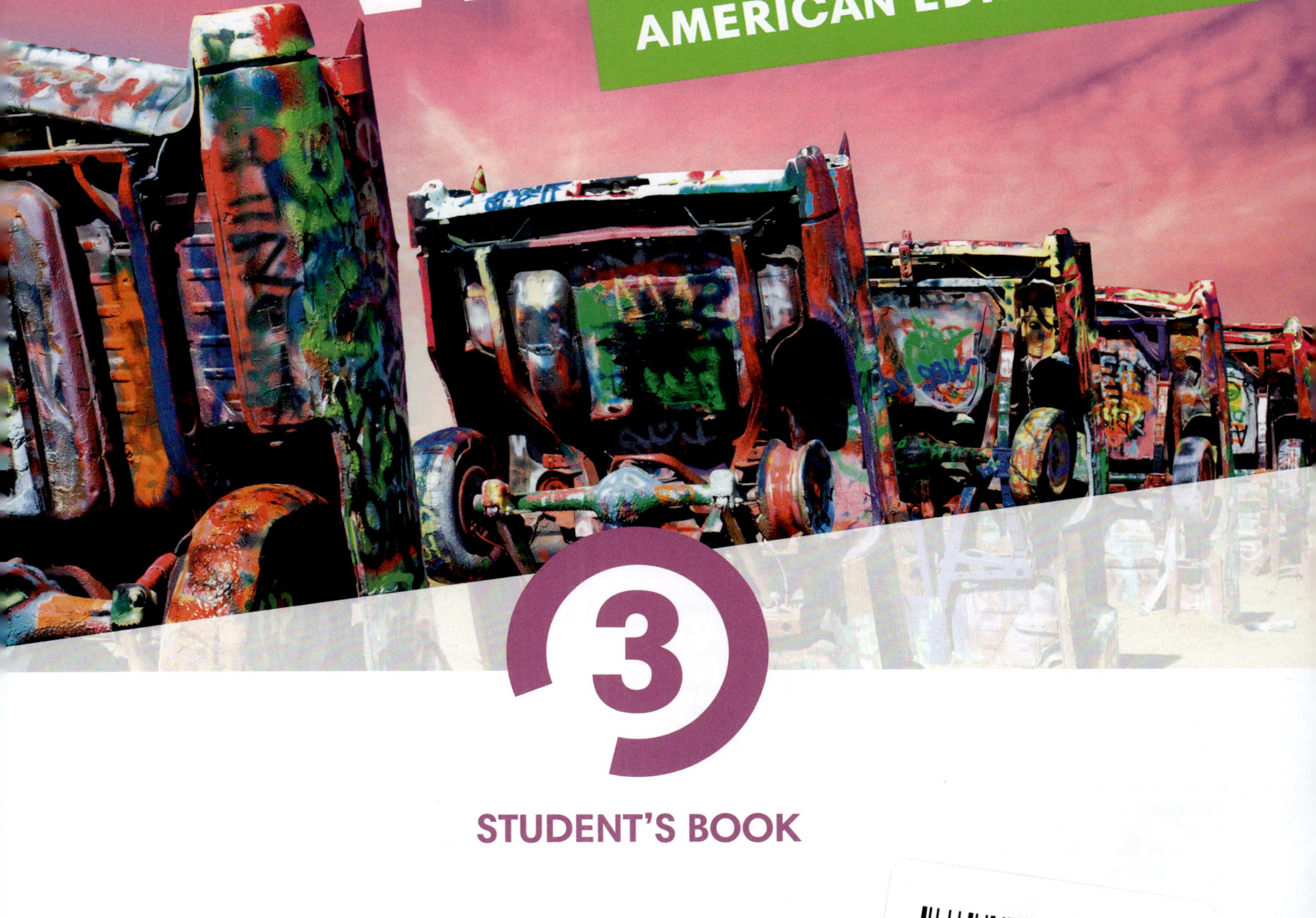

3

STUDENT'S BOOK

Carolyn Barraclough
Suzanne Gaynor

Pearson

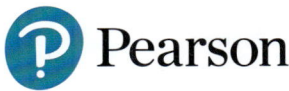

Pearson Education Limited
KAO Two, KAO Park
Hockham Way,
Harlow, Essex, CM17 9SR England
and Associated Companies throughout the world

www.english.com/widerworld

© Pearson Education Limited 2020

The right of Carolyn Barraclough and Suzanne Gaynor to be identified as authors of this work has been asserted by them in accordance with the Copyright, Designs and Patents Act, 1988.

All rights reserved; no part of this publication may be reproduced, stored in a retrieval system, or transmitted in any form or by any means, electronic, mechanical, photocopying, recording, or otherwise without the prior written permission of the Publishers.

First published 2020
Fourth impression 2022
ISBN: 978-1-292-39236-3

Set in Harmonica Sans
Printed in Slovakia by Neografia

Acknowledgements
The Publishers would like to thank all the teachers and students around the world who contributed to the development of Wider World, especially the teachers on the Wider World Teacher Advisory Panel:
Irina Alyapysheva, CEE; Reyna Arango, Mexico; Marisa Ariza, Spain; Alfredo Bilopolski, Argentina; Isabel Blecua, Spain; Camilo Elcio de Souza, Brazil; Ingrith del Carmen Ríos Verdugo, Mexico; Edward Duval, Belgium; Norma González, Argentina; Natividad Gracia, Spain; Claribel Guzmán, Mexico; Izabela Lipińska, Poland; Fabián Loza, Mexico; Miguel Mozo, Spain; Huỳnh Th Ái Nguyên, Vietnam; Joacyr Oliveira, Brazil; Montse Priego, Spain; Gladys Rodriguez, Argentina; Lyudmila Slastnova, CEE; Izabela Stępniewska, Poland.

The Publishers would also like to thank the teachers who contributed to the Go Getter series, as materials from Go Getter Level 1 were adapted to create Wider World Starter Level:
Anna Borek, CEE; Svetlana Chistyakova, CEE; Marina Grechanichenko, CEE; Sofija Ljilak Vukajolvič, CEE; Ece Kahraman, Turkey; Maria Soledad Saravai O'Keefe, Argentina; Bilbana Pavolvič, CEE; Jovana Popovič, CEE; Alla Sichurova, CEE; Marta Skałbania, CEE; Anna Standish, CEE; Katarzyna Szwejkowska, CEE; Renata Woldan, CEE; Ewa Wódkówska, CEE; Oksana Zinchenko, CEE.

The Publishers would also like to thank all the teachers who contributed to the develpment of Wider World American: Acacio Tavares, Adriana Felice Gimenes Camargo, Alessandra Franco, Ariane Belchior, Arlete de Simone, Cristiane Tulmann, Danilo Meris, Felipe José Batista Silva, Gil Carla Leite do Nascimento, Iara Toledo de Assis Batista, Ivy Caroline Farias Vieira, Kelly Cardoso, Liliane Reis Soares da Cruz, Marcia Aparecida Auricchio, Maria Isabel Rossignolli, Maria Luiza Corbisier, Renan Cyrino Mansur, Sávio Câmara Leite, Sueli Valente da Silva Caparroz, Vainer Eduardo Pedra. The publishers would like to thank the editors and authors Carla Maurício Vianna, Rhiannon Sarah Ball and Viviane Kirmeliene who contributed to the adaptation of Wider World American.

Image Credit(s):
123RF.com: 36clicks 23, Cathy Yeulet 87, irochka 80, lizon 50, magone 23, Pablo Hidalgo 134, Scott Griessel 87, Sergey Nivens 83; **Alamy Stock Photo:** AGF Srl 1, Andre Babiak 43, Arcaid Images 3, Ashley Cooper pics 134, dpa picture alliance 98, Fedor Selivanov 128, foodfolio 92, Hemis 54, Hero Images Inc. 165, Hugh Nutt 41, Juice Images 81, Juniors Bildarchiv GmbH 10, Losevsky Pavel 81, Mandy Collins 35, The golden marshmallow/Stockimo 10, Tom Uhlman 30, Xinhua 32; **Babar Ali:** 84; **BBC Worldwide Learning:** 20, 91, 95, 95, 95, 95, 103, 103, 103, 103; **Booker Travels:** 53; **Emile Wamsteker:** 25; **Fotolia:** audreyshot 31, emiliano85 72, gpointstudio 10, 104, James Threw 79, marek 53, Miguel Garcia Saaved 72, mitrija 71, peresanz 73, pressmaster 65, Proxima Studio 53, sdecoret 59, SeanPavonePhoto 51, ssaronow 83, theartofphoto 10, Tiramisu Studio 53, View Apart 146; **Getty Images:** Angelo DeSantis 31, GSO Images 90, Heath Korvola 100, Richard Heathcote - The FA 41, Sascha Steinbach 41, Shomos Uddin 94, Wild Shutter Imaging 95; **Imagestate:** John Foxx Collection 80; **Jubilee Sailing Trust:** 55; **Nixie Labs, Inc.:** 122; **Pearson Education Asia Ltd:** Terry Leung 80; **Pearson Education Ltd:** 81, Jon Barlow 6, 7, 8, 9, 10, 14, 16, 20, 22, 26, 30, 34, 37, 40, 42, 46, 50, 52, 56, 60, 62, 66, 70, 74, 76, 80, 82, 86, Jules Selmes 128, Studio 8 6, 8, 12, 14, 22, 24, 32, 34, 42, 44, 52, 54, 62, 64, 72, 74, 82, 84; **PhotoDisc:** 10, 20, 30, 40, 50, 60, 70, 80; **Shutterstock.com:** 29, 81, 114, 9george 120, AC Rider 37, Africa Studio 80, Alxcrs 51, Andrea Boullosa 57, beats1 57, BlueOrange Studio 51, BlueSkyImage 16, 26, 36, 46, 56, 66, 76, 86, Customdesigner 53, Dar1930 21, David Crockett 80, Dragon Images 10, 17, 27, 47, 57, 67, 77, 87, Dragonskydive 120, etraveler 25, evenfh 154, Evikka 120, Evlakhov Valeriy 102, Foto-Ruhrgebiet 25, frantic00 50, goodluz 114, Helen Bird 10, Helly Hansen 120, IndaramSoulmate 136, Laszio Szirtesi 41, littleWhale 61, 61, mamahoohooba 30, Manuel Fernandes 24, mapman 53, Marie C Fields 80, Martin Valigursky 17, Merla 57, Minerva Studio 61, Moofer 57, Naypong Studio 123, Neale Cousland 96, Nuangthong 57, Oleksandr Kostiuchenko 114, Prostock-studio 114, Seregam 126, Sergey Le 120, Sergey Peterman 13, 23, 23, 43, 53, 63, 73, 83, Shevtsovy 44, Shutter_M 75, SpeedKingz 89, StockLite 15, 25, 35, 45, 55, 65, 75, 85, StockSmartStart 37, Studio 10ne 51, Suzanne Tucker 31, Thongseedary 120, ValeStock 51, Westend61 Premium 35, Yellow Cat 120, Zaitsava Olga 65, zaniman; **Sole Power LLC:** Joseph Brown 122; **UE Ultimate Ears:** 122

Cover images: *Front:* **Alamy Images:** AGF Srl
All other images © Pearson Education

Illustration Acknowledgements
Student's Book
Tim Bradford (Illustration Ltd) p. 20, 60, 61, 70; The Boy Fitz Hammond p. 30, 40, 50; Mark Ruffle (Beehive Illustration) p. 13, 32, 45; John Lund (Beehive Illustration) p. 15, 64, 85; Maria Serrano Canovas (Plum Pudding) p. 11, 67, 71, 75.

Workbook
The Boy Fitz Hammond p. 135, 138, 144; John Lund (Beehive Illustration) p. 118, 124, 162; Maria Serrano Canovas (Plum Pudding) p. 156,

Every effort has been made to trace the copyright holders and we apologize in advance for any unintentional omissions. We would be pleased to insert the appropriate acknowledgement in any subsequent edition of this publication.

See the Wider picture

The eccentric Cadillac Ranch, Amarillo, Texas, USA

Three artists built Cadillac Ranch in 1974 beside the famous Route 66. They created the installation by half-burying 10 old Cadillacs nose down in the ground. The cars are placed at the same angle as the face of the Great Pyramid of Giza in Egypt. You can add your own graffiti, but make sure you take a photo because it will soon be painted over by someone else.

What would you paint?

CONTENTS

WELCOME UNIT Welcome to Woodley Bridge

W.1 Home and hobbies Activities and interests; Likes and dislikes; Home and furniture; Clothes and accessories; Talking about feelings; *There is/are* with *some/any*; Possessive adjectives and possessive *'s* pp. 6-7

	VOCABULARY	GRAMMAR	READING and VOCABULARY	GRAMMAR
UNIT 1 That's my world!	Talk about everyday technology pp. 10–11	Use different tenses to talk about the present • Simple Present • Present Continuous • State verbs p. 12	Identify the writer's opinion in reviews and talk about unusual objects p. 13	Use verb constructions • verb + *-ing* • verb + *to*-infinitive • verb + *-ing* or *to*-infinitive p. 14
UNIT 2 The taste test	Talk about food and drink pp. 20-21	Use the Present Perfect with *ever, never, just, already,* and *yet* • Present Perfect p. 22	Identify quotations in an article and use *make* and *do* accurately p. 23	Talk about duration of time, and be general and specific about experiences • Present Perfect with *for* and *since* • Present Perfect and Simple Past p. 24
UNIT 3 Wild nature	Talk about the weather and natural disasters pp. 30-31	Use the Past Perfect to talk about an action before another action in the past • Past Perfect p. 32	Use the title, introduction, and picture in an online diary to identify its topic, and talk about culture p. 33	Talk about an event in the past and what happened before it • Simple Past and Past Perfect p. 34
UNIT 4 The big game!	Talk about sports and sports events pp. 40-41	Talk about plans, predictions, arrangements, and schedules • The future: *will/going to/* Present Continuous/ Simple Present p. 42	Find specific information in a case study and talk about volunteering at a sports event p. 43	Talk about possible situations in the future • First Conditional + *if/unless* p. 44
UNIT 5 See the world!	Talk about vacations and traveling pp. 50–51	Talk about obligation and prohibition, and give advice • Modal verbs: *must, have to, ought to, should* p. 52	Find specific information in an article and talk about traveling p. 53	Speculate about the present • Modal verbs: *must, could, might, may, can't* p. 54
UNIT 6 Getting to know you	Talk about relationships with family and friends pp. 60–61	Talk about hypothetical situations in the present and future • Second Conditional p. 62	Identify the purpose of an informative essay and talk about friends p. 63	Identify and give additional information about people, things, and places • Defining and non-defining relative clauses p. 64
UNIT 7 No time for crime	Talk about crime and criminals pp. 70-71	Use verbs in the passive form • The passive (Simple Present and Simple Past) p. 72	Identify the genre of a text and talk about solving crimes p. 73	Use the structure *have/get something done* • *have/get something done* p. 74
UNIT 8 Think outside the box	Talk about school life pp. 80-81	Ask questions with the correct word order • Word order in questions p. 82	Identify the headings in a magazine article and talk about intelligence p. 83	Talk about hypothetical situations in the past • Third Conditional p. 84

STUDENT ACTIVITIES pp. 114-115   IRREGULAR VERBS LIST p. 116   SELF-ASSESSMENT ANSWER KEY p. 168   GRAMMAR TIME ANSWER KEY p. 169

W.2 Home and beyond Countries and languages; *was/were, there was/were*; Simple Past pp. 8-9 | WORKBOOK pp. 118-119

LISTENING and VOCABULARY	SPEAKING	WRITING	REVIEW	EXTRAS
Identify specific information from a radio show and talk about using technology p. 15	Make and respond to suggestions p. 16	Describe places and lifestyles p. 17	WORDLIST p. 18 VOCABULARY IN ACTION p. 18 SELF-CHECK p. 19	BBC CULTURE 1 Do smartphones make you smarter? ▶ *Addicted to screens* pp. 90-91 GRAMMAR TIME 1 p. 106 WORKBOOK pp. 120-125
Identify specific detail in speech and describe food p. 25	Order food in a café or restaurant p. 26	Write an email to a friend p. 27	WORDLIST p. 28 VOCABULARY IN ACTION p. 28 SELF-CHECK p. 29	BBC CULTURE 2 What do the British really eat? ▶ *Indian food Liverpool style* pp. 92-93 GRAMMAR TIME 2 p. 107 WORKBOOK pp. 126-131
Identify specific information in a conversation and talk about being in the wild p. 35	Criticize and explain when things go wrong p. 36	Design a campaign poster and write a supporting text for a campaign p. 37	WORDLIST p. 38 VOCABULARY IN ACTION p. 38 SELF-CHECK p. 39	BBC CULTURE 3 Can you believe this weather? ▶ *Severe weather* pp. 94-95 GRAMMAR TIME 3 p. 108 WORKBOOK pp. 132-137
Identify specific information in a podcast and in a conversation, and talk about sports practice p. 45	Ask and talk about plans p. 46	Write messages and make requests p. 47	WORDLIST p. 48 VOCABULARY IN ACTION p. 48 SELF-CHECK p. 49	BBC CULTURE 4 Where do they toss the caber? ▶ *The Highland Games* pp. 96-97 GRAMMAR TIME 4 p. 109 WORKBOOK pp. 138-143
Identify specific information in an interview and in a story, and talk about trips and excursions. p. 55	Clarify what I have said and ask for clarification p. 56	Write a photo story p. 57	WORDLIST p. 58 VOCABULARY IN ACTION p. 58 SELF-CHECK p. 59	BBC CULTURE 5 Where do the Brits love to go on vacation? ▶ *Adventures of a lifetime* pp. 98-99 GRAMMAR TIME 5 p. 110 WORKBOOK pp. 144-149
Identify specific information in an account and talk about pets p. 65	Explain who I am talking about p. 66	Write a short story p. 67	WORDLIST p. 68 VOCABULARY IN ACTION p. 68 SELF-CHECK p. 69	BBC CULTURE 6 Is moving good for you? ▶ *On the move* pp. 100-101 GRAMMAR TIME 6 p. 111 WORKBOOK pp. 150-155
Identify the main points of a story and talk about discovering a crime p. 75	Persuade and reassure someone p. 76	Write a crime report p. 77	WORDLIST p. 78 VOCABULARY IN ACTION p. 78 SELF-CHECK p. 79	BBC CULTURE 7 Is chewing gum a crime? ▶ *A famous robbery* pp. 102-103 GRAMMAR TIME 7 p. 112 WORKBOOK pp. 156-161
Identify specific information in dialogues and talk about awkward moments p. 85	Have a casual conversation and exchange personal information p. 86	Write an email giving information p. 87	WORDLIST p. 88 VOCABULARY IN ACTION p. 88 SELF-CHECK p. 89	BBC CULTURE 8 Can school be fun? ▶ *Two very different schools* pp. 104–105 GRAMMAR TIME 7 p. 113 WORKBOOK pp. 162-167

Contents

W

Welcome to Woodley Bridge

VOCABULARY
Activities and interests | Home and furniture | Jobs | Clothes and accessories | Countries and languages

GRAMMAR
There is/are with *some/any* | Possessive adjectives and possessive *'s* | *was/were*, *there was/there were* | Simple Past

SPEAKING
Likes and dislikes | Talking about feelings

W.1 HOME AND HOBBIES

1 canal boat
2 _____
3 _____

1 🔊 **1.02** Listen and read the text. Name the person and objects in the picture.

> My name's Tom. I'm fifteen and I'm from North Carolina in the United States, but my family and I are living in Woodley Bridge, a small town in the UK. My mom is a scientist and she's working on a project here in the UK. My dad got a job at the local hospital. He's a nurse. We have a very unusual home, a canal boat called *Ocean Princess*. It's small, but I don't have any brothers or sisters, so there's enough space for the three of us. I have a cat called Hissy. She's a little wild and she isn't very friendly!
>
> Life on a boat is fun and it's a great place for my favorite hobby, kayaking. I have my own kayak and I like going out on the canal before school. I'm interested in nature, and I love drawing and painting wildlife, too, so this is the perfect home for me.

2 Work in pairs. Mark the sentences T (true) or F (false). Correct the false sentences in your notebook.

1 [F] Tom is British.
2 [ ] Tom's parents are doctors.
3 [ ] His home isn't very big.
4 [ ] Tom has a younger brother.
5 [ ] He doesn't have any pets.
6 [ ] Tom often goes kayaking before school.

3 Read the text again. What are Tom hobbies and interests?

4 🔊 **1.03** **I KNOW!** Listen and repeat the phrases in Vocabulary A box. How many activities and interests can you add to the list in three minutes? Write them in your notebook.

Vocabulary A	Activities and interests
doing nothing going to the movies listening to music playing video games reading books or magazines taking pictures	

Welcome!

5 Use the Speaking box to tell your classmate about your favorite activities and interests.

Speaking	Likes and dislikes
I love … / I like … / I don't mind … / I can't stand … / He can't stand …	

I love taking pictures.

6 🔊 **1.04** Check that you understand the words in Vocabulary B box. Listen to Tom talking to his friend, Skye, and check (✓) the words that you hear.

Vocabulary B	Home and furniture		
bathtub ✓	bathroom ☐	bed ☐	bedroom ☐
cabinet ☐	ceiling ☐	dining room ☐	floor ☐
garage ☐	kitchen ☐	mirror ☐	roof ☐
shower ☐	wall ☐	window ☐	yard ☐

7 Study Grammar A box. Look at the picture of Tom's bedroom in Activity 6 and complete the sentences with *there is/are* or *there isn't/aren't*.

Grammar A	There is/are with some/any
	Singular / **Plural**
+	There's (there is) a bed. / There are some clothes.
−	There isn't a desk. / There aren't any stores.
?	Is there a chair? / Are there any books?

1 ___There's___ a backpack on the bed.
2 _____ any pictures on the wall.
3 _____ curtains.
4 _____ a TV.

8 Study Grammar B box. In your notebook, write sentences with possessive adjectives or possessive *'s*.

Grammar B	Possessive adjectives and possessive *'s*
's = singular	the cat's toys
s' = plural	my parents' boat
	my/your/his/her/its/our/their bedroom

9 🔊 **1.05** **CLASS VOTE** Look at the picture. Do you think the boys are family or friends? Listen and check.

10 🔊 **1.05** Listen again. Mark the sentences true (T) or false (F).
1 [F] Dan is older than Ed.
2 ☐ Dan and Ed were born in Mexico.
3 ☐ Dan and Ed don't speak Spanish.
4 ☐ Ed's in New York at the moment.
5 ☐ Dan likes the school uniform in the UK.

11 🔊 **1.06** Study Vocabulary C box, then listen and repeat the words. Circle the clothes and accessories you can see in the picture in Activity 9.

Vocabulary	Clothes and accessories	
(baseball cap)	earrings	jacket
school uniform	T-shirt	watch

12 Study the Speaking box. In your notebook, add more words to describe feelings.

Speaking	Talking about feelings
I'm … annoyed/bored/excited/frightened/irritated/nervous/relaxed/sad/shocked/tired/worried.	

13 🔊 **1.07** Listen and answer the questions in your notebook.
1 What is Dan's problem?
2 How does Dan feel about the party?

14 In pairs, describe how you usually feel:
1 before a test
2 on your birthday
3 after a party
4 on vacation

Welcome!

W.2 HOME AND BEYOND

1 🔊 **1.08** Add the words below to the correct categories in the Vocabulary box. Listen, check, and repeat.

> China   Arabic   France   Italian   Chinese
> Italy   Portugal   Eygpt   New Zealand
> Portuguese   French   English

Vocabulary	Countries and languages
Countries	**Languages**
India	Hindi
Spain	Spanish

2 🔊 **1.09** Listen and read the text. Underline three countries and two languages.

Hi or "Namaste!" My name's Alisha and I'm half-English and half-Indian. My dad's from India and my mom's from England, so I speak Hindi and English. We weren't in India last summer, but this year we're planning to be there for a whole month. I have an older brother called Damian. I'm really into computers and I want to be an IT specialist one day. I like helping my friends when they have problems. I'm not crazy about sports, but Skye and I were in a kickboxing class last year, and I really liked it.

Hi! I'm Skye and I'm 15. I live with my grandma because my parents are scientists and they are in New Zealand at the moment. Grandma and I have breakfast together, then I feed my pet snake. Yes! I have a beautiful snake called Basil. After school, I see my friends Tom, Dan and Alisha. Dan and I like running together. Sometimes we all meet at the café on the canal. In the evenings, I do my homework and Grandma makes dinner.

3 Read the text again. In your notebook, write three things about Alisha and Skye.

Alisha has an older brother.

4 Study Grammar A box. Complete the sentences with *was/were* and *wasn't/weren't*.

Grammar A	*was/were, there was/were*
Affirmative	**Negative**
He **was** on vacation.	He **wasn't** on vacation.
We **were** on vacation.	We **weren't** on vacation.
There **was** a party.	There **wasn't** a party.
There **were** lots of people.	There **weren't** lots of people.
Questions	**Short answers**
Was it fun?	Yes, it **was**. / No, it **wasn't**.
Were they at home?	Yes, there **were**. / No, there **weren't**.
Was there a party?	Yes, there **was**. / No, there **wasn't**.
Were there many people?	Yes, there **were**. / No, there **weren't**.

1 Naomi and her parents ___were___ on vacation in Spain, but the weather _____ awful.
2 _____ you at the movies last night? No, I _____ .
3 The film festival _____ fun and there _____ lots of movies to watch.
4 _____ your parents angry when you _____ late home?
5 Liam _____ only 10 years old in 1999.
6 _____ the English test difficult? Yes, it _____ . There _____ lots of difficult activities.

5 🔊 **1.10** Study Grammar B box. Listen and answer the questions in your notebook.

Grammar B	Simple Past
He **lived** in California.	
They **didn't speak** to her.	
Did you **like** the movie?	

1 What was Dan like on his first day at school?
2 Who did Dan live with until last year?
3 What language does Alisha want to learn?

6 In pairs, tell your classmate about five things that were true for you last year, but are NOT true now.

I was in a different class.
I wasn't in the basketball team.

7 In pairs, describe the picture. Make as many sentences as possible. What do you think life is like in Woodley Bridge?

8 🔊 **1.11** Listen and mark the sentences true (T) or false (F).

1. [F] The café is closed.
2. [ ] The café sells lemonade.
3. [ ] Dan doesn't have a cell phone.
4. [ ] Dan is waiting outside the café.
5. [ ] Dan likes the café.
6. [ ] There are lots of places to hang out in Woodley Bridge.

9 Complete the questions with one word in each blank.

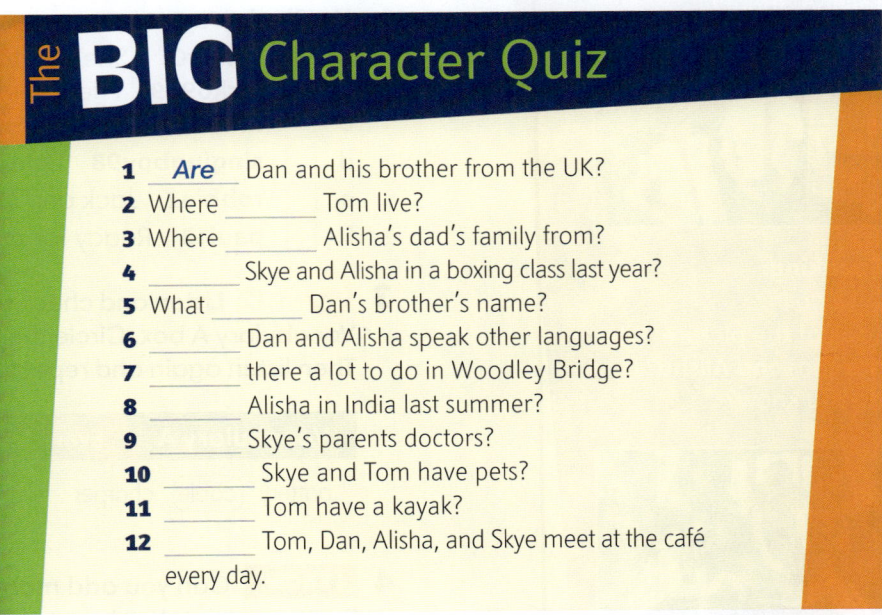

The BIG Character Quiz

1. __Are__ Dan and his brother from the UK?
2. Where _____ Tom live?
3. Where _____ Alisha's dad's family from?
4. _____ Skye and Alisha in a boxing class last year?
5. What _____ Dan's brother's name?
6. _____ Dan and Alisha speak other languages?
7. _____ there a lot to do in Woodley Bridge?
8. _____ Alisha in India last summer?
9. _____ Skye's parents doctors?
10. _____ Skye and Tom have pets?
11. _____ Tom have a kayak?
12. _____ Tom, Dan, Alisha, and Skye meet at the café every day.

10 In groups, answer the quiz about the young people from Woodley Bridge in your notebook. Use the texts in this unit if necessary.

11 In pairs, write two similar questions about yourselves. Hand the questions to your teacher and have a class quiz with two teams.

Welcome!

1

1.1 VOCABULARY Lifestyle

I can talk about everyday technology.

That's my world!

VOCABULARY
Everyday technology | Adjectives of opinion | Time

GRAMMAR
Simple Present, Present Continuous, and state verbs | verb + -ing / verb + to-infinitive

Grammar:
It's upside down
Look at the picture. What do you think Tom and Alisha are talking about?

Speaking:
Let's go in
Look at the picture. Where are Tom and Alisha? How do you know?

1 **CLASS VOTE** Do you take pictures with your cell phone? What do you take pictures of? People? Places? Food? Other things?

2 Match pictures 1–6 to sentences a–f. What do the pictures tell you about each person's life?

He/She has a cat.

a ☐ 3 **sunny01** She's up to no good again!
b ☐ **jacko999** Friends + chocolate cake #agreatday!
c ☐ **ninab98** Come on, rain! We have the right boots.
d ☐ **singingboy98** Dan's singing again! ;)
e ☐ **robbie2** Jack and I busy choosing a movie!
f ☐ **paul13** Ready for our trip!

3 🔊 **1.12** Listen and check that you understand the words in Vocabulary A box. Circle the objects you can see in the pictures. Then listen again and repeat the words.

Vocabulary A	Everyday technology
battery (cable) charger earphones plug selfie stick speaker tablet

4 **I KNOW!** Can you add more words to Vocabulary A box? Make a list in your notebook.

5 🔊 **1.13** Listen to speakers 1–4 and write the gifts. Use Vocabulary A box to help you.

1 *charger*   2 _____   3 _____   4 _____

6 Which object from Vocabulary A box would be the best gift for you? Why?

I'd like a selfie stick because my friends and I love taking pictures.

7 🔊 **1.14** Read the text. Circle the correct options. Listen and check. Is it the same in your house?

I want to listen to music, but I can't find my ¹(earphones) / plugs because my brother is using them! "They're better than mine," he says. "It's OK," I say. I can use my new ²battery / speaker that plays music *really* loud. However, when I look inside, the ³plug / battery isn't there because it's in my brother's digital camera, and guess what? His friend has it at the moment. In the end I decide to watch a funny movie on my ⁴cable / tablet, but I can't find it. "OK, where is it?" I ask him. Then I hear Mom's voice. "Are you looking for this, sweetie?" she asks. "I'm just buying some shoes, but it's nearly dead. Can you get me the ⁵battery / charger, please?" I know exactly where the charger is. I go into my brother's bedroom. On his desk there's a pile of ⁶earphones / cables that are all different lengths. And of course, there's the short black one with the right ⁷ plug / selfie stick on the end of it for my tablet!

8 🔊 **1.15** **WORD FRIENDS** Listen to people talking about their phones and check (✓) the expressions you hear.

Word Friends	
chat with friends ☐	**download** apps ☐
go online ✓	**listen** to music ☐
make a video ☐	**play** games ☐
read e-books ☐	**send/get** text messages ☐
share pictures ☐	**text** friends/parents ☐
upload videos ☐	**watch** music videos ☐

9 In pairs, ask and answer the questions.

1 How many text messages do you send and get in a day?
I send about ten text messages in a day and I get about twenty.
2 Do you read e-books?
3 When do you listen to music?
4 How often do you download apps?
5 Would you like to make a video with friends in your school?
6 What games do you play on your cell phone?
7 When do you usually text your parents?
8 What type of pictures do you usually share?

10 🔊 **1.16** Write the words in the correct column. Listen, check, and repeat.

Vocabulary B	Adjectives of opinion
all right amazing awesome awful boring cool disgusting exciting funny lovely nice noisy OK old-fashioned perfect strange terrible useful	

😊	🙂	😐	🙁	☹️
amazing awesome	cool funny	all right nice	boring noisy	awful disgusting
___	___	___	___	___

11 In your notebook, write two things for each adjective below. Then compare with a classmate.

1 useful   4 strange
2 awesome   5 awful
3 old-fashioned

12 Who in your family uses technology the most? What do they use it for?

My brother loves his gadgets, especially his tablet. He shops online, watches movies, and uses it for studying.

And YOU

1.2 GRAMMAR — Simple Present, Present Continuous, and state verbs

I can use different tenses to talk about the present.

1 CLASS VOTE Do you watch music videos? If so, what are some of your favorites?

2 🔊 1.17 Listen and read the text. What does the band do on Saturdays? What are/aren't they doing today?

___

X-RAY: The indie band with all the moves!

Hi! It's Gary here, lead singer. Today I'm writing the band's blog at a special event in a skate park. We have photographers and reporters with us, but we aren't singing at the moment. One reporter, Ali, is asking us lots of questions: "What do you normally do on Saturday afternoons? What are you doing today?" We tell Ali about our lives. We often travel from one city to the next on Saturday afternoons. Then in the evenings we usually play live in concert. We don't normally skateboard! Today there are lots of skateboarders around because we're making our new music video. They're doing some amazing tricks. I love the video!

3 Study the Grammar box, then circle the correct option about state verbs. Underline examples of the Simple Present, Present Continuous, and state verbs in the text.

Grammar: Simple Present, Present Continuous, and state verbs

Simple Present
They usually *travel* on a tour bus.
He *doesn't write* on his blog every day.
Do they *speak* English? Yes, they *do*.

Present Continuous
He's *traveling* a lot these days.
They *aren't recording* a song at the moment.
Is she *skateboarding* now? No, she *isn't*.

State verbs
We *should* / *shouldn't* use these verbs in the continuous form: *love, like, hate, know, think, see, feel, understand, want, need*

GRAMMAR TIME > PAGE 106

4 🔊 1.18 Circle the correct option. Listen and check.
1 Ali and Gary *sit* / (*are sitting*) on a bench at the skate park.
2 Gary usually *sings* / *is singing* in concerts on Saturday evenings.
3 The band members *don't often visit* / *aren't often visiting* skate parks.
4 The skateboarders *do* / *are doing* some awesome skateboard tricks at the moment.
5 Sara *always wears* / *is always wearing* her lucky blue helmet.

5 In your notebook, use the Simple Present or the Present Continuous to write questions about the text in Activity 2. In pairs, ask and answer the questions.
1 there people in the park / film / the skateboarders?
   Are there people in the park filming the skateboarders? Yes, there are.
2 Gary / work / as a reporter?
3 Ali / ask / questions at the moment?
4 the band members / usually play / live in concert on Saturdays?
5 the skateboarders / perform / in a competition today?

6 🔊 1.19 Complete the text with the correct form of the verbs in parentheses. Listen and check.

My name's Sara. I ¹ _love_ (love) skateboarding. I ² _____ (practice) at a local park every weekend. I ³ _____ (not/often/participate) in competitions because I'm from a small town.

I'm very excited today because I ⁴ _____ (perform) in a video for a famous band. At the moment we ⁵ _____ (get) ready. Lots of people ⁶ _____ (come) into the park now. My parents ⁷ _____ (sit) near the front because they ⁸ _____ (want) to take lots of pictures!

7 In pairs, tell your classmate about a hobby/sport you like. Complete the sentences to make them true for you.

I really like/love … because …
I usually/never/don't often …
I want …

Unit 1

1.3 READING and VOCABULARY — Gadget reviews

I can identify the writer's opinion in reviews and talk about unusual objects.

1 🔊 **1.20** Look at the pictures. How do you think the gadgets work? Listen and read the reviews. Check your answers.

The strangest new gadgets
by Max Stevens and Tina Wallis | Posted on May 15, 2020

Today we're going to school by bus as usual. We normally leave home at 8 a.m., but we're leaving early because we're testing some new gadgets for this month's reviews. All these gadgets are useful when you're traveling. So, what do we have?

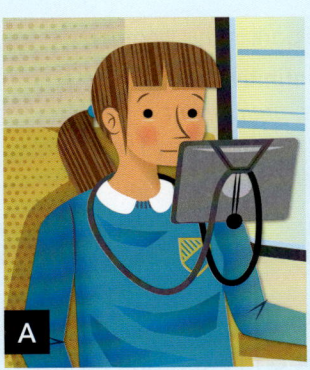

First up is the **Sospendo**. It's a strange plastic gadget which works like an extra pair of hands to hold your phone or tablet. Tina's wearing it at the moment. She won't drop her tablet, but people are staring at her. I'm sure they're thinking, "What on earth is she doing?". Tina doesn't like this gadget!

Final rating:

Next, we're trying the **Briefskate**. It's made of wood, so it looks like a normal skateboard, but you can open the top. Inside there's space for books and a cell phone or a tablet. In my opinion, it's useful and fun, but Tina and I can't skate, so we can't test it

Final rating: ☆☆☆☆☆
Well, we can't rate it if we couldn't test it!

Max

Now it's my turn. I normally take a backpack to school every day, but today I'm testing a **Defender** bag – you can wear it on your back or on your front. When it's in front of you, you can use it like a small table. I don't like it because it is ugly.

Final rating:

Right now, Max is using the **Phorce** bag. You can use it to charge your phone or tablet. I often forget to charge my phone before I leave the house, so I think this is a brilliant idea. Max loves it, too. It's our favorite gadget!

Final rating:

Tina

2 Read the reviews again. Circle the correct answers.
1 Max and Tina normally get the bus to school.
   a True (circled)   b False   c Doesn't say
2 Tina is going to school on the Briefskate today.
   a True   b False   c Doesn't say
3 The Sospendo is heavy.
   a True   b False   c Doesn't say
4 You need to put the Defender bag on a table to use it.
   a True   b False   c Doesn't say
5 Tina forgot to charge her phone today.
   a True   b False   c Doesn't say

3 What is Max's and Tina's opinion of each object? Use the adjectives below to help you.

> boring   brilliant   fun   normal
> strange   ugly   unusual   useful

Max thinks the Briefskate looks quite normal.

> **Reading tip**
> Look for examples and reasons to explain the writer's opinion.

4 **CLASS VOTE** Which of the gadgets in the reviews do you prefer?

5 In pairs, describe the things below.

> something in your backpack
> your favorite gadget

It's made of plastic. You can use it to charge your cell phone. It's boring.

Unit 1 13

1.4 GRAMMAR Verb + -ing / verb + to-infinitive

I can use verb constructions with to-infinitives and -ing forms.

1 **CLASS VOTE** Who do you speak to when you have a problem with your computer, tablet, or cell phone?

2 🔊 **1.21** Listen and read. Why does Tom want Alisha to help him?

IT'S UPSIDE DOWN

Tom: Hi, Alisha. Are you busy?
Alisha: Yes. I'm trying to finish my homework, but it's taking ages. I'd love to be outside in this weather.
Tom: Me too, but there's a problem with my computer. Dan says you're good at fixing things.
Alisha: Well, I enjoy trying. What's up?
Tom: I'm making a poster for a competition. I prefer using my own pictures, but when I upload them from my cell phone to the computer, they're upside down.
Alisha: That's weird.
Tom: It's really annoying. I want to put the posters up in town, but now I have ten pictures … upside down!
Alisha: Tom, the problem is with your settings.
Tom: Oh, so what can I do?
Alisha: I can't explain now, but I don't mind coming to your boat later.
Tom: OK … but don't forget to bring a snack. It could take a long time.
Alisha: Tom!

3 Study the Grammar box, then add the verbs in the correct place in it. Underline more examples of verb + -ing or verb + to-infinitive in the dialogue.

> enjoy   want

Grammar | verb + -ing and verb + to-infinitive

verb + -ing
After: avoid, can't stand, _____, finish, look forward to, (not) mind, miss, practice, stop, and after prepositions
I don't mind coming to your house.
She's good at fixing things.

verb + to-infinitive
After: agree, allow, ask, choose, decide, forget, hope, learn, offer, plan, try, _____, would like/love
I'd love to be in the park in this weather.

verb + -ing or to-infinitive
After: like, love, hate, prefer, start
I prefer making my own posters. / I prefer to make my own posters.

GRAMMAR TIME > PAGE 106

---

4 Circle the correct option.
1. There's a concert on TV tonight. I want watching / **to watch** it when I get home.
2. Our friends are coming to the park. We're planning meeting / to meet here after school.
3. My cousin's learning Chinese and would like visiting / to visit China one day.
4. Homemade pizza is amazing, but I'm not very good at making / to make it.
5. Naomi misses seeing / to see her friends from her old school.

5 🔊 **1.22** Listen to some of the sentences from Activity 4. What do you notice about the pronunciation of *to*? Practice saying the sentences.

6 Work in pairs. Tell your classmate five things about you. Use the verbs below.

> don't mind   forget   hate   hope   learn
> like   look forward to   miss   plan
> want   would like/love

I always forget to clean my sneakers.
I'm looking forward to going on vacation.

1.5 LISTENING and VOCABULARY — Are you technology crazy?

I can identify specific information from a radio show and talk about using technology.

1 **CLASS VOTE** Do you think you spend too much time on your cell phone or on the computer?

2 Is it time for time out? Do the quiz and compare your results with the class. Then go to page 114 to read what your answers say about you.

1 When do you first look at your cell phone or use the internet?
 a In the evening.
 b Probably around noon.
 c The minute I wake up.

2 When is it too late to text somebody?
 a On a weekday, after 10 p.m.
 b At midnight.
 c It's never too late.

3 What do you do when you have some free time?
 a I listen to music.
 b I read a book.
 c I go online.

4 How often do you check your text messages?
 a Once a day. I don't get many.
 b At school I check them between classes.
 c I check them all the time.

3 🔊 1.23 Complete the blanks in the Vocabulary box with words from the quiz. Listen and check.

Vocabulary	Time
second, _minute_, hour 6 a.m., _____ in the morning/the afternoon/_____ on a schoolday/_____/Sunday(s)/the weekend at mealtimes/_____ _____/twice/three times a day/a week/ a month/a year	

4 In pairs, ask and answer the questions. Compare your ideas with the class.

1 What's your favorite mealtime? Why?
 I love lunch because I eat with my friends.
2 What time do you go to bed on weekends?
3 What time do you do your homework?
4 What time do you get up on weekdays?
5 What do you normally do at recess?
6 What do you do the minute you wake up?

5 🔊 1.24 Listen to the first part of a radio show. What is it about? Circle the correct answer.
 a The number of families that use cell phones or tablets in their free time.
 b How much time families spend on their cell phones or tablets.

6 🔊 1.25 Listen to the second part of the show. Mark the sentences true (T) or false (F).

1 [T] Everybody in Gemma's family has a cell phone.
2 [ ] First Gemma gets up and then she checks her messages.
3 [ ] Gemma's mom uses her cell phone to read the news.
4 [ ] A phone app helps Gemma's mom when she's running.
5 [ ] Sometimes Gemma's brother doesn't hear his mom's questions.
6 [ ] Gemma thinks they should talk more in her family.

7 **And YOU** How important is technology in your life? What technology do you use and what do you like doing with it? Write five sentences in your notebook.

Technology is very important to me. It's useful because I can go online and do my homework and I can chat with friends. In my free time, I listen to lots of music …

Unit 1 | 15

1.6 SPEAKING — Making suggestions

I can make and respond to suggestions.

1 **CLASS VOTE** Do you ever watch cat videos online? Which one is your favorite?

LET'S GO IN

Tom: Hi, Alisha. Welcome to my canal boat. <u>Let's go in</u>.
Alisha: This is so cool! So, are you making your poster?
Tom: No, not now. I'm filming my cat for an online video. Like these.
Alisha: Aah! I love Ninja Cat! Your cat can be famous, too.
Tom: You could help me.
Alisha: OK, cool. Where's your cat? What's his name?
Tom: *Her* name is Hissy. She's a girl.
Alisha: Oops, sorry! So, where is she?
Tom: Er, I don't know. She usually hides from visitors.
Alisha: Why don't we look for her? Maybe she's behind the **sofa**.
Tom: I can't see her. Oh, yes, she's there, but she isn't coming out.
Alisha: What about putting some food down?
Tom: Good idea. Dinner time, Hissy!
Alisha: Look! I can see her eyes. Why don't we film her there?
Tom: Sure, why not? She looks funny.
Hissy: Hissssss!
Alisha: What's up? Oh, she doesn't like the camera.
Tom: Hissy! Where are you going? Come back!
Alisha: Don't worry! You can call the video "Moody Cat"!

 sofa
 couch

Watch OUT!

2 🔊 **1.26** Listen and read. Then answer the questions.

1 What's Alisha's opinion of the canal boat?
   She thinks it's cool.
2 What's Tom doing?
3 How does Hissy react to visitors?
4 Where's Hissy hiding?

3 Study the Speaking box. Underline more examples of suggestions in the dialogue.

Speaking	Suggestions

Making suggestions
You could look online.
Let's look for it.
What about texting her?
Why don't you charge it?

Accepting or rejecting suggestions
Yes, great idea. / Yes, why not? / OK, cool.
I'm not sure. / I'd rather not.

4 🔊 **1.27** Listen to six speakers and respond accordingly. Use the Speaking box to help you.

5 In pairs, follow the instructions.
Student A: choose a situation from the list.
Student B: respond with a suitable suggestion.

I need some information for my project.
The teacher's late.
I can't see the board.
It's really cold in here.
I can't swim.
There are too many people working in this project.
Let's plan her surprise party.

6 In pairs, plan a funny video. Discuss what you want to film and where. Make suggestions and respond to them.

a dog with a stick – in a park
my sister at dinner – at the table
a child eating pizza – at a restaurant
a man looking at his cell phone – on the sidewalk
a boy with a dog – near the lake

Unit 1

1.7 WRITING A description of your dream lifestyle

I can describe places and lifestyles.

1 **CLASS VOTE** Which of these would be your dream home?

- a modern RV
- a castle in Europe
- a beach hut on an exotic island
- a huge skyscraper
- a villa in Costa Rica
- a cottage in the mountains

2 Read the text. Which of the things below does Skye write about in paragraph 1? Which are in paragraph 2?

sports 2   home ___   hobbies ___
friends ___   place ___   daily routine ___

My Dream Lifestyle
Skye Winter-Fox

In my everyday life, I live in a house near Wisconsin with my grandma **because** my parents are in New Zealand. **But** my dream home is a beach hut in Bali. The beach hut has one bedroom and a living room. **As well as** a huge touch screen TV, there's **also** a fast internet connection **in case** I want to share videos with friends! **Although** it's small, outside there's a porch, **so** I have a perfect view of the sea.

In real life I go to Cherwell High School on weekdays. I usually swim before school and I try to write on weekends. **However**, in my dream lifestyle, I sit outside and write my novel on my laptop every morning. Then in the afternoon I swim and go surfing, **too**. Friends often visit me on weekends and we have amazing barbecues on the beach.

3 In pairs, find four differences between Skye's real life and her dream lifestyle.

In her real life Skye lives near Wisconsin, but in her dream lifestyle she lives in Bali.

4 Complete the sentences to make them true for you.

Writing	A description of your dream lifestyle

Real home and dream home
I live in _____ . / My home is in _____ .
My dream home is _____ in _____ .
It's near a beach/a cliff/_____ .
It has _____ .
Outside/Inside there is/are _____ .

Daily life and dream life
In real life I go to _____ school.
I usually/often/sometimes/never _____ .
I _____ on weekdays.
In my dream lifestyle, I often _____ in the morning.

5 Complete the blanks with the connectors in bold in the text, matching them to their function.

- Adding similar detail: *also, as well (as)*, _____ , _____
- Showing contrast: *although,* _____ , _____
- Giving reasons: *in case,* _____ , _____

6 Write a description of your dream lifestyle for a school magazine. Follow the instructions below.

Writing Time

1 **Find ideas**
Look at the Writing box. In your notebook, take notes about your real home and dream lifestyle.

2 **Draft**
Write a draft of a description of your lifestyle. Look at the description in Activity 2 to help you. Consider the structure below.
Paragraph 1: Real home and dream home
Paragraph 2: Daily life and dream life

3 **Share**
Share your text with another student for feedback. Listen to his/her opinion and suggestions. Check the spelling and grammar.

4 **Write**
Make any necessary changes to your description. Do you use the Simple Present and the adverbs of frequency correctly? Write the final version of your text.

Unit 1 17

WORDLIST Everyday technology | Adjectives of opinion | Time

alarm [n]	lead singer [n]	touch screen TV [n]
all right [adj]	lovely [adj]	trick [n]
amazing [adj]	mealtime [n]	ugly [adj]
app [n]	midnight [n]	unusual [adj]
awesome [adj]	nice [adj]	upside down [adj]
awful [adj]	noisy [adj]	useful [adj]
band [n]	noon [n]	view [n]
barbecue [n]	normal [adj]	villa [n]
battery [n]	novel [n]	
beach hut [n]	OK [adj]	
blog [n]	old-fashioned [adj]	
boring [adj]	perfect [adj]	
cable [n]	perform [v]	
castle [n]	photographer [n]	
charge [v]	photography [n]	
charger [n]	plug [n]	
cliff [n]	porch [n]	
couch [n]	poster [n]	
competition [n]	recess [n]	
cool [adj]	reporter [n]	
cottage [n]	RV (recreational vehicle) [n]	
dead (battery) [adj]	selfie stick [n]	
digital camera [n]	settings [n]	
disgusting [adj]	skate park [n]	
(dream) lifestyle [n]	skateboarder [n]	
earphones [n]	skyscraper [n]	
event [n]	smart [adj]	
exciting [adj]	sofa [n]	
fix [v]	space [n]	
fun [n]	speaker [n]	
funny [adj]	strange [adj]	
gadget [n]	tablet [n]	
heavy [adj]	technology [n]	
helmet [n]	terrible [adj]	
internet connection [n]	top [n]	

WORD FRIENDS

chat with friends
download apps
go online
listen to music
make a video
play games
read e-books
send/get text messages
share/take pictures
text friends/parents
upload videos
watch music videos
it's made of metal/wood/plastic/
  cotton/paper
it's like a/an (+ noun)
it looks (+ adjective)
it looks like a/an (+ noun)
it works like a/an (+ noun)
you can (+ verb)
you can use it like a (noun)
you can use it to (+ infinitive) /
  for (+ –ing)

VOCABULARY IN ACTION

1 Use the Wordlist to find and write in your notebook:

1. three people
   photographer, reporter, skateboarder
2. three types of houses
3. three positive adjectives
4. three types of materials
5. three gadgets

2 In your notebook, write adjectives from the Wordlist that describe:

- the town you live in
  exciting
- your school
- your favorite band
- your school backpack
- your cell phone or computer

3 Use the Wordlist to complete the sentences. In pairs, tell your classmate if the sentences are true for you.

1. I always *listen* to music on my cell phone when I walk to school.
2. I like to sing along when I _____ music videos.
3. My friends usually _____ me text messages.
4. I always _____ my parents when I'm late.
5. I only _____ online when I don't have any homework.

4 🔊 1.28 **PRONUNCIATION** Listen and decide how the final *s* is pronounced in each word. In your notebook, write the word in the correct column. Then listen and repeat the words. When do you pronounce the final *s* as /s/ and /z/?

earphones   e-books   gadgets   helmets   hours
novels   pictures   plugs   reporters   tablets   tricks

/s/	/z/
e-books	plugs

18 Unit 1

SELF-CHECK

1 Write the correct word for each definition.

1. You put these in your ears to listen to music. e _a r p h o n e s_
2. If you use a skateboard, you should wear this on your head. h _ _ _ _ _ _
3. This means the opposite of awesome. a _ _ _ _ _
4. A small house in the country. c _ _ _ _ _ _ _
5. You put this inside a gadget to give it energy. b _ _ _ _ _ _ _
6. Sixty seconds. m _ _ _ _ _ _

2 In your notebook, complete the quiz with one of the expressions in the box. In pairs, ask and answer the questions.

> in the evening   on weekends   twice a day
> at mealtimes   on a weekday   at midnight

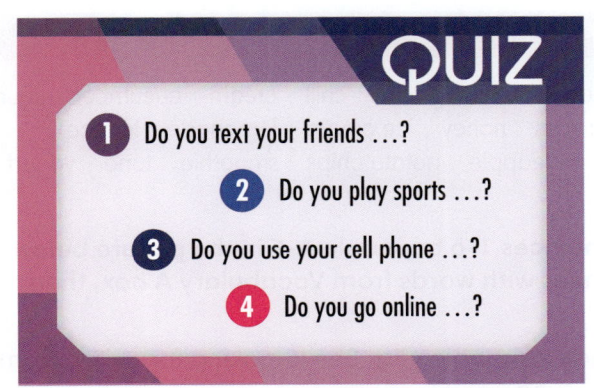

QUIZ

1. Do you text your friends …?
2. Do you play sports …?
3. Do you use your cell phone …?
4. Do you go online …?

A: *Do you text your friends at mealtimes?*
B: *I never text my friends at mealtimes.*

3 Complete the sentences with the correct form of the verbs in parentheses, then match them to the correct function (A, B, or C).

A an action in progress
B a regular action
C a state verb

1. Carla _is reading_ (read) an e-book now. [A]
2. My grandparents _____ (usually/call) us on the weekend. ☐
3. Jake _____ (not/like) music videos. ☐
4. We _____ (not/often/download) apps. ☐
5. I _____ (know) how to upload photos. ☐
6. Why _____ (you/chat) with friends now? It's very late. ☐

4 Complete the questions with the correct form of the verbs in parentheses.

1. Are you planning _to go_ (go) online later?
2. Are you good at _____ (fix) things?
3. Do you prefer _____ (live) in a village or in a town?
4. Do you want _____ (make) a video of your school?
5. Are you looking forward to _____ (see) your little brother?

5 Complete the dialogue with the words below.

> about   ~~want~~   idea   rather
> could   sure   don't   let's

A: Do you ¹ _want to_ go to the movies?
B: No, I'd ² _____ not. What's on TV tonight?
A: Er, not much … Why ³ _____ we watch *The Simpsons*?
B: I'm not ⁴ _____. What time does it start?
A: 7:30 p.m. … Oh, it's 8 p.m. now.
B: What ⁵ _____ watching soccer on PBC? It starts at 8.
A: Mmm, I don't really like soccer. I know, ⁶ _____ watch a series online!
B: Yes, great ⁷ _____. We ⁸ _____ watch *Anne with an E*.

6 In pairs, decide what to watch together. Use the TV guide to help you.

TV GUIDE

Time	NBS	PBC
7:30	The Simpsons	soccer
8:00	Teen Wolf	
8:30	This Country's Got Talent	tennis
9:00	Shark Tank	
9:30	Teen Movie Awards	basketball
10:30	Star News	gymnastics
11:00	Teen Reality Show	Golf News
11:30	The Big Bang Theory	volleyball

7 🔊 1.29 Listen, then listen again and write down what you hear.

_____
_____
_____

SELF-ASSESSMENT Think about this unit. What did you learn? What do you need help with?

2

The taste test

VOCABULARY
Food and drink | Flavors |
Describing food

GRAMMAR
Present Perfect with *ever, never, just, already, yet, for,* and *since* |
Present Perfect and Simple Past

Grammar:
I've heard it's funny!
Look at Tom and Alisha. What are they doing?

Speaking:
What can I get you?
Where are Tom and Alisha now?

2.1 VOCABULARY Food and drink
I can talk about food and drink.

1 **CLASS VOTE** Which is your favorite meal of the day? Why?

☐ breakfast   lunch   dinner   snack

2 🔊 **1.30** Study Vocabulary A box. Listen and see if you can find the items you hear in the picture. Then listen and repeat the words.

Vocabulary A	Food and drink
beef   breadrolls   cheese   chewing gum   chili   cream   cucumber   flour
fruit juice   garlic   grapes   honey   ice cream   lemonade   lettuce
nuts   peach   pear   pineapple   potato chips   smoothie   tuna   yogurt

3 🔊 **1.31** Match sentences 1-6 to people A-F in the picture below. Complete the sentences with words from Vocabulary A box, then listen and check.

1 [C] This person has a shopping list. She is looking for chili, cream, and some _tuna_ .
2 ☐ These people want to buy _____, honey, yogurt, and _____ .
3 ☐ The salesclerk is near the _____ , grapes, and _____ .
4 ☐ The old woman wants lettuce, _____, and some _____ .
5 ☐ The child is looking at the fruit juice and _____ .
6 ☐ The man is buying _____ , beef, and _____ .

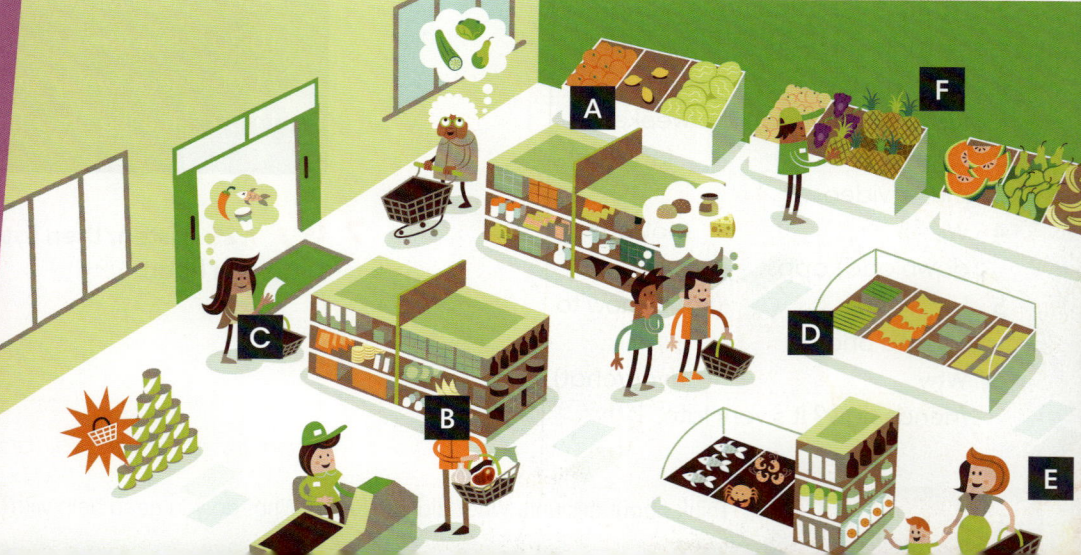

4 Copy supermarket sections 1–7 into your notebook. Then, match the words from Vocabulary A to each section.

1 Fruit *peach, …*
2 Vegetables *lettuce, …*
3 Meat and fish *beef, …*
4 Dairy *cheese, …*
5 Cereals *bread rolls, …*
6 Candy and snacks *ice cream, …*
7 Drinks *fruit juice, …*

5 **I KNOW!** Add as many words to each category in Activity 4 as you can. Compare your ideas with the class.

6 🔊 **1.32** Listen and repeat the words in Vocabulary B box. What is your favorite flavor? What other foods and drinks can have these flavors?

Vocabulary B	Flavors

chocolate   coconut   coffee   lemon
melon   mint   strawberry   vanilla
These words can be used as adjectives or nouns.
*I like **strawberries**.* [noun]
*I like **strawberry** ice cream.* [adjective]

7 🔊 **1.33** Complete the text with the words below. Then listen and check. Can you think of other food that make you feel hot or cold?

beef   chili   coffee   dishes   drink
~~ice cream~~   mint   taste

8 🔊 **1.34** Listen to three questions from a food quiz. Can you guess the answers?

1 *garlic*
2 _____
3 _____

9 In pairs, create a quiz similar to the one in Activity 8.

- Choose a food item that you like.
- In your notebook, write 2–4 facts about this food in the facts.
- DON'T include the name of the food in the facts.
- Switch clues with another pair and guess the food.

It's small and red, with lots of small seeds in the outside. It's sweet and it tastes delicious! It is used in cakes and pies.

Taste and Temperature

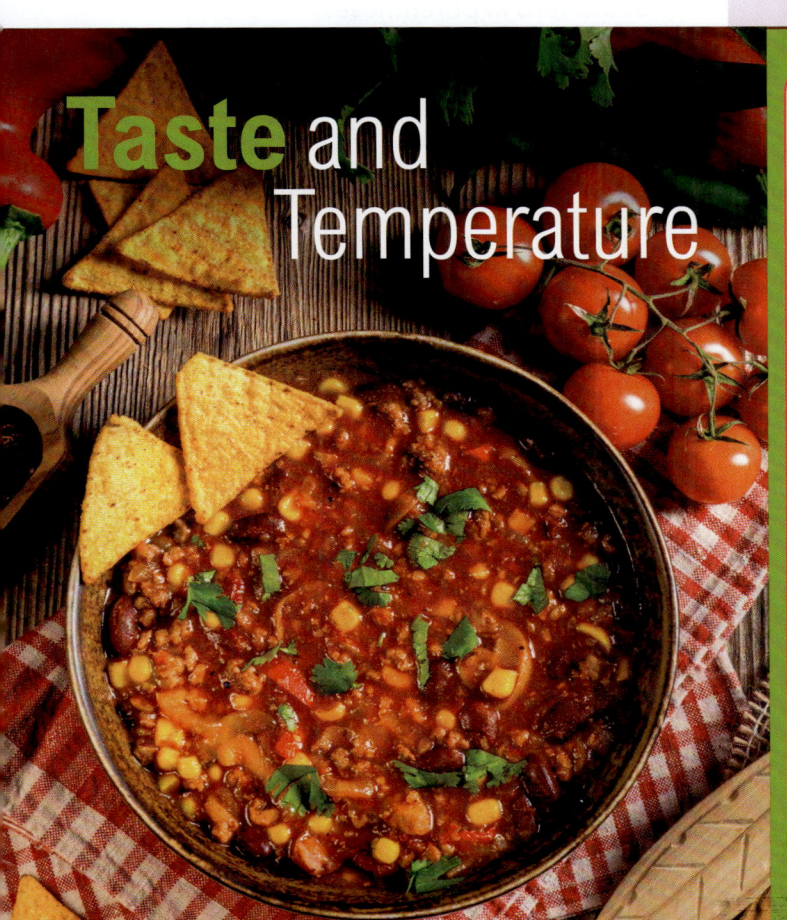

People usually enjoy ¹ *ice cream* in the summer because it is cold, in the same way they enjoy hot tea or ² _____ in the winter. But did you notice that some food is not really hot or cold, but makes you feel like that? For example, in some hot countries, ³ _____ lemonade is very popular. It's a cool, refreshing ⁴ _____. But does this herb really make your mouth cold? When you ⁵ _____ mint flavors, your mouth sends a message to your brain: "Hey, that feels cold!" In fact, it's a "trick" because the temperature in your mouth doesn't change. Spicy ⁶ _____ do the opposite, they make you feel hot. Take chili con carne, for example — a famous Mexican dish with meat — usually ⁷ _____ and beans, served with rice. ⁸ _____ doesn't really make you hot. But it makes you FEEL hot.

2.2 GRAMMAR   Present Perfect with *ever*, *never*, *just*, *already*, and *yet*

I can use the Present Perfect with *ever*, *never*, *just*, *already*, and *yet*.

1 **CLASS VOTE** Which strange food would you like to try?

> cheeseburger ice cream   pizza with bananas
> cucumber and garlic smoothie

2 🔊 1.35 Listen and read, then answer the questions in your notebook.

1 Where are Tom and Alisha? *at a market*
2 Who is Oliver Jenkins?
3 What type of store does Oliver Jenkins have?
4 What flavor ice cream does Alisha try first?

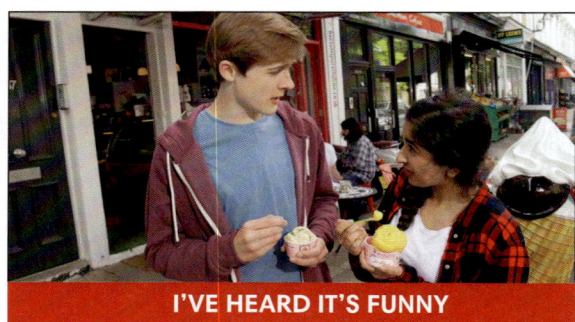

I'VE HEARD IT'S FUNNY

Tom: I've never seen so much food. Ah, smell that pizza!
Alisha: Yes, I've already had some! This market is great for Chinese food, too. Have you ever eaten noodles?
Tom: Yes, I have. Dad's cooked them at home.
Alisha: Tom, look! That's Oliver Jenkins, the famous TV chef. Have you seen his **programme**?
Tom: No, but I've heard it's funny.
Alisha: Maybe he's brought some nice food?
Tom: Well, he's just opened an ice cream parlor. Let's go and see. Maybe we can try some.
Alisha: Look. There's cheeseburger **flavour** or chili or pea-and-mint. He's used weird flavors!
Tom: You bet!
Alisha: I hate peas, but cheeseburger flavour sounds OK. What about you?
Tom: I haven't decided yet ... What's it like?
Alisha: Yuck! That's disgusting. Hang on, let's try another. Mmm, chili. Now, that's the best ice cream I've ever eaten!

 programme / flavour    program / flavor   **OUT of class**

3 Study the Grammar box then circle the incorrect option. Underline examples of the Present Perfect in the dialogue.

Grammar	Present Perfect

Have you **ever tried** pizza with banana?
I**'ve never eaten** so much food.
He**'s just made** a new TV program.
I**'ve already tried** it.
I **haven't finished yet**.
Have you **done** it **yet**?
We use the Present Perfect to talk about *experiences* / *continuous past actions* / *recent past actions*.

GRAMMAR TIME > PAGE 107

4 Complete the sentences with the correct form of the words in parentheses.

1 Alisha *has already eaten* (already/eat) some pizza.
2 _____ Tom _____ (ever/cook) noodles at home?
3 Alisha and Tom _____ (just/see) Oliver Jenkins.
4 Tom _____ (never/watch) Oliver Jenkins on TV.

5 Complete the text with the Present Perfect form of the verb in parentheses.

> Hi Ed,
> Sorry I ¹ *haven't called* (not call) you.
> I ² _____ (have) a bad cold and
> I ³ _____ (not speak) to anyone.
> ⁴ _____ (you/decide) about the summer yet? I hope I can come and see you.
> See you,
> Dan

6 In your notebook, write about a place where you like to eat with friends.

1 What's it called?
2 Who have you been there with?
3 What food have you tried?

It's called Marco's and I've been there with ...

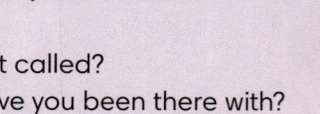

2.3 READING and VOCABULARY   An article

I can identify quotations in an article and use *make* and *do* accurately.

1 CLASS VOTE   Do you watch cooking TV programs?

2 Read the title and the first paragraph of the article. What does the title refer to?
  a Jolene's cooking class at school.
  b Jolene's experience on a TV show.

Reading tip
Identify key words in articles - they can give you the necessary information to understand the main idea in the text.

3 ▶ 1.36 Listen and read the article. Circle the correct answers.
  1 Why can't Jolene go out with her friends tonight?
     a She wants to study at home.
     b She wants to upload some pictures on Twitter.
     (c) She wants to bake more cupcakes.
     d She wants to relax at home.
  2 Why has Jolene chosen to study food technology?
     a Because she wants to avoid disasters in the kitchen.
     b Because she loves all kinds of science.
     c Because she wants to discover what happens when you cook food.
     d Because it goes well with math and chemistry.
  3 What happened during the school cooking competition?
     a Jolene got angry with the other students.
     b Jolene had a disaster with her cake.
     c The other students left and went home.
     d Jolene's oven gloves caught fire.
  4 How does Jolene's family help?
     a They go and watch every show.
     b They can help Jolene to stay calm.
     c They tell her when she's making mistakes.
     d They help her with her schoolwork.

4 WORD BUILDING   Find nouns from the verbs below in the text. Make sentences with each noun in your notebook.
  1 contest   *contestant*
  2 compete _____
  3 appear _____
  4 build _____
  5 win _____
  6 weigh _____

5 WORD FRIENDS   Find the phrases in the text. Write *make* or *do* in the correct place in the box.

Word Friends   *make* and *do*
  _____ : a cake   a decision   time   a mess   mistakes
  _____ : (my/your/his/her) homework   my/you/his/her best

"I have loved every minute of it!"

She's done her homework, but there's no time for 17-year-old Jolene to relax with friends tonight. Jolene is the youngest contestant in a national cooking competition, *The Great American Baking Show*, and she has to practice for the next show. Every week she has to impress the judges with different recipes. Next week it's cupcakes. She's already made 24 cakes today, but she hasn't finished yet. Since her first appearance on the show, Jolene has posted messages and pictures on Twitter. Her profile says: "I only have friends because I make good cake. Seriously." So when did this passion begin?

Jolene started baking when she was about seven years old. She often made a mess in the kitchen and the results weren't always good. At school she made a decision to study math, chemistry, and food technology because she says, "I've always loved food, but I've never understood the science behind it." It hasn't always been easy. Once she set her oven gloves on fire during a school cooking competition and the whole building was evacuated. But the judges announced that Jolene was one of the winners. She was very happy!

What about Jolene's family? Her parents have watched her on TV every week. They know that the competition is getting tough and that Jolene is tired. Jolene wants to do her best and hates making mistakes, so it's important that they keep her calm. They are proud that she has made time for both her schoolwork and the TV show. Everyone is enjoying the competition although, as Jolene says with a smile, "We have all put on a little weight!"

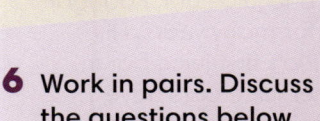

6 Work in pairs. Discuss the questions below.
  • Have you ever made a cake?
  • Have you ever made a big decision?
  • How do you feel when you make mistakes?
  • When do you usually do your homework?

2.4 GRAMMAR Present Perfect with *for* and *since*; Present Perfect and Simple Past

I can talk about duration of time, and be general and specific about experiences.

1 **CLASS VOTE** What's your favorite flavor for a fruit juice or smoothie?

2 🔊 1.37 In pairs, answer the questions. Then listen and read the text. Check your answers.

1 Amanda is traveling from the USA to Brazil. What do you think will surprise her?

_____

2 How many types of fruit are there in Brazil?

_____

3 Study the Grammar box, then fill in the blanks with *for* and *since*. Underline more examples in the text of the Present Perfect and the Simple Past.

Grammar	Present Perfect and Simple Past

Present Perfect with *for* and *since*
I've lived in Rio **for** many years. (a period of time)
They've had this bar **since** 1970. (a point in time)

Present Perfect and Simple Past
We**'ve been** to Sao Paulo.
We **went** to Sao Paulo in 2012.

_____ : two o'clock   Monday   last weekend   1958
_____ : five minutes   a few hours   a long time

GRAMMAR TIME > PAGE 107

4 In your notebook, use the prompts to write sentences in the Present Perfect. Add *for* or *since*.

1 I / not / have / a candy bar / a month.
   I haven't had a candy bar for a month.
2 My family / own / this café / 2010.
3 We / not eat / any food / breakfast time.
4 This cooking program / be / on TV / a few months.

5 🔊 1.38 Complete the dialogue with the Present Perfect and the Simple Past. Listen and check.

Mia: ¹ *Have* you had any fruit juice yet today?
Miguel: No, I ² _____ had any yet, but I'd like some now.
Mia: ³ _____ you ever tried sugar apple juice?
Miguel: Yes, I ⁴ _____ some yesterday. Sugar apples look like pears! They're very good for you.
Mia: ⁵ _____ you like it?
Miguel: Yes, I ⁶ _____ .

The best drink ever!

We've been in Rio de Janeiro since yesterday afternoon. I'm so excited! My parents are from Brazil, but we haven't visited the country many times. The plane tickets are very expensive! We didn't want to go sightseeing yesterday, but we went to the beach. My favorite thing in Rio is the juice bars on every street corner. I've never seen so much fruit!

The owner of one juice bar, Rodrigo, has lived in Rio for many years. His father opened Rio's first juice bar in 1958. Many other juice bars have opened since then. I found out that there are 146 different types of fruit in Brazil! Some of them are very unusual. Have you ever heard of cashew apple? It looks like a red apple, but the cashew nut grows at the top of the fruit. I've just tried it. It's amazing.

Amanda

6 In your notebook, write questions in the Present Perfect and the Simple Past. In pairs, ask and answer the questions.

Start with a general question with *ever* (Present Perfect):
Have you ever eaten / drunk … ?
Then ask about details Simple Past:
When did you try it? / Did you like it? / What was it like?

2.5 LISTENING and VOCABULARY — A dream cake

I can identify specific detail in speech and describe food.

1 **CLASS VOTE** Is it important to have a special cake on your birthday?

2 🔊 **1.39** Study the Vocabulary box using a dictionary. Circle the correct option to complete the sentences, then listen and check.

Vocabulary	Describing food
bitter bland delicious dry fresh rich sour spicy stale sweet tasty	

1 I like chili popcorn because it's so (spicy) / stale.
2 These cupcakes aren't very tasty, they're quite sweet / bland.
3 I love this fruit juice, it's really dry / delicious.
4 This cake has icing and a filling with butter, so it's very rich / bitter.
5 This milk has been in the sun too long, it tastes sour / fresh.
6 This bread is old, I think it's stale / bitter.

Is it a car? Is it a robot? No … it's a cake!

3 🔊 **1.40** Listen to Gianni talking about a very special cake. Mark the sentences true (T) or false (F).

1 ☐ Gianni saw the cake in New York.
2 ☐ The cake took a week to be made.
3 ☐ The baker didn't make the cake in his shop.
4 ☐ The cake weighed around 70 kilos.
5 ☐ Gianni didn't like the cake at all.

4 Look at the form below. In pairs, decide what kind of information is missing from blanks 1–6: words or numbers?

5 🔊 **1.41** Listen to part of a radio show with information about how to enter the Dream Cake competition and complete the form.

6 In pairs, describe the best cake you have ever had. Ask and answer the questions:
- What did it look like?
- What did it taste like?
- What flavor was it?
- Who made it?

WIN Your *Dream Cake* from *Benny's Bakery!*

Send us a picture or drawing of your ideal cake! We will make the best cake and send it to you.

① Email address: benny@ _____ .com
② Usual cost of cake: $ _____
③ Choose a flavor: chocolate, _____ , or vanilla
④ Don't forget! Tell us your _____ .
⑤ Closing date of competition: Friday, January _____
⑥ Other prizes for five runners up: 12 _____

Unit 2   25

2.6 SPEAKING — Ordering food

I can order food in a café or restaurant.

1 **CLASS VOTE** What would you like from the menu below?

2 🔊 **1.42** In pairs, discuss what you think the green cake in the picture is. Listen and check.

Annie's Café
eat in or take away!

Homemade tomato soup and bread
Grilled cheese sandwich
Salad with tuna or cheese
Chocolate cupcakes
A selection of cookies

Today's special: Green cake!
ALSO Why not try a smoothie?
Melon-and-mango or
banana-and-strawberry
OR our homemade lemonade!

3 🔊 **1.42** Listen and read the dialogue again. What do Dan, Alisha, Tom, and Skye order? Answer in your notebook.

Annie: Hi! Take a seat and I'll get you the menus. Here you are. Now what can I get you to drink?
Alisha: I'll have an apple juice, please.
Dan: Just water for me, thanks.
Tom: Could I have a melon-and-mango smoothie, please?
Annie: Of course. Are you ready to order?
Alisha: Almost. That green cake looks interesting. What's in it?
Annie: Green tea and yogurt. It's quite sweet.
Tom: Mmhh. I'd like that, please.
Alisha: Me too.
Dan: Um, I don't feel like eating sweets. I'll have a grilled cheese sandwich, please.
Annie: So that's one toasted sandwich and two slices of cake.
Tom, Dan, and Alisha: Thanks.
Skye: Hi, guys. Sorry I'm late.
Tom: We've just ordered. What do you want?
Skye: It's OK. I'll get it. Excuse me. Can I have a hot chocolate, please?
Annie: Of course. Would you like anything to eat?
Skye: Not for me, thanks.

4 🔊 **1.43** Listen to how the words in the sentences below are connected. Then listen again and repeat.
1 I'll have an apple juice.
2 I'll have a soda.

5 Study the Speaking box. Match questions 1–5 to answers a–e.

Speaking — Ordering food

Customer
I'll have … I'd like a …/a slice of …
Excuse me, can/could I have …
Just … for me, please.
Not for me, thanks.

Server
Take a seat and I'll get you the menu.
What would you like to drink?
Are you ready to order?
Would you like anything to eat?
Can I get you something?
Here you are.

1 [c] Are you ready to order?
2 [ ] What's in it?
3 [ ] What soup do you have?
4 [ ] What can I get you to drink?
5 [ ] Would you like anything to eat?

a Homemade tomato.
b I'll have a soda, please.
c Almost.
d Not for me, thanks.
e It's just fruit and yogurt.

6 In pairs or small groups, use the Speaking box to order food from the menu in Activity 1.

 Unit 2

2.7 WRITING — An email to a friend

I can write an email to a friend.

1 CLASS VOTE What food would you have at a party with friends?

2 1.44 Study the Vocabulary box using a dictionary. Then listen and repeat the words.

Vocabulary	Cooking verbs
boil chop fry mix slice	

3 Use the words in the Vocabulary box to make sentences about two types of food. Write them in your notebook.
You can boil potatoes and peas.

4 Read Alisha's email. Order the information as it appears in the text.

Hi Kalinda,

Thanks for getting in touch. It was great to hear about your field trip. The pictures were awesome.

Tom and I have just started summer break and we've decided to have a party tomorrow on his boat! He's bought lots of delicious food, including sausages and cheese. I'm making my famous chicken salad. It's really easy. First, I fry the chicken and boil some eggs. Then I slice them. After that, I chop tomatoes into small pieces and mix everything together with some mayonnaise. I can't tell you how good it is!

Anyway, I was wondering if you'd like to come. We're asking everybody to bring some fruit or some juice because we want to make smoothies with different flavors.

Let me know if you can make it.

Alisha

a ☐ Alisha talks about what's happening in her life now.
b ☐ Alisha invites Kalinda and asks her to do something.
c ☐ 1 Alisha thanks her friend and comments on her friend's news.
d ☐ Alisha asks Kalinda to reply to the invitation.

5 Study the Writing box. Underline the sentences that are in the email in Activity 4.

Writing	Email to a friend

Starting your email
How are things?
Thanks for getting in touch.

Responding to news
It was great to hear about your field trip.
I can't wait to hear more about it.

Giving your news
Tom and I have just started summer break.
We've decided to have a party.

Explain why you're writing
Anyway / By the way, I was wondering if you'd like to come.
I'm writing to ask if you'd like to come to the party.

Ending your email
Let me know if you can make it.
See you soon.

6 Write an email to a friend.

1 **Find ideas**
Follow the instructions below. Take notes in your notebook.
- thank your friend for his/her email and comment on his/her news
- explain that you're having a party and describe what food you're making
- invite your friend and suggest something he/she can make for it

2 **Draft**
Write a draft of your email. Use contractions to make your email sound friendly and informal.

3 **Share**
Share your draft with another student for feedback. Listen to his/her opinion and suggestions. Check the spelling and grammar.

4 **Check and write**
Make changes to your email. Do you use the correct style for writing to a friend? Write the final version of your text.

Writing Time

WORDLIST — Food and drink | Flavors | *make* and *do* | Describing food

appearance [n]	delicious [adj]	meal [n]	sour [adj]
baker [n]	dinner [n]	meat [n]	special [n]
beef [n]	dish [n]	melon [n]	spicy [adj]
bitter [adj]	dry [adj]	mint [n]	stale [adj]
bland [adj]	egg [n]	mix [v]	strawberry [n]
boil [v]	enter [v]	noodles [n]	sweet [adj]
bread [n]	filling [n]	nuts [n]	taste [v]
breakfast [n]	fish [n]	order [v]	tasty [adj]
building [n]	flavor [n]	oven gloves [n]	tea [n]
candy [n]	food technology [n]	pea [n]	try [v]
cheese [n]	flour [n]	peach [n]	tuna [n]
chef [n]	fresh [adj]	pear [n]	vanilla [n]
chewing gum [n]	fruit [n]	pineapple [n]	vegetables [n]
chicken [n]	fruit juice [n]	popcorn [n]	weight [n]
chili [n]	fry [v]	potato chips [n]	winner [n]
chocolate [n]	garlic [n]	recipe [n]	yogurt [n]
chop [v]	grapes [n]	refreshing [adj]	
coconut [n]	herbs [n]	rice [n]	
coffee [n]	homemade [adj]	rich [adj]	
competition [n]	honey [n]	salad [n]	
contestant [n]	ice cream [n]	sausage [n]	
cook [v]	icing [n]	serve [v]	
cooking class [n]	lemon [n]	server [n]	
cooking teacher [n]	lemonade [n]	shopping list [n]	
cream [n]	lettuce [n]	slice [n]	
cucumber [n]	lunch [n]	smoothie [n]	
cupcake [n]	mango [n]	snack [n]	
dairy [adj]	mayonnaise [n]	soup [n]	

WORD FRIENDS
make a cake
make a decision
make a mess
make mistakes
make time
do my/your/his/her homework
do my/your/his/her best
put on weight

VOCABULARY IN ACTION

1 Find in the Wordlist and write:

1 four drinks:
   fruit juice , _____ , _____ , _____

2 three types of main meal or small meal:
   breakfast , _____ , _____

3 ten adjectives to describe food:
   bitter , _____ , _____ , _____ , _____ , _____ , _____ , _____ , _____ , _____

4 four actions you do when you're cooking:
   boil , _____ , _____ , _____

5 four people:
   contestant , _____ , _____ , _____

2 Use the Wordlist to find the opposites of the words below.

1 disgusting — *delicious*
2 loser _____
3 sweet _____
4 spicy _____
5 fresh _____

3 In pairs, take turns to spell words in Activities 1 and 2.

How do you spell tasty?

It's T-A-S-T-Y.

4 🔊 1.45 **PRONUNCIATION** Listen to the underlined vowels in each word and repeat.

/ə/
van<u>i</u>lla   c<u>u</u>cumber   br<u>e</u>akf<u>a</u>st   may<u>o</u>nnaise
flav<u>o</u>r   comp<u>e</u>tition

SELF-CHECK

1 Write the correct word for each definition.

1. This person takes part in a competition.
   c <u>o n t e s t a n t</u>
2. This is a type of meat. b _ _ _ _
3. This is a synonym for tasty.
   d _ _ _ _ _ _ _ _ _
4. These are small, round fruit and can be green, red, or black.
   g _ _ _ _ _ _
5. You do this to cook food in very hot water.
   b _ _ _

2 Complete the questions. Then ask and answer the questions in pairs.

QUIZ — Favorite foods beginning with "s"

1. Some people like garlic and chili with everything! Do you like s<u>picy</u> food?
2. You have two slices of bread and butter and you want to make a s_____. What filling do you like?
3. You're buying a s_____ in a juice bar. What flavor do you choose?
4. You'd love something s_____ to eat, like cake. What do you want?
5. Your family is having a nice, healthy, green s_____ for dinner. What do you put in it?

3 Complete the sentences with *make* or *do*.

1. I often <u>make</u> cakes for my friends.
2. I never _____ mistakes in my English classes.
3. I listen to music when I _____ my homework.
4. I always clean up when I _____ a mess.
5. I _____ my best to eat healthy food.

4 Complete the dialogue with the words below.

| already | ~~yet~~ | just | for | since |

Ana: Hi, Mom! Have you made my birthday cake ¹ <u>yet</u>?
Mom: Yes, I've ² _____ taken it out of the oven. It's still warm.
Ana: Awesome! We haven't had cake ³ _____ ages! It looks amazing. What about the rest of the food? Is there any pizza?
Mom: Yes, everything's ready for the party.
Ana: Oh, you've ⁴ _____ put all the food on the table. Thanks, Mom.
Mom: I'm glad you like it. I've been in the kitchen ⁵ _____ noon!

5 In your notebook, write five questions using one word or phrase from each column.

Have/Has Did	your mom/dad	ever been in a competition?
	you	go to the supermarket last weekend?
	your brother/sister	ever made a cake?
	your friends	cook dinner yesterday?
	your teacher	ever had a picnic or a barbecue outside?
	your parents	take the family to a restaurant last year?

Did you cook dinner yesterday?

6 In pairs, ask and answer your questions from Activity 5.

7 In pairs, role-play the situation. Follow the instructions.

Student A you are a server. Ask the customer
- to take a seat, and offer to get the menu.
- if he/she is ready to order food.
- what he/she would like to drink.

Student B: you are a customer. Make your order from the menu on page 114.

8 🔊 1.46 Listen, then listen again and write down what you hear.

_____
_____
_____
_____
_____

SELF-ASSESSMENT — Think about this unit. What did you learn? What do you need help with?

3

Wild nature

VOCABULARY
Weather | Temperature
Natural disasters | In the wild

GRAMMAR
Past Perfect | Simple Past vs. Past Perfect

Grammar:
Luckily I'd left my cell phone on the bus!
Look at Dan's mom. What do you think she's talking about? Why?

Speaking:
Why did you do that?
Look at the picture. What is Dan holding? What is he going to do with that?

 3.1 **VOCABULARY** Weather and natural disasters

I can talk about the weather and natural disasters.

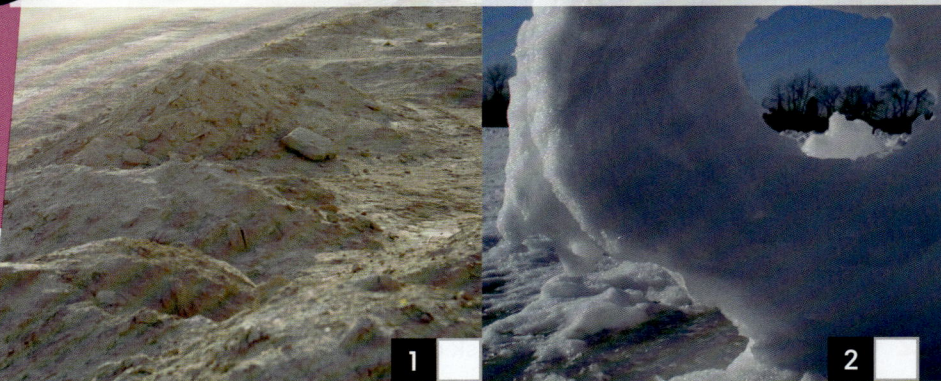

1   **CLASS VOTE**   What's your favorite season? Why? Compare your ideas.
I like fall because the trees are different colors.

2   🔊 1.46   Complete Vocabulary A box with the words from the word cloud. Listen and check.

Vocabulary A	Weather	
	Noun	Adjective
🌧	rain	rainy
❄		
☀		
🚗💨		
☁		
🌬🌳		
🧊		
⛈		

snow cloud fog wind ice storm sunny foggy cloudy sun icy stormy windy snowy

> **Watch OUT!**
> To describe the weather, we use *It's* + adjective:
> *It's rainy/foggy/windy.*
> When the weather is beginning to change, we use *get* + adjective:
> *It's getting sunny/foggy/windy/cloudy.*

3   In pairs, describe two pictures from pages 30 and 31.
It's very windy in picture 1 and it's cold and there's snow on the ground in picure 2.

4   Read the facts in *Did you know …?* Circle the correct option. Which facts (A-H) are shown in the pictures? Match them to the pictures (1-5). There are three extra facts.

3 A   4   5

DID YOU KNOW ... ?

A It isn't always hot and ¹*sunny* / *sun* in the desert! In January 2015, because of ²*stormy* / *stormy weather*, there was enough ³*snow* / *snowing* to build a snowman.

B Less than 1 mm of ⁴*rain* / *raining* falls every year in Arica, in Chile. It would take 100 years to fill a coffee cup.

C The "zonda" ⁵*windy* / *wind* in Argentina is a dry wind that often carries dust over the mountains. When it happens, it makes the ⁶*sunny* / *sun* look brown.

D When it's very ⁷*wind* / *windy* in hilly places, ⁸*snowy* / *snow* can move along the ground and make a snowroller.

E A mustache ⁹*cloud* / *cloudy* forms when a cloud passes over a column of air. But it doesn't happen very often!

F It's so cold in Antarctica that in some places the ¹⁰*icy* / *ice* is more than 4,000 meters thick.

G The Grand Banks are shallow areas of water on the coast of Newfoundland, Canada. They have more than 200 ¹¹*foggy* / *fog* days every year.

H It can be very ¹²*rain* / *rainy* in Kerala, India, but in 2001 the ¹³*rain* / *raining* was red because it was carrying sand from the desert. Strange, isn't it?

5 🔊 **1.47** Complete the blanks with the words below. Then listen, check, and repeat.

> boiling (hot)   cool   chilly   degrees
> freezing (cold)   minus

Vocabulary B	Temperature
¹ __boiling (hot)__	
hot	
warm	
mild	
² _____	
cold	
³ _____	
⁴ _____	
It's 35 ⁵ _____.	
It's ⁶ _____ 10 today.	

6 🔊 **1.48** Listen to three weather forecasts and complete the blanks below.

1 New York: _____ _____
2 Rio de Janeiro: _____ _____ _____
3 Krakow: _____ _____ _____

7 🔊 **1.49** Study Vocabulary C box. Listen and repeat the words.

Vocabulary C	Natural disasters
avalanche drought earthquake flood hurricane tsunami	

8 Match the sentences to the words from Vocabulary C box.

1 The water is going into the houses. People are moving upstairs. __flood__
2 There's a lot of snow and it's coming down the mountain very quickly. _____
3 People can't grow plants because the ground is dry and hard. _____
4 The building is shaking. _____
5 The beach is empty. People are going up the mountains before the wave arrives. _____
6 It's very windy. Everybody is inside and the doors and windows are closed. _____

9 In pairs, choose one of the natural disasters from Vocabulary C box. Describe the problems it can cause in the area you live.

> go outside   grow food   stay indoors
> trees fall down   water leaves a (place)
> windows break

In our area, there are floods. People need to stay indoors until the water leaves the streets and ...

Unit 3 31

3.2 GRAMMAR Past Perfect

I can use the Past Perfect to talk about an action before another action in the past.

1 **CLASS VOTE** Do you enjoy storms? Why? / Why not?

2 🔊 1.50 Listen and read the text. In your notebook, write three unusual facts about the color, place, and frequency of the lightning it describes.

Venezuela's Special Storms

On a stormy night in 1595, foreign sailors were preparing to attack Venezuela. People in Venezuela had seen the ships and heard about the attack. They were afraid. But when morning came, everyone was surprised. Nothing <u>had happened</u>! The sailors hadn't attacked. Why? Well, during the storm they had seen some strange pinkish lightning. The local people had experienced the lightning many times, but the sailors had felt scared. They had decided not to attack. A storm had saved Venezuela! This took place over Lake Maracaibo on the Catatumbo River. It is an area famous for its special storms. Nowadays Lake Maracaibo holds a Guinness World Record as the place with the most lightning bolts per square kilometer.

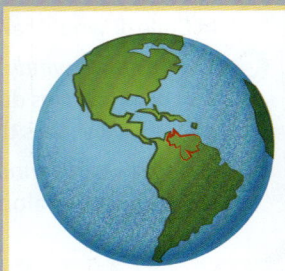

3 Study the Grammar box and complete the sentences. Then underline examples of the Past Perfect in the text.

Grammar	Past Perfect

Had you already **seen** a storm?
We **hadn't been** to Venezuela before.
People **had seen** the lightning.

We use the Past Perfect with *after*, *already*, *before*, and *yet*.

- We form the Past Perfect with the past form of _____ + the _____ of the main verb.
- The Past Perfect describes an action _____ another action in the past.

GRAMMAR TIME > PAGE 108

4 Complete the sentences with the Past Perfect.
1 The avalanche ___had started___ (start) earlier than expected.
2 It _____ (be) freezing cold for days when we arrived in New York.
3 Amy wanted to tell us the end of the movie, but we _____ (already/read) the spoilers online.
4 The movie _____ (not be) released in theaters.

5 Look at the chart. Then complete the sentences about Maria and her brother, Ryan. Use the Past Perfect.

In 2018…

	Maria	Ryan
meet their younger cousin	✓	✓
join the swim team	✓	✗
learn to code	✗	✓
start high school	✓	✗

1 Maria and Ryan ___had met___ their younger cousin.
2 Maria _____ the swim team.
3 Maria _____ to code.
4 Ryan _____ high school.

6 Use the prompts to write questions in the Past Perfect in your notebook. Then answer them.
1 Maria / start high school
Had Maria started high school?
Yes, she had.
2 Ryan / learn to code
3 Ryan / join the swim team

7 Work in pairs. Think back to the first day of this school year. What had you done before the first day? Use the options below to help you.

vacation school supplies studies
family clothes

Unit 3

3.3 READING and VOCABULARY — An online diary

I can use the title, introduction, and picture in an online diary to identify its topic and talk about culture.

1 **CLASS VOTE** What do you do when it is cold outside? Vote for the top three ideas.

2 Look at the title, introduction, and picture in the online diary. What do they tell you about its topic?

Reading tip

The title, introduction, and pictures in a text can tell you a lot about its topic. Always analyze them carefully before you start reading a text.

3 🔊 **1.51** Listen and read the diary. Then answer the questions in your notebook.
1. What did Ari's family do to feel warm? *They drink soup/kakosupa.*
2. Why do students call their teacher by his/her first name?
3. What do all young students learn to do?
4. What happened before the volcanic eruptions?
5. Where did Ari go on Saturday?
6. When can you see the Northern Lights?

---

arisolinediary.com

I love living in Iceland. I hope my diary inspires you to visit my country one day! *Ari*

Wednesday: It's the end of winter now, but it's absolutely freezing tonight, about −10°C. My sister and I did some knitting. Like all children here, we learned to knit at elementary school, but we're not very good at it. Mom makes great jumpers for us, though. I helped my dad make some *kakosupa* – it's cocoa soup, like hot chocolate – lovely, thick, and really warm!

Thursday: Our math teacher, Jakob, gave us a very difficult test this morning. By the way, I'm not completely crazy – it's normal here to use your teacher's first name, because most of us don't have a last name, we take our father's name. So, for example, my dad's name is Jón, so my sister is Eva Jónsdottir (Jón's daughter) and I'm Ari Jónsson (Jón's son).

Friday: The news programs tonight were full of information about the latest volcanic eruptions here. They were really interesting. There were a lot of small earthquakes before the eruptions. Eva found some pictures online. They are totally amazing!

Saturday: I spent the whole afternoon with my friend's family at a natural thermal pool. We didn't swim, though. We sat in the open air and talked for hours. It's a normal way to relax in Iceland.

Sunday: I took some great pictures of the Northern Lights. You can only see them when the sky is dark. Spring and fall are good times, sometime between 5 p.m. and 2 a.m., when there are no clouds. I waited for ages, and they started at about 10 p.m. It was an awesome display, and pretty long, too – about fifteen minutes.

4 **WORD FRIENDS** Look at the highlighted words in the text. Complete the chart with the correct adverb.

adverb + regular adjective		adverb + strong adjective	
very	cold	_____	freezing
	good	_____	amazing
	difficult	_____	crazy

Watch OUT! In some contexts, you can use *really* and *pretty* with both adjective types.

5 Circle the correct option.
1. Wow! The volcano is (absolutely) / very amazing!
2. These pictures are totally / very good.
3. *Kakosupa* is really / totally delicious.
4. This place is completely / very special.
5. The view is very / absolutely spectacular.

6 In your notebook, write sentences about the things below. Compare with a classmate.

- the place where you live
- a TV program
- your favorite hobby
- a food or drink

3.4 GRAMMAR Simple Past and Past Perfect

I can talk about an event in the past and what happened before it.

1 **CLASS VOTE** What's the first thing you do when you arrive home after a trip?
- eat something   take a shower   unpack my bag
- talk to friends online   fall asleep

2 🔊 1.52 Listen and read. What did Dan forget to do when he got home last night?

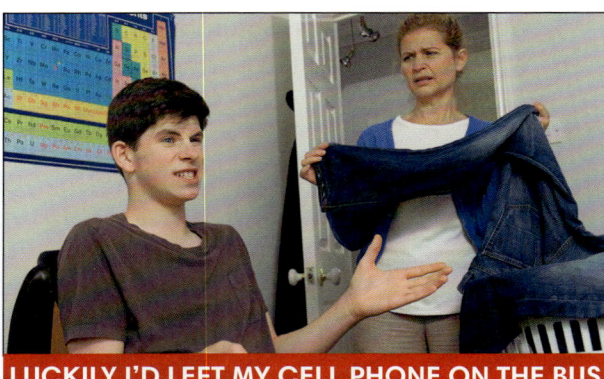

LUCKILY I'D LEFT MY CELL PHONE ON THE BUS

Mom: What's that funny smell? Ugh! Dan! You <u>didn't empty</u> your bag last night.
Dan: Oh, sorry, Mom. I thought I <u>had emptied</u> it before I went to bed. But I guess I hadn't done it …
Mom: Wait a second … these aren't your jeans.
Dan: Yeah, they're Tom's. He lent them to me because my jeans had gotten wet.
Mom: Mmhh. How …?
Dan: Oh, well, we had finished our work in the field and had decided to go for a walk when we came across a river. I'd just jumped onto a big rock when …
Mom: When you fell in?
Dan: That's right. Luckily I had left my cell phone on the bus before we got off. Can you imagine if it had gotten that wet?
Mom: Mmhh …

> *Can you imagine if …?*   **OUT of class**

3 Study the Grammar box, then circle the correct words to complete the sentences. Underline examples of the Simple Past and the Past Perfect in the dialogue.

| Grammar | Simple Past and Past Perfect |

Mark **had canceled** the party before I **arrived**. By the time the plane **landed**, the rain **had stopped**.

1 The Past Perfect always shows how an event is related to another event in the *present* / *past*.
2 Use the Past Perfect for the *earlier* / *later event* and the Simple Past for the *earlier* / *later* event.

GRAMMAR TIME > PAGE 108

4 Circle the correct option.
1 We *ate* / (*had eaten*) lunch when Dad *came* / *had come* home with pizzas.
2 The rain *had started* / *started* before we *had gotten* / *got* to the beach.
3 Emma had taken 100 pictures *after* / *by the time* we got there.
4 I *had already seen* / *already saw* the movie online when Dan *had suggested* / *suggested* watching it on TV.

5 Complete the email from Dan's brother with the Simple Past or Past Perfect forms of the verbs in parentheses.

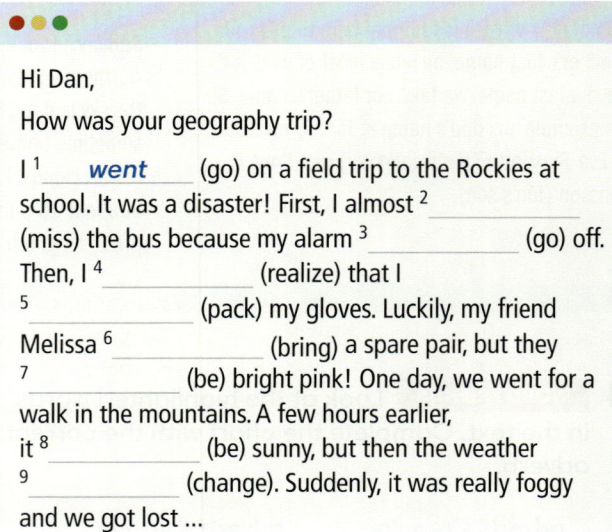

Hi Dan,
How was your geography trip?
I ¹ _went_ (go) on a field trip to the Rockies at school. It was a disaster! First, I almost ² _____ (miss) the bus because my alarm ³ _____ (go) off. Then, I ⁴ _____ (realize) that I ⁵ _____ (pack) my gloves. Luckily, my friend Melissa ⁶ _____ (bring) a spare pair, but they ⁷ _____ (be) bright pink! One day, we went for a walk in the mountains. A few hours earlier, it ⁸ _____ (be) sunny, but then the weather ⁹ _____ (change). Suddenly, it was really foggy and we got lost …

6 In pairs, discuss funny things that happened on a school field trip or on vacation.

I went skiing and fell over. I had put my skiis on the wrong way!

Unit 3

3.5 LISTENING and VOCABULARY   In the wild

I can identify specific information in a conversation and talk about being in the wild.

1 **CLASS VOTE** Do you enjoy being outdoors? Why? / Why not? Compare your ideas with the class.

2 🔊 **1.53** Look at the pictures from the *Go Wild!* camp. Decide if sentences 1–3 are true (T) or false (F). Listen and check.
1. [T] The *Go Wild!* camp is a summer camp.
2. [ ] The *Go Wild!* camp is for families.
3. [ ] The *Go Wild!* camps are in different locations.

3 🔊 **1.54** **WORD FRIENDS** Listen to Abigail telling Max about her experience with *Go Wild!* Circle the correct option.
1. (make) / build a fire
2. sit / sleep outside
3. make / build a shelter
4. learn about / listen to the wildlife
5. see / watch the stars
6. look for / find wild animals
7. grow / discover unusual plants

4 🔊 **1.55** Listen to how the words are connected in the phrases below.
1. m**a**ke **a** fire
2. slee**p o**utside
3. look for wil**d a**nimals
4. discove**r u**nusual plants

Speak UP!

5 🔊 **1.55** Listen again and repeat.

6 🔊 **1.56** Listen to Abigail and Max again. Match the activities from Activity 3 to the days of the week in Abigail's diary. There are two extra activities.

Monday	*make a shelter*
Tuesday	_____
Wednesday	_____
Thursday	_____
Friday	_____

7 🔊 **1.56** Listen once more and answer the questions in your notebook.
1. Why didn't Abigail sleep outside in the end?
2. Why didn't Abigail listen to the wildlife?
3. Why weren't there any spiders in the camp?
4. Why do you think Max has a headache?

8 🔊 **1.57** Study the Vocabulary box using a dictionary. Write the words in the correct category. Listen, check, and repeat.

Vocabulary	In the wild
bat bear cave leaf (leaves) path sky spider star sunset waterfall wildlife	

- elements of landscape: _____, _____, _____, _____, _____, _____, _____
- animals: _____, _____, _____, _____

9 **I KNOW!** Work in groups. Can you add more words to each category in Activity 6? Write them in your notebook.
- elements of landscape: *mountain, …*
- animals: *tiger, …*

10 Circle the correct option.
1. My favorite season is fall, when the *stars* / (*leaves*) fall off the trees.
2. We walked into the *cave* / *waterfall*, where it was cold and dark.
3. In the distance, there was something big and brown. A *bear* / *spider* was standing and looking at us.
4. At the end of the day, there's an amazing *path* / *sunset* over the lake.
5. The sun was shining and the *sky* / *star* was blue. It was a perfect day to go out on the boat.

11 Choose the correct verb to make the sentence true for you. Write a short paragraph. Then share it with a classmate.

I'd love/hate to go on a Go Wild! camp because …

And Y?U

Unit 3 35

3.6 SPEAKING — Criticizing

I can criticize and explain when things go wrong.

1 **CLASS VOTE** How do you feel about snakes?

I'm scared of them.   I don't like them.
I'm fine with them.   I think they're great!

WHY DID YOU DO THAT?

Dan: Phew! I ran all the way here.
Skye: But it's so hot today! What were you thinking? Do you want a drink?
Dan: Oh, yes. Thanks.
Skye: Can I introduce you to Basil?
Dan: Who's Basil?
Skye: He's my pet. Close your eyes … Surprise!
Dan: Urgh! What did you do that for? I hate snakes!
Skye: Oh, I didn't realize. I didn't mean to scare you. I brought Basil outside because I was cleaning his tank. Snakes like warm places. Twenty-nine degrees is just right. But they need a shady place to cool down.
Dan: Me too! Can we go to the pool yet?
Skye: Yes. Alisha texted. She and Tom are almost here.
Dan: Great. I brought my water gun for a water fight.
Skye: Cool. Get them when they come round the corner … ready?
Grandma: Oh! I'm soaking wet! Why did you do that?
Skye: Oh, Grandma. I'm so sorry. We thought you were Tom.
Grandma: Well, just be more careful next time!

2 🔊 **1.58** Listen and read. Answer the questions in your notebook.
1 How did Skye scare Dan?
   She showed him her pet snake.
2 Who were Skye and Dan waiting for?
3 What happened to Skye's grandmother?

3 🔊 **1.59** Complete the dialogues with the phrases from the Speaking box. Listen and check.

Speaking	Criticizing
Criticizing	**Explaining**
What did you do that for?	I didn't mean to.
Why did you do that?	I didn't realize.
What were you thinking?	I really wanted (to) …
Just be more careful next time.	I thought you were / it was …

1 A: Why did you cut in line? I was here first.
   B: Oh! I _____ to cut in. I _____ you were standing in the line.
2 A: I was so angry. I just shouted at the teacher.
   B: _____ for?
   A: I didn't see who it was. I _____ another student!
3 A: You did the wrong activity for homework! What _____?
   B: Oh, sorry!

4 In pairs, role-play the situations. Follow the instructions.
• I had an argument with a family member.
• I copied my homework from a friend.
• I didn't buy my friend a birthday gift.

A: Say what happened and give extra information.
B: Criticize your classmate's actions.
A: Explain your reasons.
B: Give your opinion or say if you understand now.

5 In pairs, tell your classmate about a time when you had a problem.

3.7 WRITING — A campaign poster

I can design a campaign poster and write a supporting text for a campaign.

1 **CLASS VOTE** Have you ever participated in a school campaign? If so, what for?

2 In pairs, look at the posters below. What do they want to achieve?

Poster 1: Some people have nothing and nowhere to go. Everybody can help. **Donate to the victims of the floods.**

Poster 2: Don't be a trash monster! Trash belongs in the trash can.

Watch OUT! In campaign posters, we often use the Imperative to encourage people to take action.

3 Read the supporting text for Dan's campaign. Which poster from Activity 2 is it about?

Poster _____

My campaign
By Dan

The purpose of this campaign is to persuade everybody at school to throw their trash in the trash can. There have been several floods in our local area this year. In my opinion, this is because there is a lot of trash on the street. Did you know that if trash blocks a street drain, the water has nowhere to go. So the water stays on the street and causes a flood. Street floods are a problem for everyone – it is a fact that people have lost furniture, cars and even their houses in floods.
To sum up, I believe that we can all do our part and make our community a better place.

4 Study the Writing box. Underline examples in the supporting text.

Writing — A supporting text for a campaign

Introducing a campaign
The purpose of this campaign is …
This campaign is for/against …

Expressing your opinion
In my opinion, …
I believe that …

Giving facts
Did you know that …?
It is a fact that …

Summarizing
In conclusion …
To sum up …
In summary, …

5 Design a campaign poster and write a short supporting text for the campaign. **Writing Time**

1. **Find ideas**
Choose a topic for your campaign. Think about what needs to change around your school or where you live. Take notes in your notebook. If possible, find some facts to include in your text.

2. **Draft**
Come up with a strong message and a powerful image (drawing or picture) for your poster, and write a draft of the supporting text. Use the Writing box to help you. Remember to keep the poster message brief. Try to use the Imperative.

3. **Share**
Share your drafts (poster and text) with another student for feedback. Listen to his/her opinion and suggestions. Check the spelling and grammar.

4. **Check and write**
Make changes to your poster and supporting text. Is language use correct? Design the final version of your poster and write the final version of your supporting text.

WORDLIST
Weather | Temperature | Natural disasters | In the wild

Antarctica [n]	icy [adj]	summer [n]
area [n]	island [n]	sun [adj]
avalanche [n]	lake [n]	sunny [adj]
bat [n]	land [n]	sunset [n]
beach [n]	landscape [n]	sunshine [n]
bear [n]	leaf (leaves) [n]	supporting text [n]
boiling [adj]	light [n]	temperature [n]
camp [v]	lightning [n]	thermal pool [n]
campaign [n]	lightning bolt [n]	thick [adj]
cave [n]	mild [adj]	thunder [n]
chilly [adj]	minus [prep]	tsunami [n]
cloud [n]	mountain [n]	volcanic eruption [n]
cloudy [adj]	move [v]	warm [adj]
coast [n]	natural disaster [n]	waterfall [n]
cold [adj]	Northern Lights [n]	water fight [n]
column [n]	open air [n]	wave [n]
conditions [n]	outdoor [adj]	wet [adj]
cool [adj]	path [n]	wild [adj]
create [v]	plants [n]	wildlife [n]
degrees [n]	rain [n]	wind [n]
desert [n]	rainy [adj]	windy [adj]
drought [n]	river [n]	winter [n]
dry [adj]	rocks [n]	
dust [n]	sailor [n]	
earthquake [n]	sand [n]	
erupt [v]	save [v]	
fall [n]	season [n]	
fire [n]	shady [adj]	
flood [n]	shallow [adj]	
fog [n]	sky [n]	
foggy [adj]	snake [n]	
freezing [adj]	snow [adj]	
grow [v]	snowman [n]	
ground [n]	snowy [adj]	
happen [v]	spider [n]	
hot [adj]	spring [n]	
hurricane [n]	star [n]	
ice [n]	storm [n]	
Iceland [n]	stormy [adj]	

WORD FRIENDS
absolutely freezing
completely crazy
pretty long
really interesting
totally amazing
very difficult
soaking wet
weather forecast
make/build a fire
sit/sleep outside
make/build a shelter
learn about/listen to the birds
see/watch the stars
look for/find wild animals
grow/discover unusual plants

VOCABULARY IN ACTION

1 Use the Wordlist to find and write in your notebook:
1. five weather words *cloud, ...*
2. three words to describe temperature
3. four natural disasters
4. three things you can do outdoors
5. three countries

2 In pairs, use the Wordlist to discuss things that are:
1. totally amazing
2. completely crazy
3. very difficult
4. absolutely freezing

3 In your notebook, write sentences with three words and/or phrases from the Wordlist.

4 1.60 **PRONUNCIATION** Listen and underline the stress in the sentences below. Where does the stress fall when there is just an adjective, and where does it fall when there is an adverb with the adjective?

It was freezing in the park.
It was absolutely freezing in the park.

5 1.61 Listen and repeat.

That test was really difficult.
My hair is soaking wet.
I think he's really interesting.
What a totally amazing party!

SELF-CHECK

1 Write the correct word for each definition.
1. A small creature with eight legs.
   s _p_ _i_ _d_ _e_ _r_
2. A very cold area around the South Pole.
   A _ _ _ _ _ _ _ _ _ _
3. A natural disaster that makes the land move.
   e _ _ _ _ _ _ _ _ _ _
4. A storm with very strong, fast winds.
   h _ _ _ _ _ _ _ _ _
5. Very hot. b _ _ _ _ _ _ _
6. Animals and plants that live in natural conditions. w _ _ _ _ _ _ _ _

2 Look at the pictures and write the words.

1. _clouds/cloudy_   2. _____   3. _____
4. _____   5. _____   6. _____

3 Complete the text with the Past Perfect form of the verbs in parentheses.

Hi Dan,
I had an amazing time in Turkey. We only spent four days there, but by the end of the trip I ¹ _had visited_ (visit) a thermal pool and ² _____ (have) a special Turkish massage. I ³ _____ (watch) the sunset on the beach. Dad and I ⁴ _____ (make) a fire. Oh, and I ⁵ _____ (try) lots of different Turkish foods! Unfortunately, I ⁶ _____ (not go) sightseeing and I ⁷ _____ (not meet) any local people. How was your trip?
See you soon,
Anna

4 Complete the sentences with the Past Perfect form of the verbs in parentheses.
1. It _hadn't started_ (not start) to snow when I _left_ (leave) the house.
2. When I _____ (find) Jack and Emma, they _____ (already/make) a shelter.
3. We _____ (not see) bears before until we _____ (travel) across Canada.
4. The family _____ (already/eat) breakfast when the tsunami _____ (happen).
5. We _____ (hear) some strange noises when we _____ (decide) to go outdoors.

5 Complete the dialogues with the phrases below.

> I thought it was mine.   What did you do that for?
> Just be more careful next time.   I didn't mean to.

A: Hey, you've written in my notebook.
¹ _____.
B: Sorry, ² _____ because it's the same color.
A: You left your new cell phone at school!
B: ³ _____ But it's OK. Gemma has it.
A: ⁴ _____.

6 In pairs, role-play the situations below.
- I borrowed my friend's jacket and now it's dirty.
- I forgot to invite a friend to my party.

7 🔊 1.62 Listen, then listen again and write down what you hear.

_____
_____
_____
_____

SELF-ASSESSMENT Think about this unit. What did you learn? What do you need help with?

4 The big game!

VOCABULARY
Sports | Sports events | Phrasal verbs with *up*

GRAMMAR
The future: *will*/*going to*/Present Continuous/Simple Present | First Conditional + *if*/*unless*

Grammar:
We're having a competition. Look at the picture. What are Tom and Skye holding? Why?

Speaking:
What are you up to?

4.1 VOCABULARY Sports and sports events

I can talk about sports and sports events.

MAYFIELD SUMMER SPORTS CAMPS
Click on an icon to find out more.

1 **CLASS VOTE** In groups, suggest the names of three athletes for "sports personality of the year" in your country. Compare your ideas with the class and vote for the top athlete.

2 🔊 **1.63** Study Vocabulary A box. Match the pictures to the names of sports. Then listen, check, and repeat.

Vocabulary A		Sports					
badminton	☐	basketball	6	climbing	☐	diving	☐
gymnastics	☐	handball	☐	horseback riding	☐	ice hockey	☐
ice-skating	☐	kayaking	☐	skateboarding	☐	snowboarding	☐
surfing	☐	table tennis	☐	volleyball	☐	yoga	☐

3 🔊 **1.64** Listen to people taking part in the Mayfield Sports Camp. Complete the blanks with the names of sports.

1. Katia _diving_
2. Max and Heather _____
3. The red and blue teams _____
4. The green team _____
5. Alexia and Tim _____
6. Leo _____

4 **I KNOW!** How many words can you add to Vocabulary A box in two minutes? Write in your notebook.

5 Use Vocabulary A box and the words from Activity 4 to give three examples of each type of sport.

- indoor sports
- outdoor sports
- team sports
- individual sports
- water sports
- winter sports

6 🔊 **1.65** **WORD FRIENDS** In your notebook, write the activities that go with verbs 1-6. Listen and check.

> a sport (x2)   ball games or competitive games
> ~~soccer practice~~   karate, yoga, gymnastics
> swimming, walking, climbing, skiing

1 have *soccer practice*
2 do
3 play
4 go
5 practice
6 take up

7 In your notebook, write sports from Vocabulary A box (or your own list) that …
- you play or do in your PE classes.
- you practice outside school.
- you watch on TV.
- you would like to take up in the future.

8 🔊 **1.66** Study Vocabulary B box. Listen and repeat the words. Then circle the words you can see in the pictures in Activities 8 and 9.

Vocabulary B	Sports events
fans field game goal locker room mascot score scoreboard seats stadium team uniform	

Stadium tour

Meet Super Duck!

9 🔊 **1.67** Complete the text with words from Vocabulary B box. Listen and check.

Mascot for the day!

Yesterday afternoon I was a mascot for the English soccer ¹ *team*. There were twelve of us – mascots, boys and girls, – and we had a tour of the famous Wembley ² _____ in London in the morning. Before the game, we went to get ready in the ³ _____.

I was very excited because they gave each of us a gift, a new white-and-red ⁴ _____ to wear!

Finally, we walked along the tunnel in pairs, with each mascot next to a player. Then we came into the stadium, and we stood on the beautiful green ⁵ _____. The crowd made a lot of noise because there were thousands of ⁶ _____. When the game started, we sat in special ⁷ _____ at the front. By the end of the game, the score on the big ⁸ _____ was 2–1. England won!

10 Would you like to be a team mascot? Why? / Why not? What sport and what team would you choose?

And YOU

I'd like to be a team mascot because I'm a big sports fan. I'd be a soccer mascot for my favorite team, FC Barcelona.

Unit 4

4.2 GRAMMAR The future: *will/going to*/Present Continuous/Simple Present

I can talk about plans, predictions, arrangements, and schedules.

1 **CLASS VOTE** Do you regularly practice sports or exercise at home?

2 🔊 **1.68** Listen and read. What sports do Tom and Skye mention?

Skye: Oh, you've got weights. Cool!
Tom: Yeah, we're having a competition at the kayak club next month. I'll be one of the youngest, so I'm going to prepare well for it.
Skye: They aren't very heavy!
Tom: They don't have to be heavy, but you have to use them every day. It doesn't take long. Look, I'll show you. You lift your arms like this, and repeat about ten times.
Skye: Here, let me have a quick go. Hey, my swimming practice starts next week. These exercises will help.
Tom: Why don't you stay and do some more?
Skye: Sorry, Tom, I can't. I'm meeting Dan for a run.
Tom: Oh, OK, I'll exercise by myself, then. Catch you later!

WE'RE HAVING A COMPETITION

Watch OUT!
🇬🇧 You've got 🇺🇸 You have

3 Study the Grammar box, then match A–D to 1–4. Underline different ways of talking about the future in the dialogue.

A *will* + verb | B *going to* + verb
C Present Continuous | D Simple Present

Grammar	The future *will/going to*/Present Continuous/Simple Present
1 **D**	**Predictions/Decisions made at the moment of speaking** **I'll exercise** by myself, then.
2 ☐	**Plans/Predictions based on what we know now** She'**s going to** train for the competition.
3 ☐	**Arrangements** We'**re having** a sports day at school on Tuesday.
4 ☐	**Scheduled activities** The judo classes for beginners **start** next month.

GRAMMAR TIME > PAGE 109

4 Complete the sentences with the future form of the verbs in parentheses.

1. Next year, the soccer club _is going to have_ (have) new locker rooms. GOING TO
2. The fans _____ (not be) happy with the result. WILL
3. The basketball game _____ (start) in ten minutes. SIMPLE PRESENT
4. We _____ (go) to Nick's house after the game. PRESENT CONTINUOUS
5. _____ (you/buy) your tickets for the game online? GOING TO

5 Complete the text with the words below.

> are offering   ~~are you doing~~
> begins   is going to help
> will be   will need   won't have

What ¹ *are you doing* this summer? If you don't have any plans, join us at your local park. Fitness in the Park is a new idea that ² _____ you to get fit and make friends. The fun ³ _____ on June 10 with a special yoga class for beginners. All you ⁴ _____ is comfortable clothes and a bottle of water. Each day for four weeks we ⁵ _____ a different activity for you to try. We think it ⁶ _____ the best summer ever! Don't miss out. We ⁷ _____ enough places for everyone.

6 In your notebook, complete the sentences to make them true for you. Compare with a classmate. **And YOU**

1. Tonight I'm going to …
2. Tomorrow the weather will be …
3. In 2050, I will …
4. When I'm 18, I won't …

Unit 4

4.3 READING and VOCABULARY   A case study

I can find specific information in a case study and talk about volunteering at a sports event.

1 **CLASS VOTE** Do you regularly go to sports events? What is the most popular event in your region?

2 Read the website. When is the Force4Sport festival?

Force4Sport

You're not into sports, but you like watching them. Why not <u>take up</u> volunteer work at the Force4Sport summer festival? You decide the hours you want to volunteer and the job you'd like to do – from helping competitors to <u>cleaning up</u> the stadium. Click on our <u>case studies</u> to find out more.

3 🔊 1.69 Look at the volunteer's pass. Then listen and read the case study. Complete blanks 1–6 in the pass.

Volunteer's PASS

Name: Danielle Marley   Age: 16
Type of event: ¹ *gymnastics competition*
Start date for the event: ² _____
Length of competition: ³ _____
No. of days as volunteer: ⁴ _____
Volunteer role: set up spectators' area and
⁵ _____
Previous experience: ⁶ _____

Reading tip

To find specific information in a text in order to do an activity, read the items in the activity before reading the text. Predict the type of information you'll need to look for.

4 **PHRASAL VERBS** 🔊 1.70 Look at the Vocabulary box, then listen and repeat the words. Underline them in the texts in Activities 2 and 3.

Vocabulary	Phrasal verbs with *up*
clean up end up give up	
pick up set up take up	

5 Use the phrasal verbs in Activity 4 to complete the sentences.

1. Let's ___set up___ a gym in the garage and we can train there.
2. I don't want to _____ horseback riding, but it is very expensive.
3. The team isn't doing well. They could _____ losing the game.
4. Emma loves trying new sports. She's just decided to _____ karate.
5. I have to _____ the tickets. I paid online and they're at the ticket office.
6. There are clothes all over the floor. I want everybody to _____ the locker room.

Danielle Marley, 16

My cousins volunteered two years ago and talked non-stop about it. I <u>ended up</u> applying to volunteer this year and I'm really excited. I'm going to help at a gymnastics competition at our local sports stadium. I did gymnastics when I was younger, but gave up a few years ago because I didn't have enough time. The event starts on July 17 and it lasts for two weeks. I'm only doing the first week, from Monday to Friday. On the first day I'm going to help set up the spectators' area. After that, I'm going to take pictures for the website. I'll have a digital camera to take action shots and some team pictures. I'm picking it up this afternoon, so that I can practice with it. I've already won photography competitions, so I think I'll do a good job. I'm excited about volunteering because I enjoy watching sports. Force4Sport will be "the" sports event this summer!

6 **And YOU?** Would you like to be a volunteer at a sports event? Use the ideas below to write true sentences in your notebook. Share your ideas with your classmates.

I would/wouldn't like to be a volunteer because …

- watch/learn about different sports
- get free tickets
- take great pictures
- crowds at the stadium
- not earn money for hard work

Unit 4   43

4.4 GRAMMAR — First Conditional

I can talk about possible situations in the present and future.

1 Work in pairs. Look at the picture in Activity 2. Use the words below to describe what the girl is doing.

> walk   fall   balance   rope

2 🔊 **1.71** Listen and read the poster. Who is slacklining perfect for?

SLACKLINING CLUB

Have you ever thought of slacklining?

If you like gymnastics, you'll love this modern sport! The only equipment you need is a rope or "line" about five centimeters wide. Place line about 50 centimeters above the ground. If you fall, you won't hurt yourself, and if you improve, you will try some new tricks. You can do slacklining anywhere, but you need a tree or something strong to fix the line.

Are you a climber, a surfer, or a skateboarder? Slacklining can help your balance. Also, if you don't enjoy team sports, this will be a good choice for you. So, if you want to try something different, come along. Will you like this sport? You won't know unless you try!

WHERE? Greendale Park
WHEN? Saturdays, at 3 p.m.

---

3 Study the Grammar box, then complete the sentence. Then underline examples of First Conditional structures in the poster.

> **Grammar** — First Conditional + *if/unless*
>
> You **won't know if** you **don't try**!
> You **won't know unless** you **try**!
>
> Time clauses with *when* are constructed similarly.
> **When I'm** back home, **I'll watch** some slacklining videos.
> Use *unless* + a verb in the _____ form to have a similar meaning to *if* + verb in the negative form.
>
> GRAMMAR TIME > PAGE 109

4 Match phrases 1–4 to phrases a–d to make sentences.

1. [c] If you do slacklining, …
2. [ ] You won't do any special tricks …
3. [ ] I won't go to the slacklining club …
4. [ ] You'll see people slacklining …

a unless you're very good.
b if you go to the park on Saturday.
c you will improve your balance.
d unless a friend comes, too.

5 Read the news headline and complete the sentences with the correct form of the verbs in parentheses.

> **Riverside Sports Center to close next week for renovation work!**

1. If they ____*close*____ (close) the sports center, we ____*won't play*____ (not play) handball for ages!
2. I _____ (not stop) playing badminton if they close it.
3. We _____ (not have) karate practice unless the teacher _____ (find) a new place.
4. I _____ (go) swimming every week if they _____ (build) a pool at the new center.
5. If there _____ (be) tennis courts, I _____ (take up) tennis.
6. We _____ (join) the new gym if it _____ (not be) too expensive.

6 **And YOU?** In your notebook, finish the sentences to make them true for you. In pairs, discuss your ideas.

> What will you do if there's a new sports center in town?
>
> I'll take up tennis.

1. If there's a new sports center in town, …
2. If my friends are free tonight, …
3. If I get some money for my birthday, …
4. I … unless the weather's nice on the weekend.

Unit 4

4.5 LISTENING and VOCABULARY A young soccer player

I can identify specific information in a podcast and in a conversation, and talk about sports practice.

1 **CLASS VOTE** Should a 16-year-old play sport professionally or wait until he or she is older? Why?

2 🔊 **1.72** Listen to the sports podcast. Circle the correct answers.

1 What number soccer shirt did Tom Santana play for Brazil in?

A 19   B 76   C 36

2 What does he like to do in soccer?

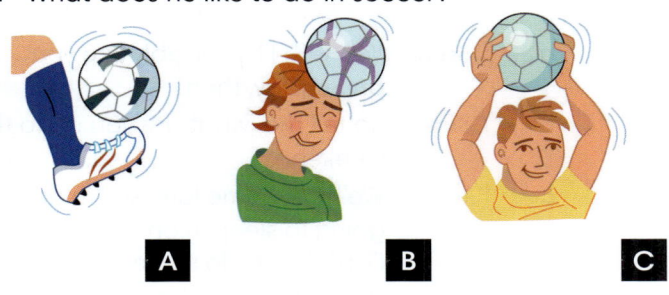

A   B   C

3 🔊 **1.73** Listen to Avril and Ben talking about Tom Santana. Mark the sentences true (T) or false (F). Correct the false sentences in your notebook.

1 [T] Ben would be afraid to live in a different country.
2 [ ] Avril thinks Tom will learn Spanish quickly because he'll take up classes.
3 [ ] Tom will have lots of free time when he finishes soccer practice.
4 [ ] Ben thinks it will be difficult for Tom to be without his family.
5 [ ] Tom's dad is going to be his coach.
6 [ ] Ben says Tom will be rich if he plays well.

4 🔊 **1.57** Listen again to three sentences from the dialogue in Activity 3, paying attention to how the contracted form of *will* is pronounced. Then listen once more and repeat.

Speak UP!

1 He'll have to leave his country.
2 That'll be quick because he'll be with Spanish people all day.
3 If he scores lots of goals, he'll earn lots of money.

5 **WORD BUILDING** Study the chart and read the sentences below. Write *V* if the underlined word is a verb, *NA* if it is a noun (action), and *NP* if it is a noun (person).

Verb	Noun (action)	Noun (person)
train	training	trainer
run	running	runner
play	–	player
practice	practice	–
coach	–	coach
race	race	–
score	score	–
kick	kick	–

1 Jack was too tired to finish the <u>race</u>. *NA*
2 Do you know who <u>scored</u> the goals? ___
3 There's no volleyball <u>practice</u> today. ___
4 The team is <u>practicing</u> very hard. ___
5 Their <u>coach</u> doesn't look very happy. ___
6 He's useless! He can't <u>kick</u> the ball at all. ___

6 Complete the text with one word in each blank. Use Activity 5 to help you.

Interschool Handball Victory 28–33

Well done to all handball ¹p_players_ who joined us on Saturday! It was a great game and an amazing ²s_____. Handball ³p_____ will be on Tuesday next week. As you know, Ms. Taylor will ⁴c_____ the team from now on. She would also like to offer extra ⁵p_____ on Saturdays for anybody who is interested.

7 Imagine you are an athlete. Would you like to practice/play in a different country? Discuss in pairs. Use the ideas below to help you.

And YOU

- family and friends
- earn money
- the weather
- meet other teams/players
- learn another language

I wouldn't like to …
It would be nice to …

Unit 4

4.6 SPEAKING — Talking about plans

I can ask and talk about plans.

1 In pairs, look at the picture. What do you think is happening?

2 🔊 1.74 Listen and read, then check your answer to Activity 1. Mark the sentences true (T) or false (F).
1. [F] Dan is going to run.
2. [ ] The event isn't a competition.
3. [ ] There will be two hundred volunteers.

WHAT ARE YOU UP TO?

Alisha: So, is this the Wild Run course you organized?
Dan: Yep. Well, a lot of people helped, of course.
Alisha: Well done! But why is it called a Wild Run? I hope there aren't any wild animals?
Dan: Of course not! It's just a fun run! What are you up to before it starts?
Alisha: Not a lot.
Dan: Well, if you come with me, I'll explain it all. Over two hundred people are running here later, so I need to check everything. First, they're going under a net.
Alisha: Seriously? It's really muddy!
Dan: Yeah. Try it! Yeah, that's it.
Alisha: Well, if they don't like dirt, they won't enjoy this run!
Dan: Come on. Then they're crossing a stream and running up that hill.
Alisha: Oh, no! It's fun, but I'm tired already! What happens after the run?
Dan: Well, when you all finish, we'll give you a medal. Then we're going to have a barbecue.
Alisha: Great. I'll need a medal. Wish me luck!

3 🔊 1.75 Study the Speaking box. Then order the sentences below. Listen and check.

Speaking — Talking about plans

Asking
What are you up to today/on the weekend?
Do you have plans for tonight/after the run?
What are you doing on Sunday/next Monday?

Answering and following up
I'm visiting my grandma/going to the movies.
First (of all) I'm going to/I'm seeing …
Then … / After that … / Later …
I don't have any plans. / I don't know yet.
What about you?
And you?
What are your plans?

a [ ] Sam: Yes, OK. I'll probably see you on Sunday, then.
b [1] Sam: So tell me, what are you up to this weekend?
c [ ] Tara: We'll get home late, so I'm definitely going to sleep in on Sunday … Then I'll probably do some homework. We could go to the movies after that, if you like?
d [ ] Tara: Well, first I'm visiting my grandparents on Saturday morning. Then we're going to a basketball game together. It starts at 4 p.m.
e [ ] Sam: That's nice. Do you have any plans after that?

4 In pairs, ask and answer questions about your plans for the weekend. Use the ideas below to help you.
- sports and activities
- family and friends
- homework
- trips
- shopping
- relaxation
- entertainment
- special events

And YOU?

5 Tell the class about some of your classmate's plans.

Linda is going to see her friends on Saturday afternoon. Then they're going to the shopping mall in the evening.

4.7 WRITING — A message making a request

I can write messages and make requests.

1 **CLASS VOTE** How do you and your friends usually send messages to each other? How long does it usually take you to reply?

> text messages   emails   notes on paper
> posts/messages on social media
> audio messages

2 Read the texts. What types of messages are they?

1 _____
2 _____

1
> Hey! Thanks 4 your help on Saturday. I had a gr8 time at the race, but it was fast! Glad I trained 4 it. Left my sneakers in the locker room :(Would u mind keeping them at your house? If it's OK with u, I'll pick them up on the weekend. Skye

2

GROUP CHAT

Hi,

Just a quick message to thank you all for competing on Saturday. More than 200 runners entered the race and we think everybody enjoyed themselves. We're now planning another race, which will take place at Northfield Park next month. Details will be on our website soon. I also have some great pictures of the event. If you'd like a picture of you with your medal, could you please send it before June 30?

All the best,

Dan

2 mins ...

3 Read the messages again and answer the questions.

1   What does Dan want the runners to do?
_____
2   What does Skye want Dan to do?
_____

4 Order the information in Skye's message.

☐ Skye asks Dan to do something.
☐ Skye introduces the topic of the race.
[1] Skye thanks Dan.

5 Study the Writing box. Underline the phrases from it in the texts in Activity 2.

Writing | A message making a request

Greeting
Hi ... / Hi, there / Hiya / Hey ...

Thank the other person
Thanks for your note/message/gift ...
Thanks for inviting me/writing/sending/coming ...
Just a quick message to thank you for ...

Introduce the topic
I had a great time at the race ...
I really enjoyed meeting the ...

Making a request
If you'd like ..., could you please ... ?
Would you mind ... ?
If it's OK with you, could we ... ?
Would it be possible to ... ?
Let me know if that's OK.

Ending
Bye! / See you! / All the best. / See you later.

---

6 You were a runner at the Wild Run. Write a private message to Dan.

Writing Time

1 ❗ **Find ideas**
In your notebook, take notes about how you could ...
1   thank Dan for his message
2   describe what you did at the race
3   ask him to do something for you

2 📄 **Draft**
Write a draft of your message. Use the Writing box to help you. Pay attention to the structure of your text.

3 🔗 **Share**
Share your note with another student for feedback. Listen to his/her opinion and suggestions. Check the spelling and grammar.

4 ✅ **Check and write**
Make changes to your message. Write the final version of your text.

Unit 4

WORDLIST

Sports | Sports events | Phrasal verbs with *up*

athlete [n]
badminton [n]
balance [n]
basketball [n]
clean up [phr v]
climbing [n]
coach [v/n]
compete [v]
competition [n]
competitor [n]
crowd [n]
diving [n]
end up [ph v]
equipment [n]
event [n]
exercise [n]
fall [v/n]
fan [n]
field [n]
fitness [n]
game [n]
get fit [phrase]
give up [phr v]
goal [n]
gym [n]
gymnastics [n]
handball [n]
head a ball [phr v]
horseback riding [n]
ice hockey [n]
ice-skating [n]
improve [v]
individual sports [n]
indoor sports [n]
judo [n]
karate [n]

kayaking [n]
kick [v/n]
lead (in the lead) [n]
lift [v]
locker room [n]
lose [v]
mascot [n]
medal [n]
net [n]
outdoor sports [n]
PE [n]
pick up [phr v]
play [v]
player [n]
pool [n]
practice [n]
race [v/n]
register [v]
rope [n]
run [v/n]
runner [n]
running [n]
score [v/n]
scoreboard [n]
screen [n]
seat [n]
set up [phr v]
skateboarder [n]
skateboarding [n]
skiing [n]
slackline [n]
soccer shirt [n]
sneakers [n]
snowboarding [n]
spectator [n]
sports camp [n]

sports center [n]
sports festival [n]
stadium [n]
surfer [n]
surfing [n]
swimming [n]
table tennis [n]
take up [n]
team [n]
team sports [n]
tennis court [n]
ticket [n]
train [v]
trainer [n]
training [n]
tricks [n]
uniform [n]
volleyball [n]
volunteer [v/n]
walking [n]
water sports [n]
weights [n]
whistle [n]
win [v]
winter sports [n]
yoga [n]

WORD FRIENDS

do karate, yoga, gymnastics
go swimming, walking, climbing, skiing
have (a sport) practice
play ball games or competitive games
practice (a sport)
take up (a sport)

VOCABULARY IN ACTION

1 Use the Wordlist to find and write in your notebook:
  1 five places where you can do sports
     gym, ...
  2 six different people
  3 three sports for which you need a ball
  4 two pieces of sports equipment
  5 two things you wear to do sports
  6 three types of sports
  7 three verbs that are the same as nouns

2 In pairs, ask your classmate about the spelling of one word in each category in Activity 1.

  How do you spell "weights"?

  It's W-E-I-G-H-T-S.

3 Circle the correct option. Use the Wordlist to check your answers. In pairs, say if the sentences are true for you.
  1 I often (go) / *play* swimming.
  2 I never *take up* / *have* any new sports.
  3 I sometimes *go* / *play* basketball at school.
  4 I'd like to *do* / *have* karate.
  5 I *go* / *have* swim practice twice a week.

4 🔊 1.76 **PRONUNCIATION** Look at the underlined vowels in each word. Do you think we say them as one syllable or two? Listen and check.

c**oa**ch   g**oa**l   tr**ai**ner   w**ei**ght   s**ea**t   t**ea**m

Unit 4

SELF-CHECK

1 Write the correct word for each definition.
1. This person can work at events, but isn't paid any money. **v o l u n t e e r**
2. You can sit on this in a stadium, movie, or theater. **s _ _ _ _**
3. If you want to be good at a sport, you must do this: **p _ _ _ _ _ _ _ _**
4. This is the object which shows spectators how each person or team is doing. **s _ _ _ _ _ _ _ _ _ _ _**
5. If you win a race, you get this. **m _ _ _ _ _**

2 Read the word groups. Choose the odd one out. Give a reason for your decision.

1	player	competitor	coach	(score)
2	karate	tennis	volleyball	soccer
3	do karate	practice judo	play volleyball	give up tennis
4	kayaking	horseback riding	diving	swimming
5	net	race	uniform	ball

3 Complete the sentences with the future form of the verbs in parentheses. Match the sentences to their function below.
1. [c] I _won't get_ (not get) a medal, but I hope to do well. (WILL)
2. [ ] My favorite team _____ (play) at the stadium on Saturday. (GOING TO)
3. [ ] The karate class _____ (finish) at 8 p.m. (SIMPLE PRESENT)
4. [ ] _____ (come) to the championship final next week? (PRESENT CONTINUOUS)
5. [ ] Thank you! I'll be happy to come. I _____ (get) the tickets for us all, then. (WILL)

a plan
b decision at the moment of speaking
c prediction
d arrangement
e timetable

4 Complete the questions with the correct forms of the verbs in parentheses.
1. What sport will you try if you _____ (go) to summer sports camp?
2. Will you meet me when school _____ (finish)?
3. If you _____ (have) some free time during the winter, where will you go?
4. What will you do if someone _____ (give) you some money for your birthday?

5 Circle the correct option.

A: What are you doing for Sports Day tomorrow?
B: ¹(First) / Then I'm watching the races. ²Then / Later I'm taking part in a soccer game. After that I'm going to try karate, I think. What about you?
A: ³Then / First I'm taking part in the street dance display. ⁴First / After that I'm not sure. I'll probably watch the volleyball competition ⁵later / then.
B: What are your plans for the evening?
A: I'm definitely going to take part in the sports quiz. And you?
B: I'm playing live music with one of the bands. ⁶First / Then I'll probably go to the barbecue, too.

6 In pairs, make your own dialogue. Use the language in Activity 5 and the sports day program.

School sports day

Time	Events	Display
3 p.m.	soccer competition	skateboard display
4 p.m.	volleyball competition	gymnastics display
5 p.m.	try-it-yourself sessions: karate slacklining yoga skateboarding	
Evening 6 p.m. – 8 p.m.	live music with school bands barbecue sports quiz (teams of four–six people)	

7 🔊 1.77 Listen, then listen again and write down what you hear.

_____
_____
_____
_____
_____
_____
_____

SELF-ASSESSMENT Think about this unit. What did you learn? What do you need help with?

5 See the world!

VOCABULARY
Types of vacation | At the hotel |
Equipment | Travel: confusing words

GRAMMAR
Modal verbs: obligation, prohibition, and advice | Modal verbs: speculation |
Time clauses

Grammar:
When should we go?
Look at the picture. What are Skye and her Grandma talking about?

Speaking:
I didn't catch that!
Look at Dan. What is he doing? Why?

5.1 VOCABULARY Travel
I can talk about vacations and traveling.

1 **I KNOW!** How do you prefer to travel? Look at the pictures below. How many types of transportation can you name for each? Make a list in your notebook.

by sea    by road    by rail    by air

Watch OUT! We say *by sea/road/rail/air* and *by boat/car/bus/train/plane*, but **on** *foot*.

2 Match questions 1–5 to responses a–e. In pairs, ask and answer the questions.

Speaking   Traveling phrases

1 ☐ Excuse me, is the bus/train station near here?
2 ☐ What time does the bus/train arrive/leave?
3 ☐ What platform does the train arrive at/leave from?
4 ☐ Excuse me, how do I get to the airport?
5 [a] I'd like a bus/train ticket to Paris, please.

a Single or return?
b At 9:15 a.m.
c There's a bus service every half hour.
d Platform 6.
e Yes, it's at the end of the road.

3 🔊 2.01 Study Vocabulary A box. Match the words to pictures 1–7. Then listen, check, and repeat.

Vocabulary A   Types of vacations

☐ activity camp   [1] backpacking vacation   ☐ beach vacation
☐ camping trip   ☐ city break   ☐ cruise   ☐ sightseeing vacation

50 Unit 5

My travel blog

4 🔊 **2.02** Listen and match dialogues 1–5 to the types of vacations in Vocabulary A box.

1 _backpacking vacation_ 2 _____
3 _____ 4 _____
5 _____

5 In pairs, describe:
1 three things to do at an activity camp.
2 four countries to visit on a cruise.
3 three things to see on a sightseeing vacation.

6 🔊 **2.03** Study Vocabulary B box. Use the words to complete the text. Listen and check.

Vocabulary B	At the hotel

check in/out   double room(s)   facilities   floor   guests
pool   ~~reception~~   reservation   single room(s)   view

We arrived late last night at the hotel. Nobody was working in the ¹ _reception_, so we couldn't ² _____ to our rooms. In the end, Mom called the hotel from her cell phone! The manager arrived, but there was a problem with our ³ _____. We needed two ⁴ _____ because there are four of us, but the hotel only had two ⁵ _____.

In the end, we found us another hotel and here we are, in a better place! We're on the top ⁶ _____ and there's a beautiful ⁷ _____ of the city. It has great ⁸ _____ and I can't wait to use the ⁹ _____ and the gym. There are lots of ¹⁰ _____ and they're all speaking different languages ... I'm very excited to be here!

7 In pairs, discuss the last time you traveled. Use the questions below to help you.
- Where did you go?
- Where did you stay?
- What facilities were there?

I went to Buenos Aires with my family and we stayed in a big hotel. We had a view of the city, but we didn't have a pool.

8 🔊 **2.04** Study Vocabulary C box using a dictionary. Listen and repeat the words. Then describe them in pairs.

Vocabulary C	Equipment

backpack   flashlight   guidebook
map   passport   sleeping bag
suitcase   sunscreen   sunglasses   tent

A: _This has your personal information and a picture, and you must take it when you travel to another country ..._
B: _It's a passport!_

9 Work in pairs. Choose a vacation from the options below. In your notebook, make a list of things you should take with you.
- a backpacking vacation with friends
- a city break in Rome
- a cruise around the Caribbean
- an activity camp in the mountains

Unit 5

5.2 GRAMMAR Modal verbs for obligation, prohibition, and advice: *must, have to, ought to, should*

I can talk about obligation and prohibition, and give advice.

1 **CLASS VOTE** How important is good weather on vacation?

2 🔊 **2.05** Listen and read. Why is Skye disappointed?

_____
_____

Grandma: Skye, we ought to talk about our visit to New Zealand.
Skye: Have you bought the plane tickets yet?
Grandma: No, I'll get them soon, but I have to know the exact date you finish school.
Skye: Classes finish on 16 June, but I have to be here for Sue's birthday party on 29 July.
Grandma: Yes. You must not miss that! Should we go the first week of July, then?
Skye: Perfect. Do Mom and Dad have to work in July?
Grandma: They don't have to work every day. It rains a lot in July, so they ought to have some free time to be with us.
Skye: Wait a second. What do you mean, it rains? I wanted a beach vacation.
Grandma: Sorry, Skye. In July it's winter in New Zealand.

WHEN SHOULD WE GO?

OUT of class
🇬🇧 16 June   29 July
🇺🇸 June 16   July 29

3 Study the Grammar box, then complete the headings with the words below. Underline examples of modal verbs used for obligation and prohibition in the dialogue.

| advice   lack of obligation   obligation and prohibition |

Grammar Modal verbs – *must, have to, ought to, should*

_____
You **must** visit us in Miami.
You'll **have to** take warm clothes.
You **must not** be late for the flight.

_____
We **ought to** ask them about their plans.
You **shouldn't** take too much luggage.

_____
They **don't have to** go by car.

GRAMMAR TIME > PAGE 110

4 Circle the correct option.
1 I'm going to China soon. I (*have to*) / *must not* buy a guidebook.
2 You can never find your passport. You *should* / *shouldn't* put it in a safe place.
3 *Do we have to* / *Should we* get a visa to travel to France?
4 The plane leaves at 9 a.m., but we *must not* / *don't have to* be there until 7 a.m.
5 I *shouldn't* / *ought to* pack my bags. We leave in an hour.
6 It's going to be very hot at the beach. We *must* / *must not* forget the sunscreen.

5 🔊 **2.06** Complete the text with the modal verbs below. Listen and check.

| don't have to   have to   must
| must not   ~~ought~~   should |

Mountain fun
Are you looking for adventure this summer? Then you ¹ **ought** to try our mountain activity camp. You ² _____ bring any special equipment because we provide everything. You ³ _____ be between 14 and 17 years old and have your parents' permission. All you ⁴ _____ bring are enough clothes for a week of camping, hiking, and climbing and, of course, you ⁵ _____ forget a warm coat for evenings around the camp fire. Book a place now and you ⁶ _____ hear from us before the end of the month.

6 In your notebook, finish the sentences to make them true for you. Compare your ideas with the class.

1 When you're on a beach vacation, you should …
  When you're on a beach vacation, you should use sunscreen.
2 On a plane, people must not …
3 When I'm on vacation with my parents, I don't have to …
4 At an activity camp, you have to …

And YOU?

5.3 READING and VOCABULARY
An article about traveling

I can find specific information in an article and talk about traveling.

1 **CLASS VOTE** Do you agree that travel is important in a person's life? Why? / Why not?

2 Read the text quickly. Order pictures A–D as you find the words for the items in the article.

1 ☐ 2 ☐ 3 [A] 4 ☐

A   B   C   D

www.livinglifeoutside.com

Most travelers know that learning a new language can make a vacation more fun. But what about *frontside, lipslide, kickflip*? What sort of language is this? It's the international language of the skateboarding world, and a language that teens like Booker Mitchell from New York know well. It has helped him to explore different places around the world and meet local people in different countries. Booker knows he's lucky to have parents who have always traveled with him. He's made videos of his trips since he was young. With the help of his mom, who's a film-maker, Booker has made videos that share his experiences of skateboarding and surfing with the rest of the world.

Booker loves traveling and enjoys the feeling of adventure that goes with it. He doesn't think you should travel with a lot of luggage, and says the most important thing is to feel comfortable wherever you are. His favorite place to sleep is in a hammock, even if he's at home in New York! Of course, like the rest of us, there are some things Booker has to travel with. In his case, it's a skateboard or surfboard, a video camera, and a notebook.

Does Booker sometimes go on vacation at the last minute? No way! Planning a trip is really important. Before every trip, he makes a list of where he wants to go sightseeing and why. He learns about the culture, food, music, and scenery. He thinks that's the best way to enjoy a place.

Back at home, Booker rides his skateboard to school. He never takes the same route, and always listens to a different song on his cell phone. He likes to see the different things that are happening around him. "Life is fascinating, no matter where you live", he says. "You just have to look at it the right way."

3 🔊 **2.07** Listen and read the text again. Answer the questions in your notebook.
1. What has skateboarding language helped Booker to do?
   It's helped him to explore different places around the world and meet local people in different countries.
2. Why does Booker think he's lucky?
3. What does Booker like about traveling?
4. What does Booker always travel with?
5. How does Booker get to school?

Reading tip
Underline important information in the text to help you do reading comprehension activities.

4 Complete the sentences with one word in each blank.
1. Booker's _mother_ has helped him with his skateboarding and surfing videos.
2. Booker doesn't think it's right to take much _____ when you travel.
3. It's important for Booker to _____ where he wants to go on a trip.
4. At home, Booker always uses a different _____ to get to school.

5 **WORD FRIENDS** Find the words in the text and complete the Word Friends. Use the words in the correct form.

Word Friends	Travel phrases
learn	a new language
_____	different places
_____	local people
_____	an experience
_____	a trip
_____	on vacation/sightseeing

6 Booker doesn't think people should travel with a lot of luggage. What about you? Talk in pairs.

And YOU

I take a huge suitcase. I always pack too many clothes.
I don't take much, and I often forget things. Last year I forgot my swimsuit!

Unit 5 53

5.4 GRAMMAR Modal verbs for speculation: *must, could, might/may, can't*

I can speculate about the present.

1 **CLASS VOTE** Look at the picture in the blog post in Activity 2. Is this a fun place to sleep in? Why? / Why not?

2 🔊 **2.08** Listen and read the blog post and the comments. In pairs, discuss the advantages and disadvantages of hanging tents.

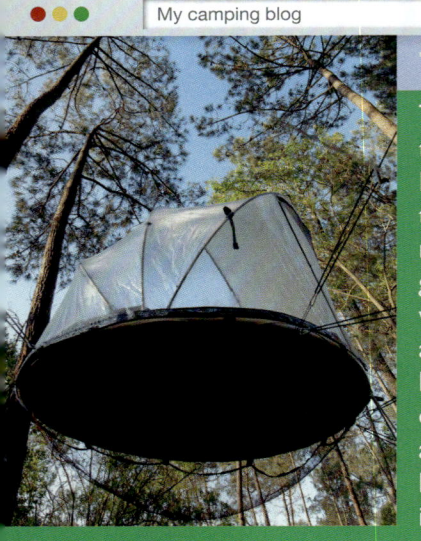

My camping blog

TENTS

This month I've discovered these amazing tree tents. It might be difficult to find them in the stores at the moment, but I think they're going to be popular. They're warm and comfortable, and great fun. I slept in one last weekend, in the middle of a forest, and it was awesome! Take a look and let me know what you think in the comments section.

JO123 6:30 p.m.	They don't look very big. It can't be easy to stand up in them if you're tall.
TENTFAN 7:10 p.m.	It might be fun to sleep up in the air, but it must be difficult to go to the bathroom in the middle of the night!
TIMABC 8:00 p.m.	They are cool! But they must be expensive because I haven't seen many of them.
CAMPER 8:30 p.m.	They may look cool, but I think they could be really uncomfortable because they move around with the wind.

---

3 Study the Grammar box, then complete the sentences. Underline examples of modals for speculation in the blog post and comments

> **Grammar** Modal verbs – *must, could, might, may, can't*
>
> **must**
> It **must be** cold outside. People are wearing jackets.
>
> **could/might/may**
> It **might be** difficult to travel with this suitcase because it's very big.
>
> **can't**
> That **can't be** our tent. It's the wrong color.
>
> • We use *must* and _____ when we have logical reasons to believe something is true or untrue.
> • We use _____, *might*, and _____ when we think something is true or untrue, but we are not sure.
>
> GRAMMAR TIME > PAGE 110

4 Circle the correct option.

A: That's a strange tent! It looks like a balloon.
B: Oh, that ¹(must)/ can't be the new tree tent. I've seen it on the internet.
A: I'd love to get one. Is it expensive?
B: It ²can't / could be expensive because my uncle has one, and he doesn't have much money.
A: Is there a campsite near here?
B: I'm not sure. There ³might / must be one near the lake. I've seen people there in the summer.
A: Can we borrow your uncle's tree tent?
B: OK, but today ⁴could / can't be a bad time. I think he's going on vacation with it!

5 Rewrite the sentences using the verbs from the Grammar box. Sometimes more than one answer is possible.

1. I'm sure this is Ellie's tent. That's her backpack.
   This ___must___ be Ellie's tent. That's her backpack.
2. They're very quiet. Maybe they're sleeping.
   They _____ be sleeping.
3. I'm sure this isn't the same campsite.
   This _____ be the same campsite.
4. I'm sure the map is on the table. I put it there.
   It _____ be on the table. I put it there.
5. Here's a guidebook, but maybe it's the wrong one.
   Here's a guidebook, but it _____ be the wrong one.

6 🔊 **2.09** Listen to the sentences in Activity 5. Which verb is stressed: the modal or the main verb?

Speak UP!

7 What do you think of these ideas for unusual vacation accommodation? Use the Grammar box to help you.

- a canal boat
- a tree house
- an ice hotel
- a castle

It could be noisy in a tree house in a forest because of all the animals.

And YOU

54 Unit 5

5.5 LISTENING and VOCABULARY — Jess lives the dream!

I can identify specific information in an interview and in a story, and talk about trips and excursions.

1 In pairs, describe the picture. What do you think is happening?

They're on a boat.
It might be a sailing vacation.

2 🔊 **2.10** Listen to the first part of the interview. What does Nicky do?

3 🔊 **2.11** Listen to the second part of the interview. Mark the sentences true (T) or false (F).
1. [F] Nicky was working in South America when she met a girl who couldn't see.
2. [ ] The girl was on vacation with her family.
3. [ ] Special bikes are popular with kids who don't usually ride a bike.
4. [ ] Nicky thinks the journey is more important than the vacation.
5. [ ] Hotel staff don't always realize how difficult staying in a hotel is for blind guests.
6. [ ] The winter vacations are the most popular.

4 🔊 **2.11** Work in groups of three. Listen to the interview again. In your notebook, write down:
- four activities mentioned in the interview
- three types of vacations
- three problems that blind people might have

5 🔊 **2.12** Listen to Jess's story. Answer the questions in your notebook.
1. How old is Jess and where does she come from?
   She's sixteen years old and she comes from New Zealand.
2. What type of vacation did she go on?
3. What did Jess want to do during the trip?

6 In pairs, discuss why this sort of vacation is important for people with disabilities. Compare your ideas with the class.

It's an adventure.
It might help them to make new friends.

7 🔊 **2.13** Study the Vocabulary box, using a dictionary if necessary. Then read the sentences and circle the correct word. Listen and check.

Vocabulary	Travel: confusing words
excursion journey travel (noun) travel (verb) trip voyage	

1. It was a three-hour car (journey)/ excursion to the beach.
2. The *trip / voyage* across the Atlantic took two months and the cabins were comfortable.
3. Air *travel / journey* is very expensive at the moment.
4. The school is organizing a two-day *travel / trip* to Boston.
5. Let's get tickets for the afternoon *journey / excursion* to the castle.
6. I'd love to *travel / voyage* to the North Pole one day.

8 In pairs, discuss the best trips and excursions for foreign students in your area. Compare your ideas with the class.

And YOU

They could go on an excursion to the waterpark.
They could visit the capital city, but it's a long journey.

5.6 SPEAKING — Understanding a conversation

I can clarify what I have said and ask for clarification.

1 **CLASS VOTE** Do you like packing when you go on vacation or do you prefer somebody else to do it for you? Why?

I like doing it because I know I'll pack the right things.

2 Look at the picture and identify the items. In pairs, discuss if you would take them when going on vacation.

I DIDN'T CATCH THAT

Dan: Tickets, yes. Passport, yes … Hi, Ed. I'm just in the middle of packing for New York, but I can't see you. The camera's not working.
Ed: That's OK. I can see you. What time …?
Dan: Sorry, I didn't catch that. You're breaking up.
Ed: What I said was, what time does your plane leave?
Dan: At seven, but I have to be at the airport at four in the morning! Now, what should I pack?
Ed: You just need lots of sports clothes and …
Dan: Oh, this is really annoying. I didn't get the last part, Ed. What did you say?
Ed: I was just saying that you should bring things for the beach.
Dan: OK. How about these?
Ed: No way! Dan, promise me …
Dan: Sorry, can you say that again?
Ed: Don't bring those smelly sneakers.
Dan: What was that?
Ed: Forget it, Dan. I'll see you tomorrow …

3 🔊 **2.14** Listen and read the dialogue. Answer the questions in your notebook.

1 What's Dan packing for?
He's packing for a trip to New York.
2 What time does Dan have to be at the airport?
3 What type of clothes should Dan take?
4 What doesn't Ed want Dan to take?

4 Complete the dialogues with the phrases from the Speaking box. In pairs, say the dialogues.

Speaking — Understanding a conversation

Asking for clarification
Sorry, I didn't catch that.
Sorry, can you say that again?
What was that?
Sorry, I didn't get the first/last part.
Could you speak louder/more slowly?

Clarifying
What I said/asked was …
I said that …
I was just saying …
I just wanted to ask you about …

1 A: Hi, Maria! There's a school trip to Venice this year.
B: *Sorry, can you say that again*?
A: _____ there's a trip to Venice this year.
2 A: I think we need a visa for our vacation.
B: _____?
A: _____ we need a visa for our vacation.

5 In pairs, role-play the situations. Follow the instructions.

And YOU

A You're at the train station and your train is late. Call your friend and explain what's happening.

B Your friend calls from the station, but it's noisy. You want to know what time she is arriving.

A: *Hi, it's me. I'm at …*
B: *Could you speak louder?*

Unit 5

5.7 WRITING A photo story

I can write a photo story.

1 Look at the photo story. Then circle the correct option.

A photo story usually …
a tells multiple stories.
b focuses on one person, place, or situation.
c includes only images, and no text.

2 All photo stories have a beginning, a middle, and an end. Read the captions to these pictures and number them in the correct order (1–4).

PHOTO STORY

My first time on a European train! <u>Before I return home</u>, I'll have traveled through eight different countries on these trains.

And so my trip begins! <u>As soon as I board the plane</u>, I'll be saying goodbye to my life in the United States for the next eight months.

First stop, Geneva! <u>After I eat this fondue</u>, I'm going to try some Swiss chocolate. Can't wait!

Interrail is a popular way to travel through Europe. <u>When you buy a ticket</u>, you choose how many different countries you want it to cover. It obviously takes longer than a plane ride, but I'm seeing so much interesting scenery <u>while I'm traveling</u>.

3 Underline the time clauses in the photo story.

> **Watch OUT!**
> We use the present tense in future time clauses with *when, while, before, until, as soon as*.
> **When I'm** there, I'll buy the tickets.
> I'll have a party **after I finish** school.
> **Before we go,** we'll look at the map.
> I'll call you **as soon as I arrive**.
> Put a comma (,) after the time clause if it comes first in a sentence.

4 Study the Writing box. Find examples of the language below in the photo story in Activity 1

> **Writing A photo story**
>
> **Introducing the picture**
> Here, I'm meeting some local children.
> This picture shows how scared I am.
> In this picture, you can see where I stayed.
> **Using concise language in picture captions**
> A beautiful sunset.
> The end of another awesome day.
> Finally at my destination!
> **Using time clauses**
> On my way to my next destination. It'll be ten hours before I get there!
> I went to sleep as soon as I arrived.

5 Write a photo story. **Writing Time**

1 **Find ideas**
Choose pictures of a trip that you took, or of a place you would like to travel to. Decide the order of your photo story and, in your notebook, take notes for the captions.

2 **Draft**
Write a draft of the captions for your photo story. Use Activity 1 and the Writing box to help you. Try to include time clauses.

3 **Share**
Share your photo story with another student for feedback. Listen to his/her opinion and suggestions. Check the spelling and grammar.

4 **Check and write**
Make changes to your photo story. Are your captions concise? Do they tell a story? Write the final version of your text.

WORDLIST
Types of vacation | At the hotel | Equipment | Travel: confusing words

accommodation [n]	culture [n]	noisy [adj]	tent [n]
activity camp [n]	disability [n]	the North Pole [n]	ticket [n]
adventure [n]	double room [n]	notebook [n]	top [n]
airport [n]	excursion [n]	organization [n]	train station [n]
annoying [adj]	facilities [n]	pack [v]	transportation [n]
arrive at [v]	fascinating [adj]	passport [n]	travel [n/v]
the Atlantic [n]	film-maker [n]	platform [n]	traveler [n]
backpack [n]	floor [n]	pool [n]	tree house [n]
backpacking vacation [n]	flashlight [n]	popular [adj]	tree tent [n]
balloon [n]	forest [n]	provide [v]	trip [n]
beach vacation [n]	guest [n]	purpose [n]	unusual [adj]
blind [adj]	guidebook [n]	reception [n]	view [n]
book [v]	hammock [n]	report [n]	visa [n]
break-in [n]	hanging tent [n]	reservation [n]	visit [v]
break up [v]	hiking [n]	return ticket [n]	visually impaired [adj]
burglary [n]	hotel [n]	route [n]	voyage [n]
bus service [n]	ice hotel [n]	safe [adj]	winter vacation [n]
bus station [n]	illegal [adj]	sailing vacation [n]	
cabin [n]	impossible [adj]	scenery [n]	**WORD FRIENDS**
camera [n]	inactive [adj]	school trip [n]	learn a new language
camping [n]	incident [n]	ship [n]	explore different places
camping trip [n]	investigation [n]	sightseeing vacation [n]	meet local people
campsite [n]	irregular [adj]	single ticket [n]	share an experience
castle [n]	island [n]	single room [n]	plan a trip
CCTV [n]	journey [n]	sleeping bag [n]	go on vacation
check in [n/v]	key [n]	smelly [adj]	go sightseeing
check out [n/v]	leave from [v]	special need [n]	on foot
city [n]	lock [n]	suitcase [n]	by sea/road/rail/air
city break [n]	luggage [n]	summer vacation [n]	by boat/car/plane/train/bus
climbing [n]	manager [n]	sunscreen [n]	
country [n]	map [n]	sunglasses [n]	
cruise [n]	mast [n]	swimsuit [n]	

VOCABULARY IN ACTION

1 Use the Wordlist to find and write in your notebook:
1. five different means of transportation
   bus, ...
2. five things that you would take on vacation
3. three things that you could do on vacation
4. two facilities you might have at a hotel

2 In pairs, discuss the differences between the words below.
1. a voyage / a cruise
2. a visa / a passport
3. a sightseeing vacation / a city break
4. a camping vacation / a backpacking vacation
5. a single ticket / a return ticket

3 Use the Word Friends to complete the sentences. Write the words in the correct form. In pairs, say if the sentences are true for you.
1. You don't have to ___plan___ a trip, but it can be fun to think of all the things you can do.
2. You need a lot of money to _____ sightseeing in that city.
3. It's best to _____ different places by bus.
4. An activity camp is a good place to _____ experiences.
5. It's easy to _____ a new language when you have to use it every day.

4 🔊 **2.15** **PRONUNCIATION** Sentence stress falls on the important information in a sentence. Underline the stressed words in the sentences. Listen, check, and repeat.
1. The children <u>enjoyed</u> the <u>activity</u> camp, but the <u>weather</u> was <u>awful.</u>
2. I'd love to sail across the Atlantic in the future.
3. We stayed on a campsite near the river.
4. They were waiting at the bus station for two hours.
5. Don't forget to take the map and the guidebook with you.

SELF-CHECK

1 Write the correct word for each definition.
1. The area you see from a place. **v** _i_ _e_ _w_.
2. This helps you to see things in the dark.
   f _ _ _ _ _ _ _ _ _
3. A big bag you put things in for your vacation.
   s _ _ _ _ _ _ _ _
4. The place where you wait to get on a train.
   p _ _ _ _ _ _ _ _ .
5. Put things in bags ready for a journey.
   p _ _ _ _
6. A place where you stay on vacation, e.g., a hotel. **a** _ _ _ _ _ _ _ _ _ _ _

2 Complete the text with the words below.

> travel   learn   meet   go   pack   plan

HOW MUCH OF A TRAVELER ARE YOU?
Do you like exploring new places or would you rather stay closer to home?
1. What's the first thing you __pack__ in your bag when you're getting ready to travel?
2. Would you try to _____ a new language before visiting a different country?
3. What's the best way to _____ local people when you're on vacation?
4. When you _____ sightseeing, do you always take pictures?
5. What type of trip would you like to _____ for this summer?
6. Who would you rather _____ to another country with, family or friends? Why?

3 In pairs, ask and answer the questions. Tell the class about your classmate.
The first thing Anna packs is her make-up!

4 Circle the correct option.
1. When you're on vacation, you *must* / (*ought to*) buy food in local stores.
2. On a hot sunny day, you *don't have to* / *must* put on lots of sunscreen.
3. When you visit a new country, you *should* / *must not* try to learn the language.
4. You *don't have to* / *have to* go to a travel agency. You can buy your tickets online.
5. It's a long train journey. We *must* / *must not* forget to take lots of food and water.

5 Match sentences 1–6 to sentences a–f.
1. ☐ I got a postcard from Julia.
2. ☐ a That can't be my backpack.
3. ☐ It's a bit cloudy to go to the beach.
4. ☐ The maps might be in the reception.
5. ☐ It's a very long journey for the children.
6. ☐ Let's have a camping vacation.

a. It's the wrong color.
b. Hotels often put them there.
c. It could be too cold to swim.
d. They must be very bored.
e. Sleeping in a tent could be fun.
f. She's on vacation.

6 In pairs, speculate about the situations below.
1. Your friends have arrived at the airport, but there aren't any taxis.
2. You're going on vacation tomorrow, but you can't find your tickets.
3. You arrive at your hotel, but there aren't any rooms.

7 In pairs, role-play the situations. You and your classmate are in a noisy café at a train station. Follow the instructions.

A
- Say hello and ask why your friend is at the station.
- Explain that you couldn't understand what he/she said. Ask him to say it again.
- Tell your friend that you didn't hear the first or the last part.
- Tell your friend to have a good trip.

B
- Explain where you're traveling to and why.
- Repeat what you said.
- Repeat the part that your friend didn't hear.

8 🔊 **2.16** Listen, then listen again and write down what you hear.

_____
_____
_____
_____

SELF-ASSESSMENT Think about this unit. What did you learn? What do you need help with?

6 Getting to know you

VOCABULARY
Phrasal verbs | Talking about friends

GRAMMAR
Second Conditional | Defining and non-defining relative clauses

Grammar:
I'd come if I was free
Look at Alisha and her brother, Damian. Why are they wearing these clothes?

Speaking:
Who's the guy at the back?
Look at the picture. What are Tom, Alisha, and Skye talking about?

6.1 VOCABULARY — Family and friends

I can talk about relationships with family and friends.

"Miss Baker, I have something to tell you about my project. My dad helped me a little. Any mistakes are his."

A

1 CLASS VOTE You are going on a day out. Choose one person you would like to spend the day with.

grandfather   grandmother   teacher   neighbor   aunt   uncle   cousin

2 WORD BUILDING Read the texts. Use the words in bold to complete the definitions (1–3).

My **great**-grandmother, Julia, is ninety and she's my **grand**mother's mother. Julia was adopted.

I have a younger **half**-brother. He's my father's son from his second marriage.

I really like my **step**sister. Some people say we look alike, although we aren't related by blood.

1 The prefix *great* describes a family relative who is two generations away from you. Add an extra _____ for each extra generation.
2 The prefix _____ describes a brother, sister, or parent who is related to you by marriage, but not by blood.
3 The prefix _____ describes a brother or sister who is related to you through one shared parent.

3 Look and read cartoons A–C. Guess the relationships between the people and give reasons for your answers.

parent, stepparent, and neighbor   **B**
parent, child, and teacher   ☐
great-grandparent and great-grandchild   ☐

Unit 6

Oh, they're not all our children! These are my nieces, Clara and Sara. This is David's son, Max, and these are Max's friends, Tom and Tara.

When I was your age, things were very different. We only had ONE screen, and the whole family gathered around it to spend a nice evening all together!

B

C

4 🔊 **2.17** Listen and repeat the phrasal verbs in the Vocabulary box. Then, in pairs, check their meaning in a dictionary. The personality test can also help you understand them.

Vocabulary	Phrasal verbs
deal with (a problem)	go out
fall out with	hang out with
get along (with)	put up with
go ahead	

5 Do the personality test, then discuss your answers with a classmate. What do you have in common?

6 🔊 **2.18** **WORD FRIENDS** Circle the correct option to complete the text, then listen and check. Who do you agree with? Jessica or Mark?

Should friends have a lot in common?

JESSICA: Yes! My friend Sarah and I ¹(share)/get loads of interests. We both like horseback riding and movies. We ²have/get the same sense of humor, too. We ³share/spend a lot of time together and we're like sisters. My singing can ⁴share/get on her nerves sometimes, but we never ⁵see/have arguments.

MARK: I disagree. I'm completely different from my friend Mike, but we ⁶enjoy/see each other's company. When I ⁷enjoy/get to know people, I find them more interesting if they ⁸come/have from different backgrounds. Mike loves to ⁹spend/see time on his own, so we don't ¹⁰have/see each other often, but when we meet, we have fun.

PERSONALITY TEST

1 **Can you put up with being on your own?**
a Yes.
b No.
c It's OK.

2 **Do you like to go out and meet new people?**
a I find it difficult.
b I love it.
c I like it.

3 **Do you ever fall out with other people?**
a Never.
b Sometimes.
c Not often.

4 **Do you get along with big groups of people?**
a I find it difficult.
b I love it.
c I like it.

5 **Are you good at dealing with friendship problems?**
a No.
b Yes.
c Not always.

6 **Do you like to hang out with just a small group of friends?**
a Yes.
b No.
c It's OK.

7 **Are you the first one in your group to go ahead and try new things?**
a Never.
b Yes, I hate things to be boring!
c Sometimes.

8 **Is it important for you and your friends to laugh at the same things?**
a Yes, I like my friends to be similar to me.
b No, but they must be fun to be with.
c No, I get along with everyone.

Go to page 114 to read about your answers.

7 Should friends do lots of things together? In pairs, discuss your opinions.

And YOU

Unit 6

6.2 GRAMMAR Second Conditional

I can talk about hypothetical situations in the present and future.

1 **CLASS VOTE** Which of these family events do you prefer? What do you like/dislike about them?

- a meal   a wedding   a short visit/vacation

2 🔊 **2.19** Listen and read. Why does Alisha need to take tissues?

I'D COME IF I WERE FREE

Damian: Alisha? I can't tie this bow tie. If mom wasn't busy, she'd help, but …
Alisha: I can do it. There you go. The bow tie's nice, but you look like a server! And your hair's a mess. It would look much better if you had some gel in it. Here.
Damian: Get off! Leave me alone. Anyway, you look like a giant cream cake.
Alisha: *(cell phone rings)* Skye! Swimming? Oh! I'd come if I were free, but we have a family wedding. My aunt's getting married and I'm her bridesmaid. I can't talk now, I'm getting ready. Sorry. Bye!
Mom: Damian! Alisha! Hurry up. We're leaving in five minutes.
Alisha: Nooo! I'm not ready yet! *(sneezes)* Hold this for me.
Damian: What's up? Your eyes are really red.
Alisha: I know! I'm allergic to these flowers. *(sneezes)* I keep sneezing!
Damian: If I were you, I'd take some tissues. Loads of tissues!
Alisha: Agh! What a nightmare.

3 Study the Grammar box, then circle the correct option. Underline examples of the Second Conditional in the dialogue.

Grammar	Second Conditional

If I **were** you, I **would go** to the wedding.
I**'d come** if I **were** free. (but I'm not free)
What **would** you **do if** you **were** me?
We use the Second Conditional to talk about *real / unreal* situations in the *present / future*.

GRAMMAR TIME > PAGE 111

4 Use the verbs in parentheses to write Second Conditional sentences.

1 If she ___had___ (have) enough time, she ___would help___ (help) him.
2 If you _____ (listen) carefully, you _____ (understand) the lesson.
3 _____ (you/go) to the beach if _____ (you/be) free today?
4 He _____ (not be) here if he _____ (not want) to.
5 What _____ (you/do) if _____ (you/win) a lot of money?
6 I _____ (call) your mom if I _____ (be) you.
7 Where _____ (you/go) if you _____ (have) money to travel anywhere in the world?
8 The students _____ (take) the test tomorrow if they _____ (can) choose another day.

5 🔊 **2.20** Listen to the sentences in Activity 4, paying attention to intonation. Then practice saying them in pairs.   **Speak UP!**

6 In pairs, finish the sentences to make them true for you.   **And YOU**

1 If my friend called when I was busy, …
2 If I didn't like my clothes, …
3 If there was a big wedding in our family, …
4 If I were late for a family meal, my parents …
5 I'd be very worried if …
6 It would be a nightmare for me if …

If my friend called when I was busy, I'd probably talk to her. What about you?

Unit 6

6.3 READING and VOCABULARY An informative essay

I can identify the purpose of an informative essay and talk about friends.

1 **CLASS VOTE** Is it important to have a special day to celebrate friendship? Why? / Why not?

> **Reading tip**
>
> If you identify the purpose of a text, you will better understand it.

2 Read quickly the informative essay. What is its purpose?
- a To discuss the pros and cons of Friendship day.
- b To educate the reader about Friendship day.

3 🔊 **2.21** Listen and read the essay. Mark the sentences true (T) or false (F).
1. [F] Joyce Hall owned a company in the UK.
2. [ ] In the 1930s, people celebrated Friendship Day in the USA by giving cards.
3. [ ] The decision to spread the celebration to more countries was made in Paraguay.
4. [ ] The United Nations encouraged younger people to take part in Friendship Day celebrations.
5. [ ] The "Invisible Friend" game involves writing a message to your friends.

4 🔊 **2.22** Study the Vocabulary box. Find more examples in the essay and write them below. Then listen, check, and repeat.

> **Vocabulary** Talking about friends
>
> **words related to** *friends*
> classmates   best friends   _____
> _____
>
> **antonyms for** *friends*
> enemy   _____
>
> **phrases with** *friends*
> have a friend   be friends   _____

5 Complete the sentences with the words from the Vocabulary box.
1. At first I felt like a ___stranger___ here.
2. Of all my friends, Ezra is my _____ because he understands me.
3. She was nervous about the new school, but it was easy to _____.
4. My dad sometimes plays tennis with his _____ from the office.
5. He started high school early, so his _____ are older than him.

Friendship Day

by Jyoti Singh
9th grade - The Eagle School, India

The idea of a special friendship day has several origins. An American woman, Joyce Hall, owned a greetings card company. In 1930 she planned a Friendship Day to create more business. She thought, "If people had a new celebration, they would buy more cards." The first Friendship Day in the United States was on August 2. Many Americans sent cards, but then this tradition died out after a few years.

However, a different idea of Friendship Day has been celebrated in some South American countries since 1958. It began with a group of friends in Paraguay. They decided to celebrate friendship and understanding on July 30 every year. One man in the group, Ramon Artemio Bracho, wanted to do more. He wanted to turn strangers into friends. He worked hard to start celebrations in other countries. Thanks to his work, people in India and China took up the idea. Friendship Day was growing.

In 2011, the celebration became International Friendship Day when the United Nations agreed to support it, as a good way to encourage peace by getting different cultures to communicate more. They set up activities for children and teenagers of mixed nationalities, such as fun runs or friendly games. The hope is that these events help people to respect one another's culture and to make new friends.

In some countries, people have a meal together, call friends or use social media to send messages. In Paraguay, the "Invisible Friend" game is played one week before the special day. All names of classmates or co-workers are written on pieces of paper and put in a box. Then everybody takes one piece with a name and buys a small gift for that person, wraps it and writes the name on it. When you get your gift on Friendship Day, you don't know who bought it!

6 **And YOU** How do you like Jyoti's essay? Did it achieve its purpose? Why? / Why not?

6.4 GRAMMAR Defining and non-defining relative clauses

I can identify and give additional information about people, things, and places.

1 🔊 **2.23** Listen and read the puzzle, then write the house numbers next to each name. Which is the house where nobody lives?

32 Lucy ☐ Molly ☐ Paddy ☐ Frank Jones ☐ Mr. and Mrs. Morris

PARK STREET PUZZLE
Who lives in these houses?

1 Lucy lives in one of the apartments above the café.
2 One of Lucy's friends lives in a house which has a big tree in the yard.
3 In front of another friend's house, there is a small space where he leaves his bike.
4 Mr. and Mrs. Morris, who are Lucy's grandparents, live next door to her.
5 Mrs. Morris loves colourful flowers, which she grows in window boxes.
6 Lucy doesn't know the man who has just moved to the house with a pink roof.
7 The man's cat loves the balcony, where it can watch the birds.

2 Study the Grammar box, then number the sentences. Underline examples of relative clauses in the puzzle.

Grammar	Defining and non-defining relative clauses

1 Defining relative clauses
The man **who** (that) moved to Park Street is Frank.
Molly lives in a house **which** (that) is a hundred years old.
That's the café **where** the children often buy ice cream.

2 Non-defining relative clauses
Frank, **who** moved to Park Street, has a cat.
Molly's house, **which** has a tree in the garden, is very old.
There's a café on the street, **where** we buy ice cream.

Be careful!
The woman that/who grows flowers is Mrs Morris.
Mrs Morris, ~~that~~/who grows flowers, is Lucy's grandma.

☐ This type of clause gives additional information. The sentence still makes sense without it.
☐ This type of clause gives essential information to help us understand the sentence.

GRAMMAR TIME > PAGE 111

3 Circle the correct option.
1 The children (who)/ which are in the park live nearby.
2 Here's the office where / which my mom works.
3 Frank Jones's cat, which / where is five years old, loves hunting.

4 Use relative pronouns to combine the sentences. Write them in your notebook.
1 Lucy has a good friend. **She** lives near Park Street.
   Lucy has a good friend who lives near Park Street.
2 In Molly's yard there's a tree. **It**'s 100 years old.
3 There's a park. The children play **in it**.

5 In your notebook, rewrite the sentences adding non-defining relative clauses.
1 Mrs Morris is sixty-seven. (who/be/ Lucy's grandmother)
   Mrs Morris, who is Lucy's grandmother, is sixty-seven.
2 Paddy uses his bike every day. (which/ be/new)
3 Number 24 is a beautiful house. (where/ Molly/live)

6 Make a true and a false sentence about your house/city. In pairs, say if your classmate's sentences are true or false. **And YOU**

6.5 LISTENING and VOCABULARY A friend in need ...

I can identify specific information in an account and talk about pets.

1 **CLASS VOTE** Can an animal be your friend or part of your family? Why? / Why not?

2 Look at the pictures. How do you think the dogs help these people? What else can dogs do to help people?

Charlie and Grace 1
Milo and Ash 2

3 Look at questions 1–4. What do you think Grace will talk about? Discuss in pairs.

1 What does Grace think of her morning routine?
  a It was boring.   b It was sad.   (c) It was slow.
2 How did Grace feel when people couldn't help her?
  a stressed   b frustrated   c angry
3 What does Charlie do to help with Grace's morning routine?
  a helps her get out of bed   b washes her feet
  c puts her socks on
4 Based on Grace's account, which adjective best describes Charlie?
  a busy   b funny   c smart

4 🔊 **2.24** Listen, confirm your guesses, and answer the questions in Activity 3.

5 Look at the notes of Ash's account. In pairs, try to complete them with the words below.

> assistance dog   a year   family   people   pictures
> puppy trainer   sad   stepmom

- A ¹ _puppy trainer_ teaches young dogs special skills.
- ² _____ usually help people with special needs.
- Ash and his stepmom keep the dogs for ³ _____ .
- He feels ⁴ _____ when the dogs leave for their owners.
- New dog owners send Ash and his stepmom ⁵ _____ and messages.
- Ash and his ⁶ _____ trained Milo to help him.
- It's difficult for Ash to meet new ⁷ _____ . Milo helps him feel more confident.
- Ash feels that Milo is part of his ⁸ _____ .

6 🔊 **2.25** Listen and check your answers in Activity 5.

7 🔊 **2.26** **WORD FRIENDS** Match the meaning of *get* (1–6) to the correct words below. Listen and check.

> arrive/reach   become   bring/fetch
> buy   find   receive

Word Friends

Get can have several meanings:
1 get a cell phone = _buy_
2 get a job = _____
3 get home = _____
4 get a message/phone call/an email = _____
5 get someone's socks/book/a drink (for someone) = _____
6 get better/worse   get dressed
  get married   get old(er)   get ready
  get upset/angry/scared/stressed/bored/excited = _____

8 Circle the correct option.

1 My brother wants to get (a job) / ready as a police officer.
2 I've just got *dressed* / *a text* from my grandpa!
3 Shall I get *a glass of water* / *married* for you?
4 The train was late, so we didn't get *home* / *a new TV* until midnight.
5 Can you get my *jacket* / *home* on the table, please? It's cold outside.
6 If Alex doesn't get *angry* / *help* with his math homework, he'll have a bad grade in the test.

9 **And YOU** In pairs, tell your classmate about one of the situations below. Describe how you felt and the reasons why you felt that way.

- a time you got a pet
- a time you got bored, scared, angry, or stressed
- a time you got an important message/email/phone call

6.6 SPEAKING Identifying people

I can explain who I am talking about.

1 🔊 **2.27** Look at the Vocabulary box. How do you say these words in your language? Listen and repeat.

Vocabulary	People at a wedding
bride bridegroom bridesmaid guests pageboy	

2 🔊 **2.28** Listen and read. What four people are mentioned in the dialogue?

_____

_____

WHO'S THE GUY AT THE BACK?

Tom: Hey! What are you two up to?
Alisha: I'm just showing Skye the **photos** from the wedding.
Tom: Oh, yeah. This one's really funny. You were stressed because you had a bridesmaid's dress that looked like a cream cake!
Alisha: Hey! Give it back.
Skye: Come on, guys. Let's see the other photos.
Tom: Yeah, it'll be a laugh!
Alisha: Yeah, right! So, that's my Auntie Leena and my new Uncle Andy in the middle, of course. Then there's my little cousin.
Tom: Which one?
Alisha: The cute one who's wearing the white shirt. He got really bored. He was pulling faces all the time.
Skye: Aww! Who's this guy at the back?
Alisha: Where? Oh, that's, um, Adam. He's the bridegroom's stepbrother.
Skye: Right ... He looks nice. Very good looking, too.
Tom: Who? Let's see. Pass it here. Oops!
Alisha: Tom! Now look what you've done!

OUT of class

🇬🇧 photo   🇺🇸 picture

3 Answer the questions.
1 What does Tom think about the pictures?
   He thinks they are funny.
2 What is the bridegroom's name?
   _____
3 How did Alisha's little cousin behave during the wedding?
   _____
4 Who is Adam?
   _____

4 Work in pairs. Choose a picture from page 114 and describe a person in it. Follow the instructions. Use the language in the Speaking box.
- Select a person in the picture to describe.
- Your classmate asks you questions.
- Answer the questions with one piece of information at a time.

Speaking	Identifying people

Talking about people in a picture
She's/He's standing/sitting/talking to ... / playing with ...
She's/He's wearing ...
She's/He's in front of/behind/next to/on the left/on the right/near/in the middle/ at the front/at the back.

Asking
Who's this/that boy/girl on the left who is wearing ...
Which one/girl/boy/man/woman/guy?

Explaining
The one who is ...
The cute/tall one.
Which one do you mean?

A: *Who are you thinking of?*
B: *A person who is wearing/looks ...*
A: *Where is this person?*
B: *She's/He's in front of/behind ...*

5 Work in pairs. Show your classmate a picture where there are people he/she doesn't know. Ask and answer questions.

And YOU

Unit 6

6.7 WRITING A short story about friendship

I can write a short story.

1 Look at the pictures. In pairs, discuss what you think is happening.

2 Read the text and name each person in Activity 1.

A friend in need …

Last week I was feeling stressed about my science homework. I asked my friend Nick for help. "I'd explain it if I was free, but I'm pretty busy." Nick and I get along well, and he's good at science, so I was disappointed.

Next, I ran into another friend leaving the science lab. "Sorry, Tom. If I understood the homework, I'd help you," said Christina, "but it's difficult."

Just then, Aris heard us. He is popular, but we don't speak often because I fell out with him once because he was so bossy. "I can help," he offered.

That day, Aris explained the science homework to me carefully. Afterwards, we sat and chatted. We got to know each other and found we have a lot in common. I think we'll be good friends from now on.

3 Read the text again. Match events a–e to parts 1–5.
1. [d] Setting the scene
2. [ ] The first event
3. [ ] The second event
4. [ ] The main event (the climax)
5. [ ] The solution or outcome

a Christina can't help him.
b Aris and Tom become friends.
c Nick can't help him.
d Tom has a problem.
e Tom has a surprise offer of help.

4 Study the Writing box. Complete blanks 1–7 with phrases from the text.

> **Writing A short story**
>
> **Starting your story and setting the scene**
> My birthday was an awesome day.
> Have you ever had a really difficult day?
> ¹ *(Last week) I was feeling stressed about …*
>
> **Introducing your characters**
> Nick and I got along well …
> 2 _____
>
> **Using time words and phrases to show order of events**
> Last week … / Next … / Afterwards …
> 3 _____ 4 _____ 5 _____
>
> **Using direct speech**
> "I'd explain it if I was free, but I'm quite busy."
> 6 _____
>
> **Ending your story**
> I never want to do that again!
> 7 _____

5 Write a story with the title: *A friend in need.*

Writing Time

1. ❗ **Find ideas**
   In your notebook, take notes for your story. Think about the order of events, considering the parts in Activity 3.

2. 📄 **Draft**
   Write the draft of your story. Make sure you include the five parts in Activity 3, use direct speech and relevant past tenses.

3. 🔗 **Share**
   Share your story with another student for feedback. Listen to his/her opinion and suggestions. Check the spelling and grammar.

4. ✓ **Check and write**
   Make changes to your story. Have you set the scene and organized the order of events? Write the final version of your text.

Unit 6 67

WORDLIST — Family and friends | Phrasal verbs | Talking about friends

adopted [adj]
allergic [adj]
assistance dog [n]
aunt [n]
baby [n]
balcony [n]
behind [prep]
best friend [n]
bossy [adj]
bow tie [n]
bride [n]
bridegroom [n]
bridesmaid [n]
buddy [n]
by blood [n]
celebrate [v]
celebration [n]
cerebral palsy [n]
chat [v]
classmates [n]
communicate [v]
confident [adj]
cousin [n]
co-worker [n]
crowd [n]
deal with (a problem) [phr v]
disability [n]
disappointed [adj]

enemy [n]
fall out (with) [phr v]
friendship [n]
friendship band [n]
generation [n]
get married [v]
get along with [phr v]
go ahead [phr v]
go out [phr v]
great-grandfather [n]
great-grandmother [n]
greeting card [n]
group [n]
guest [n]
half-brother [n]
hang out (with) [phr v]
in front of [prep]
laugh at (sb/sth) [v]
marriage [n]
married [adj]
nationality [n]
near [prep]
neighbor [n]
nightmare [n]
next to [prep]
on the left [prep phr]
on the right [prep phr]
origin [n]

pageboy [n]
peace [n]
puppy trainer [n]
put up with [phr v]
related [adj]
relation [n]
relative [n]
respect [n]
roof [n]
sneeze [v]
socks [n]
solution [n]
stepmom [n]
stranger [n]
stressed [adj]
surprise [n/v]
tickle [v]
tissues [n]
train [v]
uncle [n]
wedding [n]
wheelchair [n]
window box [n]

WORD FRIENDS
be friends
come from similar/different backgrounds
enjoy each other's company
get (your/his/her) socks/book/a drink (for someone)
get a job
get a message/phone call/an email
get a cell phone
get better/worse
get dressed
get home
get married
get on someone's nerves
get old(er)
get to know
get ready
get upset/angry/scared/stressed/bored/excited
have a friend
have an argument
have something in common
have the same sense of humor
make friends
see each other after school/on weekends, etc.
share an interest in
spend time with/spend time on your own

VOCABULARY IN ACTION

1 Use the Wordlist to find and write in your notebook:
1. four words related to friends   *best friend, ...*
2. four phrasal verbs
3. six adjectives
4. five nouns that are NOT people

2 Circle the correct answers.
1. Which person is the same generation as you?
   a your grandfather
   b your mother
   (c) your half-brother
   d your aunt
2. What phrase can be used about people who have a good relationship?
   a fall out (with)
   b get along well (with)
   c have arguments
   d get on someone's nerves

3. Which person is related to you by blood?
   a half-sister
   b stepdad
   c adopted sister
   d classmate

3 In pairs, use the Wordlist to describe your relationship with a person in your family.

4 🔊 2.29 **PRONUNCIATION** Listen to the underlined letters and decide how they are pronounced. Listen again and repeat.

/d/, /t/ or /ɪd/?
bor**ed**   crow**d**   dress**ed**   marri**ed**
rel**ated**   stress**ed**

SELF-CHECK

1 Complete the words in the sentences.
1. Your father's mother's mother is your
   g<u>r e a t</u>-g<u>r a n d m o t h e r</u>.
2. At a wedding, two people will do this:
   g _ _ m _ _ _ _ _ _ _
3. If you spend time with friends, you do this.
   h _ _ _ o _ _
4. If you practice speaking English, you
   g _ _ b _ _ _ _ _ _ quickly.

2 Match phrases 1–5 to phrases a–e to make sentences.
1. [d] My best friend is standing in front
2. [ ] My brother and I get
3. [ ] Luckily, we don't often have
4. [ ] I sometimes get
5. [ ] My mom and dad both have

a angry with my baby sister.
b along very well.
c the same sense of humor.
d of me in the picture.
e big arguments.

3 Circle the correct answers to complete the song lyrics.

If you ¹_____ your friends about your problem, they would help you. (but you don't tell them)
If you didn't keep quiet, they ²_____ understand. (but you don't say anything)
Just ask them, "What would you do if you ³_____ me?" (you'll be surprised)
If you just ⁴_____ up, they would hold your hand.

So, would you listen if your friends ⁵_____ problems? (of course you would)
What would you do if you ⁶_____ them cry? (you'd go and help them)
So, next time you feel worried, you should speak out. Share things with your friends. Give it a try.

1	a tell	b telling	(c) told
2	a would	b will	c won't
3	a were	b was	c are
4	a open	b opened	c opens
5	a had	b have	c has
6	a seen	b saw	c see

4 Complete the text with one word in each blank. Then add commas for any of the non-defining relative clauses.

You and your ancestors

For every person on the planet, there are two people ¹ <u>who</u> are their biological parents, four grandparents, and eight great-grandparents. Below is a diagram ²_____ shows one person's ancestors for four generations. The top row, ³_____ has 16 people shows your great-great-grandparents. It's interesting to think of all the different places ⁴_____ they lived and the people ⁵_____ they married. If you go back 200 years in time to the 19th century, you'll probably find as many as 128 ancestors! So a stranger ⁶_____ you pass on the street could be your long-lost cousin!

great-great grandparents
great grandparents
grandparents
parents
Luisa

5 Complete the dialogue with questions a–c.

A: Where's Will?
B: ¹ <u>b</u>
A: Oh, I've found him. He's holding a book.
B: ²_____
A: He's at the front.
B: ³_____
A: Yes, that's right.

a Is he the one who is wearing glasses?
b I don't know. Which one is Will?
c There are two people holding books. Which one do you mean?

6 🔊 2.30 Listen, then listen again and write down what you hear.

_____
_____
_____
_____

SELF-ASSESSMENT Think about this unit. What did you learn? What do you need help with?

7

No time for crime

VOCABULARY
Criminals | The law |
Action verbs | Solving crimes

GRAMMAR
The passive (Simple Present and Simple Past) | *have/get something done*

Grammar:
Murder in the dark
Tom is making a list. What do you think it is for?

Speaking:
Dress rehearsal
Look at the picture. Who do you think the man wearing glasses and a hat is?

7.1 VOCABULARY Crime

I can talk about crime and criminals.

1 🔊 **2.31** Look at the picture and circle the criminals. Then use words in Vocabulary A box to complete the sentences. Listen and check.

Vocabulary A	Criminals
burglar pickpocket robber shoplifter ~~thief~~ vandal	

1 The ___thief___ is wearing a brown hat.
2 The _____ is holding a necklace.
3 The _____ are wearing earphones.
4 The _____ is running.
5 The _____ can't get out of the window.
6 The _____ is chatting on her cell phone.

2 **WORD FRIENDS** Complete the sentences with the verbs below.

breaks into   ~~commits~~   damages   robs   steals

1 A criminal is someone who ___commits___ a crime.
2 A shoplifter is someone who _____ things from a store.
3 A bank robber is someone who _____ a bank.
4 A burglar is someone who _____ apartments or houses.
5 A vandal is someone who _____ buildings or other things in public places.

3 🔊 **2.32** Use a dictionary to complete the chart with the names of the crimes. Then listen and check.

Person	Crime
(bank) robber	1 ___(bank) robbery___
burglar	2 _____
pickpocket	3 _____
shoplifter	4 _____
thief	5 _____
vandal	6 _____

Unit 7

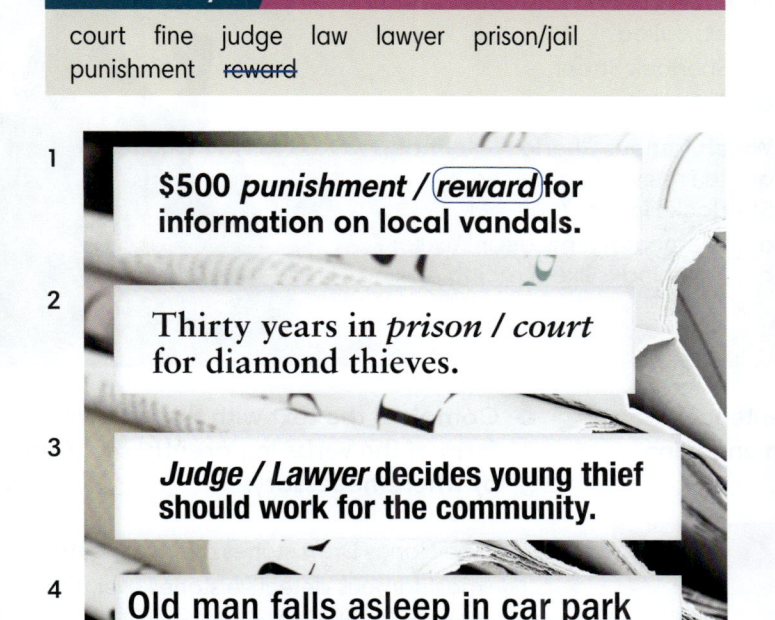

4 In pairs, discuss which crimes you have heard or have read recently about.

5 🔊 **2.33** Study Vocabulary B box, using a dictionary if necessary. Circle the correct option to complete the news headlines.

Vocabulary B	The law
court fine judge law lawyer prison/jail punishment ~~reward~~	

1. $500 *punishment* / *(reward)* for information on local vandals.
2. Thirty years in *prison* / *court* for diamond thieves.
3. *Judge* / *Lawyer* decides young thief should work for the community.
4. Old man falls asleep in car park and gets a *fine* / *reward* of $50.
5. Ex-criminal goes back to school to study and become a *lawyer* / *court*!

6 🔊 **2.34** Match the pictures to the words from Vocabulary C box. Listen and check.

Vocabulary C	Action verbs
[1] chase [ ] climb [ ] push [ ] escape [ ] pull [ ] jump [ ] fall [ ] trip	

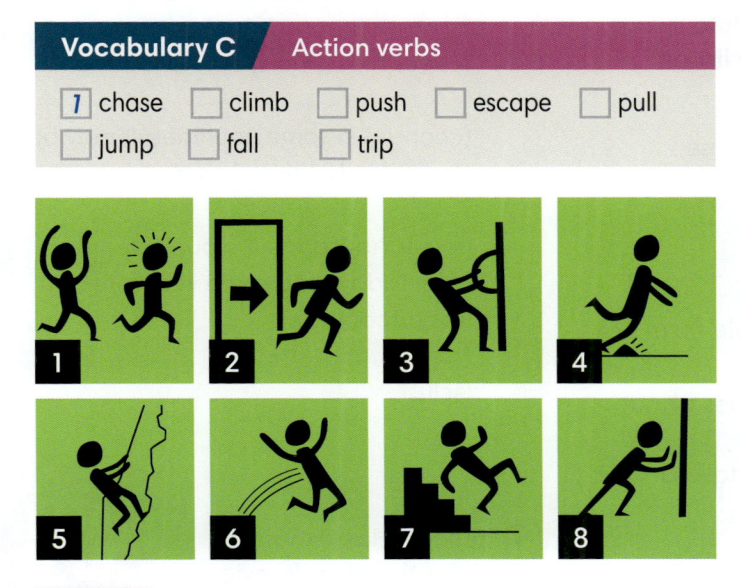

7 **I KNOW!** Add more action verbs to Vocabulary C box. Write them in your notebook.

8 In pairs, make sentences with the words in Vocabulary C box.

It's easy to trip when you can't see where you are walking.

9 Complete the text with the words below.

> jumped   were chasing   ~~fell~~   tripped
> to escape   pulled   pushed

Crazy crimes!

The thief without a belt
A vandal ¹ ___fell___ and hurt his leg while police officers ² _____ him last night. The vandal told the police he ³ _____ because his new pants were too big and fell down.

The hungry thief
A woman was walking with a fast-food meal when a thief ⁴ _____ out of a bush. He ⁵ _____ her to the ground and ran off with her burger.

A good phone connection
A shoplifter had a problem when he tried ⁶ _____ with an expensive cell phone. He ⁷ _____ the cell phone off the shelf, but didn't notice it had a security cable that was two meters long. He got to the door, then suddenly realized he couldn't go any further.

10 In pairs, choose three action verbs and write a funny crime story in your notebook.

And YOU?

7.2 GRAMMAR   The passive (Simple Present and Simple Past)

I can use verbs in the passive form.

1 CLASS VOTE What do you know about Sherlock Holmes?

2 🔊 2.35 In pairs, ask and answer the quiz questions. Listen and check.

Show what you know … The Sherlock Holmes Quiz

1 The Sherlock Holmes detective stories were written 100 years ago by
   a Arthur Conan Doyle.
   b Agatha Christie.

2 Holmes had a famous assistant. What was he called?
   a Doctor Who.
   b Doctor Watson.

3 The stories were first published
   a in a book.
   b in a magazine.

4 Sherlock's apartment is located at number 221B of a famous London street, called
   a Sherlock Street.
   b Baker Street.

5 Which famous Sherlock Holmes', quote is never really used by Sherlock Holmes?
   a "Elementary, my dear Watson."
   b "My mind is like a racing engine."

3 Study the Grammar box, then complete the sentences with the words *action* and *past participle*. Then underline examples of the passive in the quiz.

Grammar	The passive

Simple Present
Those words are not used.

Simple Past
The detective stories were written by a British author.

- We use the passive when what happens - the _____ - is more important than who does it - the agent. We use *by* to introduce the agent.
- To form the passive, we use a form of *be* + _____.

GRAMMAR TIME > PAGE 112

4 Copy the chart into your notebook. Then complete it with the past participle form of the verbs below. The list on page 116 will help you.

catch   make   see   use   watch   ask   hide   chase

infinitive	past participe
catch	caught

5 Complete the sentences with the past participle form of the verbs in parentheses.
1 CCTV cameras are ___used___ (use) to find clues about many crimes.
2 The thief was _____ (catch) because she talked about her crime on social media.
3 Yesterday evening two car thieves were _____ (chase) by the police in fast cars.
4 Sometimes CCTV films are _____ (watch) by special detectives.

6 Complete the text with the passive form of the verbs in parentheses. Add *by* where necessary.

The Nancy Drew stories are among the most famous detective stories ever. The first stories about Nancy Drew
1 ___were published in the 1930s___
(publish/in the 1930s). Different series have appeared since that time. The books
2 _____
(create/for teenagers). The Nancy Drew detective stories
3 _____
(write/several different authors). The name Carolyn Keene
4 _____,
(use/all the authors) but Nancy's name
5 _____
(change) in some countries. It may be surprising, but this old series
6 _____
(read/thousands of young people) even today, and each year lots and lots of copies
7 _____
(sell).

7 Tell the class about a detective story/movie you know.

And YOU

7.3 READING and VOCABULARY — A TV review

I can identify the genre of a text and talk about solving crimes.

1 **CLASS VOTE** Have you watched any Sherlock Holmes movies or TV series?

2 Look at the text. Circle its genre.

a story   a TV review   an article

Reading tip

Language use and visual clues can help you identify the genre. In the text below, does the author give opinions or mainly facts/information?

A Sherlock Holmes for the 21st Century

By Taylor Donovan, TV critic

The BBC series, *Sherlock*, starring Benedict Cumberbatch, has been a big hit. There have been over 250 movies about the famous detective, so what's different about the new series?

Many Sherlock Holmes movies, like the original stories, are set in the shadows of Victorian London. In those days, the best technology was a magnifying glass to look for fingerprints. However, the BBC series is set in the 21st century, and this adds a fresh perspective and helps to create some smart twists in the plot of each story.

In this modern version, Sherlock has a cell phone and a website. He can get information about suspects and witnesses online. He can even check CCTV cameras to look for extra clues, so his job has changed a lot. His friend Dr. John Watson, who is played by Martin Freeman, still helps and writes blog posts about Sherlock's cases, and you can find them online!

Isn't it strange that Sherlock is over 100 years old, but still popular? One reason can be the fact that Holmes solves crimes with the power of intelligence, which challenges viewers in every episode. Cumberbatch, who plays the role of the detective in the series, explains that playing Sherlock is "a form of mental and physical gymnastics". His acting in the series has been flawless and several critics have acclaimed the British actor as the best Sherlock Holmes ever.

Genre(s): Mystery & Suspense
Network: BBC 1
Stars: Benedict Cumberbatch and Martin Freeman

5.0 RATING ★★★★★

3 🔊 **2.36** Listen and read the text. Circle the correct answer.

1. What has changed for Sherlock in the 21st century?
   a. He doesn't use a magnifying glass anymore.
   b. He has new ways of solving crimes. *(circled)*
   c. He's no longer friends with Dr. Watson.
2. How can viewers of the series get further information about the cases solved by Holmes?
   a. They can send a message to the cast.
   b. They can access Holmes's website.
   c. They can read Watson's blog posts.
3. Why is Sherlock still popular?
   a. Because he's been around a long time.
   b. Because he challenges viewers.
   c. Because he looks great on screen.
4. What do critics think of Benedict Cumberbatch as Sherlock Holmes?
   a. They think his acting has been the best for the role so far.
   b. They think Cumberbatch is really fit.
   c. They think Martin Freeman should play the role.

4 🔊 **2.37** Complete the sentences with words from the Vocabulary box. Listen and check.

Vocabulary — Solving crimes

case   CCTV camera   clue   detective   fingerprints   magnifying glass   ~~suspect~~   witness

1. The police caught the __suspect__ because he posted pictures on the internet.
2. The burglar didn't wear gloves, so she left _____ on the window.
3. The detectives are working on a very difficult _____.
4. My mom saw a pickpocket, so police asked her to be a _____.

5 Which of these skills are you good at? Would you like to be a detective? In pairs, discuss the ideas below.

- spotting clues
- thinking quickly
- noticing little things
- using technology

And YOU

7.4 GRAMMAR *have/get something done*

I can use the structure *have/get something done*.

1 Discuss in groups. Is there a drama club at your school? If so, who participates in it? If there isn't, would it be a good idea?

2 🔊 **2.38** Listen and read. What role is Dan playing in *Murder in the Dark*?

MURDER IN THE DARK

Alisha: *Murder in the Dark* … that's a great poster for the play, Tom. Did you design it?
Tom: Yes, but I want to have some pictures taken for it.
Alisha: The camera on my cell phone is really good. I'll take the pictures and you can have the posters printed later.
Tom: Thanks!
Alisha: What's happening with the costumes?
Tom: Dan's going to have a jacket made by his aunt. I gave him my dad's old coat … but he didn't like it. He's so fussy! He wants to have his hair styled today, so that he looks like a real detective. He's taking it very seriously. The play should be called *Detective Dan*, not *Murder in the Dark*!
Alisha: Hmm … What about the furniture?
Tom: Dad's made these for us. I had them painted this morning.
Alisha: Wow, they're great!
Tom: Careful! The paint's still wet!

3 Study the Grammar box, then circle the correct option. Underline examples of *have/get something done* in the dialogue.

Grammar	*have/get something done*

She wants to have some pictures taken today.
She has her hair cut at Shortcuts.
We had the costumes made for us.
You can have the poster printed downtown.
I'm going to have my face painted for the play.

In spoken English, *get something done* is more common. We use *have/get something done* when **we do the action / someone else does the action for us**.

GRAMMAR TIME > PAGE 112

4 Match phrases 1–6 to phrases a–f to make sentences.

1 [e] I'm not happy with my hair. I …
2 [ ] When I do English activities, I always …
3 [ ] Your coat's dirty. You must …
4 [ ] I love that picture. I should …
5 [ ] I can't see what's written on the board. I'm going to …
6 [ ] If I buy the gift here, I can …

a have it printed for my room.
b have my eyes tested.
c have it cleaned.
d have it wrapped.
e had it cut on the weekend.
f have them checked by the teacher.

5 Complete the sentences with the correct form of *have* and the verbs in parentheses.

1 The burglar made a mess in the house, but we're going to **have** it **cleaned** (clean).
2 We need to catch the robber. Let's _____ some posters _____ (print) with his picture on.
3 The detective always _____ a coffee _____ (bring) to him when he arrives at work.
4 That girl chased the criminal and then she _____ her picture _____ (take) for the newspaper.
5 I never leave my bike without a lock. I don't want to _____ it _____ (steal).

6 In pairs, say if the sentences are true for you. Correct the false sentences.

1 I have my bedroom cleaned on weekends.
2 I have my lunch made every day.
3 I never have my hair colored.
4 We sometimes have pizza delivered to our house.

No, I don't have my bedroom cleaned on weekends. I clean it myself on Saturday!

7.5 LISTENING and VOCABULARY A burglary

I can identify the main points of a story and talk about discovering a crime.

1 **CLASS VOTE** How can social media help the police to find criminals?

2 🔊 **2.39** Listen to the first part of the podcast and look at the pictures. What do you think happened?

3 🔊 **2.40** Listen to the second part of Katrina's story. Order the events.

- A ☐ The police went to the burglar's house.
- B ☐ Katrina found out her laptop was missing.
- C ☐ 1 Katrina and her mom discovered the burglary.
- D ☐ A friend told Katrina about a conversation in the park.
- E ☐ Katrina showed the smartwatch box to the police.
- F ☐ The police took fingerprints and pictures of the crime scene.
- G ☐ Katrina and her friend started looking on social media.

4 **WORD FRIENDS** Study the phrases below using a dictionary. Circle the correct option.

> arrest a criminal   interview a witness   look for clues
> search the area   solve a crime   take fingerprints

1 Detectives can (solve a crime) / take fingerprints more quickly when there's a good witness.
2 The police want to *interview a witness* / *arrest a criminal* who saw somebody go into the house.
3 We believe the police are going to *search the area* / *arrest a criminal* this evening, but they won't say who it is.
4 The crime took place near the forest, and police officers are *solving a crime* / *searching the area* now.
5 The police couldn't *take fingerprints* / *interview a witness* because the burglar was wearing gloves.
6 The detective is *arresting a criminal* / *looking for clues* at the crime scene, but she hasn't found anything yet.

5 🔊 **2.41** Listen to the last part of the podcast. Complete the notes.

> Date of burglary: ¹ October 2nd
> Time of burglary: between
> ² _____ and _____
> Items stolen: ³ _____
> _____
> _____
> Text: ⁴ _____
> Reward: ⁵ $ _____

6 In pairs, tell your classmate what you would do in the situations below.

1 You have your cell phone stolen downtown.
   I'd call the phone company, then I would tell all my friends …
2 You see a person who is shoplifting.
3 You see some people vandalizing a wall near your school.

Unit 7   75

7.6 SPEAKING — Persuading and reassuring

I can persuade and reassure someone.

1 In pairs, look at the picture. What do you think is happening?

2 🔊 2.42 Listen and read the dialogue, then check your answer to Activity 1. Then answer: Who is at the door?

DRESS REHEARSAL

Miss Jones:	OK, this is our first dress rehearsal for *Murder in the Dark*. We'll start with scene two, after the murder.
Alisha:	I'm so nervous. I can't remember my lines!
Miss Jones:	It's all right, Alisha. I know you can do it. Just take a deep breath.
Alisha:	OK, I'll try.
Miss Jones:	Great. Off you go. Skye, could you give me a hand, please?
Tom:	Come on, Alisha! You'll be fine.
Lady Harrington (Alisha):	Oh, poor Sir Hugo! What happened? Was he killed by the fall?
Butler (Tom):	Or … was he murdered?
Lady Harrington (Alisha):	Pardon, Jeeves?
Butler (Tom):	Nothing, Lady Harrington. Don't worry. The police will be here soon …
Miss Jones:	Hello? Can I help you?
Stranger:	Excuse me, I'm here about the crime.
Miss Jones:	Oh, my! A crime? What happened?
Tom:	Miss Jones, it's Dan!
Miss Jones:	Dan? I didn't recognize you!
Dan:	Do you like my costume? I had it made specially for the play!

3 🔊 2.43 Study the Speaking box. Complete the dialogues with one word in each blank. Listen and check.

Speaking — Persuading and reassuring

Persuading
Come on.
Please!
Just try it.
Why don't you try?

Responding
OK, I'll try.
I don't know.
I suppose I can do it.

Reassuring
Don't worry! — It's all right. / OK.
You'll/It'll be fine.
I know. / I'm sure. / Of course you can do it.
Just practice a little more/try again.

1
- A: Could you come to a rock concert with me?
- B: I don't ___know___ … I don't really like rock music.
- A: Please! *The Wild Monsters* are playing.
- B: I _____ I can come, but I don't have much money.
- A: Don't _____! I'll pay for your ticket.

2
- A: Let's go to the fish restaurant.
- B: I never eat fish.
- A: _____ on. _____ try it. It's really good.

3
- A: I can't play this song.
- B: I'm _____ you can do it.
- A: But it's really difficult.
- B: Just _____ a little more.

4 🔊 2.44 Listen again to how people persuaded and reassured others in Activity 3. What do you notice about their intonation? Circle the correct options.

They sound cold / empathetic and enthusiastic / sad.

Speak UP!

5 🔊 2.44 Listen once more and repeat.

6 In pairs, role-play one of the situations.
- Reassure a friend who's worried about his/her math test.
- Persuade a friend to go to a party. (he/she hates parties)

Student A: State your problem.
Student B: Persuade your classmate to do/try something.
Student A: Give a reason why you're worried.
Student B: Reassure your classmate.

7 In pairs, talk about something you find difficult to do. Persuade each other that you can do it.

I can't write a play for the drama class …

And YOU

7.7 WRITING A crime report

I can write a crime report.

1 Look at the report below. What crime is it reporting?

_____

POLICE REPORT

Case No: 234
Date: October 19, 2019
Reporting Officer: Sgt. Lisa Benson
Incident: burglary

① The purpose of this report is to make a record of an illegal incident on October 10, 2019. ② On this date, a 911 call reported a break-in at Apartment 1, 22 Redbrook Way. The incident was reported by William Brown.

③ When we arrived at the crime scene, Mr. Brown's door was open. A TV, a game console, and a laptop were missing from his living room. No other objects were reported missing. Mr. Brown was not at home at the time of the incident. There was nothing else unusual about his apartment. Mr. Brown said that it was impossible for anyone to open the door because it had many locks.

④ We considered looking at CCTV recordings to find any irregular activity, but the cameras were inactive. During investigation, I would recommend that we talk to Mr. Brown's neighbors.

2 Read the report. Match parts 1-4 to their function.
Which paragraph …
☐ summarizes the events?
☐ makes recommendations?
☒ 1 states the aims of the report?
☐ gives extra information?

3 Find examples of adjectives formed by negative prefixes in the report. Complete the chart.

negative prefix	+ adjective	= adjective with negative meaning
un-	fair, usual	unfair, _unusual_
dis-	honest, satisfied	dishonest, dissatisfied
im-	patient, possible	impatient, _____
in-	correct, active	incorrect, _____
il-	logical, legal	Illogical, _____
ir-	responsible, regular	irresponsible, _____

> _We can use prefixes before an adjective to change its meaning._
> **Watch OUT!**

4 Study the Writing box. How does the author of the report state its aims and make a recommendation? Underline the phrases in the report.

Writing A report

Stating the aims of the report
The aim/purpose of this report is to …
This report describes …

Summarize the events
On January 16, 2020, a crime took place in May Gardens …

Using neutral language
The suspect was seen …
A noise was heard …

Making recommendations
I would recommend that …
It is my recommendation that …
We should consider …

5 Write a report about an incident.

Writing Time

1 ❗ Find ideas
Take notes about the incident you learned about recently, or invent one. Think about:
- what happened
- where it happened
- who was involved

2 📄 Draft
Write a draft of your report. Think carefully about the structure of your text. Try to include adjectives with negative prefixes.

3 🔗 Share
Share your draft with another student for feedback. Listen to his/her opinion and suggestions. Check the spelling and grammar.

4 ✏️ Check and write
Make changes to your report. Write the final version of your text.

Unit 7

WORDLIST   Criminals | The law | Action verbs | Solving crimes

active [adj]
assistant [n]
(bank) robbery [adj]
brain [n]
break-in [n]
burglar [n]
burglary [n]
case [n]
catch [v]
CCTV camera [n]
chase [v]
climb [v]
clue [n]
commit [v]
correct [adj]
costume [n]
court [n]
crime [n]
crime scene [n]
criminal [n]
critic [n]
damage [v]
detective [n]
diamond [n]
dishonest [adj]
displeased [adj]
drama club [n]
escape [v]
fair [adj]

fall [v]
fine [n]
fingerprints [n]
flawless [adj]
footprints [n]
fussy [adj]
glove [n]
hide [v]
honest [adj]
illegal [adj]
illogical [adj]
impatient [adj]
impossible [adj]
inactive [adj]
incorrect [adj]
irregular [adj]
irresponsible [adj]
item [n]
jail [n]
judge [n]
jump [v]
law [n]
lawyer [n]
legal [adj]
lock [n]
logical [adj]
magnifying glass [n]
mess [n]
missing [adj]

murder [n]
mysterious [adj]
necklace [n]
patient [adj]
pickpocket [n]
pickpocketing [n]
pleased [adj]
plot [n]
police officer [n]
poster [n]
prison [n]
publish [v]
pull [v]
punishment [n]
push [v]
quote [n]
recognize [v]
record [n]
regular [adj]
rehearsal [n]
report [v]
responsible [adj]
review [n]
reward [n]
robber [n]
security cable [n]
shadow [n]
shoplifter [n]
shoplifting [n]

smartwatch [n]
spot [v]
spy [n]
suspect [n]
theft [n]
thief (thieves) [n]
trip [v]
twist [v]
unfair [adj]
unusual [adj]
usual [adj]
vandal [n]
vandalism [n]
witness [n]

WORD FRIENDS

arrest a criminal
break into apartments or houses
commit a crime
interview a witness
look for clues
rob a bank
search the area
solve a crime
steal things from a store
take fingerprints
tell the truth

VOCABULARY IN ACTION

1 Use the Wordlist to find and write in your notebook:
1. four people who steal things *thief, ...*
2. two people who work in a court
3. three verbs that describe actions in which you use your hands

2 In pairs, use the Wordlist to describe a situation that is:
1. unusual
   A criminal is hiding from a police officer in a trash can.
2. illegal
3. unfair
4. dishonest

3 Compare your ideas for Activity 2 with the class.

4 Use the Wordlist to complete the sentences. Use the words in the correct form.
1. The man escaped last night and police are __searching__ the area now.
2. He _____ a bank when he was young and spent a few years in prison.
3. It's impossible to _____ these new apartments because the locks are very strong.
4. We'd like to _____ a witness who was near here at the time of the crime.
5. The detectives are _____ for clues at the crime scene now.

5 🔊 2.45 **PRONUNCIATION** Listen and repeat the pairs of words. Is the stress the same or different when there is a prefix?

1. correct   incorrect
2. honest   dishonest
3. logical   illogical
4. legal   illegal
5. possible   impossible

SELF-CHECK

1 Write the correct word for each definition.
1. This person steals things from people's pockets or bags. **p** i c k p o c k e t
2. This person tries to discover who has committed a crime. **d** _____
3. This is a crime where a person breaks into a building to steal things. **b** _____
4. This person sees a crime and can say what happened. **w** _____
5. A piece of information that helps to solve a crime. **c** ____
6. A building where criminals go for punishment. **p** _____

2 Complete the text with the words below.

> CCTV cameras   fingerprints   ~~murders~~   reward
> shoplift   uncomfortable

Did you know …?
1. Most _murders_ happen on a Monday.
2. The most popular items that people _____ are electric toothbrushes and cell phones.
3. The best _____ are often found on soap or cheese.
4. There are about 25 million _____ around the world. On average, a person is seen 300 times a day.
5. Police in the USA offered a $5 million _____ for paintings that were stolen from an art gallery. The paintings are still missing.

3 Complete the sentences with the Simple Present passive form of the verbs in parentheses.
1. A lot of TV programs _are made_ (make) about crime.
2. The jewellery _____ (hide) in a secret place.
3. Great crime books _____ (write) by ex-detectives.
4. A lot of criminals _____ (catch) abroad.
5. Fingerprint powder _____ (use) to detect fingerprints.
6. A lot of stolen items _____ (sell) on the internet.

4 In your notebook, use the prompts to write questions in the Simple Past Passive. Then read the text below and answer the questions.
1. When/the man/arrest?
   When was the man arrested?
2. Where/the man/find?
3. What/hide/under the man's jacket?
4. Why/the cakes/steal?

Thief caught with cupcakes

Last night, police in Greenville arrested a man who was found in the kitchen of the police department. The man escaped through a window. He was hiding something under his jacket. It was a selection of cupcakes in a box. The man said he was painting the kitchen in the police department when he saw the cupcakes in the refrigerator. "I wanted to take them home for my wife's birthday," he said.

5 Complete the sentences with the correct form of *have something done* and the words in parentheses.
1. We've designed a "No Time for Crime" poster. We're going to _have it printed_ (it/print) later.
2. There was a burglary at the store, so I _____ (the locks/change).
3. The vandals wrote on the gym wall, so we want to _____ (it/paint).
4. I _____ (my hair/color) red last weekend.
5. The thieves stole our car and left it on the road. We're going to _____ (it/check) before we use it again.

6 In pairs, role-play the situations on page 114. Take turns to listen to your friend's problem. Then try to persuade and reassure him/her.

7 🔊 **2.46** Listen, then listen again and write down what you hear.

SELF-ASSESSMENT   Think about this unit. What did you learn? What do you need help with?   WORKBOOK

8 Think outside the box

VOCABULARY
School subjects | Learning and assessment | Describing students

GRAMMAR
Word order in questions | Third Conditional

Grammar:
Could you give me a hand?
Look at Tom, Alisha, and Skye. Where are they? Why do you think they are at this place?

Speaking:
How was your journey?
Look at Dan, Miguel, and Ed. Are they related? What do you think they are talking about?

8.1 VOCABULARY Education
I can talk about school life.

1  [ ] 2  [ ] 3 [ ]
4  [ ] 5  [ ] 6 [ ] 

1 CLASS VOTE What is your favorite school subject? Why?

2 🔊 **2.47** Match six words in Vocabulary A box to the pictures above. Then listen and repeat the words. Which ones are new to you?

Vocabulary A	School subjects

art biology chemistry citizenship computer science English
geography health history home economics literature math
music PE philosophy physics social studies Spanish

3 CLASS VOTE Are the subjects below taught in your school? If not, which of them would you add to the school curriculum?

cooking drama fashion design film-making gardening karate
personal finance photography public speaking yoga

4 I KNOW! Copy the chart into your notebook. Then, in pairs, add as many words as you can to each category.

Types of school	People at school	Places at school
elementary school	principal	library
	homeroom teacher	cafeteria

5 🔊 **2.48** Study Vocabulary B box. Then circle the correct options. Listen and check.

Vocabulary B	Learning and assessment

Learning
learn memorize study
Types of assessment
performance practical test project speaking test written test

1 (memorize) / *study* a poem
2 *learn* / *study* for the whole night
3 *memorize* / *learn* about the ancient Romans

80 Unit 8

6 In pairs, match pictures A–D to the types of assessment in Vocabulary B box.

A

B

C

D

7 In pairs, discuss which types of assessment you might have for different school subjects. What types do you like? What do you dislike? Why?

8 🔊 2.49 Study Vocabulary C box, then listen and repeat the words. How do you say these words in your language?

Vocabulary C	Describing students
confident   creative   hard-working   intelligent   lazy talented/gifted
good at: critical thinking   general knowledge problem-solving   teamwork

9 Use the words from Vocabulary C box to complete the text. The passages in italics will help you.

Life skills are important, too!

It's easy to think that school life is all about how ¹ _intelligent_ you are, in other words, your *ability to understand things*. However, good life skills help you more than intelligence, at school and beyond.

One key skill is how ² _____ you are. That is, *you believe that you can do things successfully*. It's important to build this skill because it helps with many areas of life. Once you believe in yourself, you can start being ³ _____, *using your imagination*, which is helpful in all subjects, not just arts.

Another life skill, which is a new school subject in some areas, is ⁴ _____. This teaches you *how to think clearly and ask questions*. Part of this subject also involves ⁵ _____. Students develop *the ability to identify a problem and work out a solution*. Also, students learn *how to work well with others*, which is all part of another key skill, ⁶ _____.

Of course, traditional skills are important, too, such as ⁷ _____, *knowing information about the world around you*. And don't forget about being ⁸ _____, which means that *you always put in a lot of effort*, as that's the secret to many people's success.

10 Read the riddles below. Which life skill is each of them testing?

1. You have two minutes to think of as many uses as possible for paper clips. _____
2. Two boys are enroling at a new school. When they fill in their forms, the principal sees that they have the same parents. He also notices that they share the same birthday. "Are you twins?" asks the principal. "No," reply the boys. Is it possible? _____

11 🔊 2.50 In pairs, solve the riddles in Activity 10. Then listen and check.

12 How would you describe yourself as a student? Which skills could you improve and how?

And YOU

Unit 8   81

8.2 GRAMMAR Word order in questions

I can ask questions with the correct word order.

1 Do you have any certificates? What were they for and when did you get them?

2 🔊 **2.51** Look at the picture. What are Tom, Alisha, and Skye doing? Listen and read to check your guesses.

_____
_____
_____

COULD YOU GIVE ME A HAND?

Alisha: Hey, Tom. <u>What are you doing?</u>
Tom: I'm getting ready for my water safety test tomorrow. I'm just checking the life vest.
Skye: Cool. Will you get a certificate?
Tom: Yeah, definitely … if I pass! Have you ever gone kayaking?
Skye: No, I haven't tried it. I went windsurfing once, though.
Tom: Did you enjoy it? Who taught you?
Skye: No, not much. My dad taught me, but it was really hard.
Tom: Could you guys give me a hand moving this?
Alisha: Sure. Is it heavy?
Tom: No, it's quite light, but you have to be careful with it.
Alisha: Where do you want it? Here, near the water?
Tom: Yeah, that's great. OK, thanks. I think I'm ready.
Alisha: Good luck!
Skye: Are you going to become an instructor?
Tom: I hope so. Maybe one day!

3 Study the Grammar box, then circle the correct option to complete the sentence. Underline examples of questions in the dialogue.

Grammar	Word order in questions

Yes/No **questions**

Inversion
You are hungry. → **Are** you hungry? Yes, I am.
You have finished. → **Have** you finished? Yes, I have.
I enjoyed it. → **Did** you enjoy it? No, I didn't.
She rides her bike. → **Does** she ride her bike? No, she doesn't.

Wh- **questions**

Question word + inversion
Why are you hungry?
Why did you enjoy it?

Subject questions
Who taught you? **My dad** taught me.

Object questions
Who did they see? They saw **Tom**.
In subject questions, we use / don't use inversion and auxiliary verbs.

GRAMMAR TIME > PAGE 113

4 In your notebook, write questions for these sentences.
1 Yes, I had pasta for dinner last night.
   Did you have pasta for dinner last night?
2 No, I left home at six thirty this morning.
3 Yes, we're going to Italy on vacation.
4 Yes, I saw two plays at the theater last week.
5 No, I'm not going to do anything tonight.

5 In your notebook, write subject and object questions about the underlined words.
1 <u>A fire</u> started <u>in the science lab</u> yesterday.
   What happened in the science lab?
   Where did the fire start?
2 <u>Class 9D</u> had <u>a math test</u> this morning.
3 <u>Everyone</u> in my class has read <u>this book</u>!
4 <u>Tom</u> saw me <u>when I was at the burger truck</u>.

6 In pairs, ask and answer the questions in Activity 4. Some of your answers may be false. Say if your classmate's sentences are true or false.

And YOU

Unit 8

8.3 READING and VOCABULARY — A magazine article

I can identify the headings in a magazine article and talk about intelligence.

1 CLASS VOTE Do you think intelligence can be measured? Why? / Why not?

2 🔊 **2.52** Listen and read the magazine article. Match headings a–d to paragraphs 1–4.
- a Why are tests so hard?
- b IQs have improved
- c A new report
- d What are the reasons?

Reading tip

In a magazine article, headings summarize the main ideas of the following section. In order to match headings to paragraphs, identify the key words in a heading and then find similiar words in the paragraph.

Bright sparks!

1 [c]

Is modern education awful? Are today's teenagers poor learners who can't think for themselves? Not according to a report from researchers in Scotland. The good news is that young people are more intelligent than their great-grandparents were!

2 [ ]

Intelligence Quotient (IQ) tests are a way of measuring general intelligence. An average score in a given population is 100 points. Scientist Steven Pinker has taken a look at IQ test results over many years and made notes about what he found. Every few years, people did better in the tests, so the test writers made changes and the tests became harder.

3 [ ]

If some average modern teenagers went back in time, their IQ score would be higher than the people around them. If your IQ is 100 now, and you traveled back to 1950, you would probably have an IQ of 118. If you went back to 1910, you would have an IQ of 130. That's better than 98 percent of other people in 1910! To look at it another way, an average person from 1910 who visited us today would have an IQ measurement of only 70.

4 [ ]

Now, why are people getting smarter? In order to find the reasons, we have to ask "How have people changed?" We have made improvements in diets and health, and because they influence the brain, this is the main reason. Answers to vocabulary, math, or general knowledge questions haven't changed so much, but we have become better at problem-solving. We have made progress with puzzle questions, such as "GLOVE is to HAND as SHOE is to what?" This is also because we live in a fast-paced digital world where we have to think and react quickly, and we can't be afraid of making mistakes.

3 Read the text again. Mark the sentences true (T) or false (F).
1. [T] Researchers believe that humans are smarter now than in the past.
2. [ ] Steven Pinker based his report on IQ tests which he took himself.
3. [ ] Test writers had to make the tests more challenging.
4. [ ] A change in lifestyle is responsible for the better test scores.

4 Write in your notebook two Wh- questions about the magazine article. Ask them to a classmate.

5 WORD FRIENDS Complete the Word Friends with *make* or *take*. Sometimes more than one answer is possible.
1. _make_ changes
2. _____ a test
3. _____ sense
4. _____ notes
5. _____ progress
6. _____ a look
7. _____ an improvement
8. _____ a mistake

6 In pairs, discuss other reasons for the test results. Use the ideas below to help you.
- We take more tests.
- More people go to college.
- We learn a lot from the internet.
- Schools are better.
- Parents talk to their children more.
- We read more books.

And YOU?

Unit 8 83

8.4 GRAMMAR Third Conditional

I can talk about hypothetical situations in the past

1 **CLASS VOTE** Do you think you would be a good teacher? Why? / Why not?

2 🔊 **2.53** Listen and read the article. What was Babar Ali's idea? Was it a good one?

Babar Ali – the youngest principal in the world

Babar Ali is probably the youngest head teacher in the world. His school has hundreds of students and he is opening other branches.

But how did it all start? One day Babar was walking back from school when he saw some children in his neighborhood who couldn't afford to go to school. He decided to help them and started teaching children in his backyard. The school grew and soon people started talking about it.

If Babar Ali hadn't seen those children in his neighborhood, he wouldn't have opened his own school! If the children had had more money, they would have been in school, like Babar. But none of them could pay for school books, uniforms, or transportation, so they couldn't study.

Some of Babar's original students have started to work with him as teachers. They are happy to work at the school. If Babar hadn't had his good idea, their lives wouldn't have changed.

Imagine you enter a school in India, and you meet the principal, who is a man in his twenties!

3 Study the Grammar box, then circle the correct option to complete the sentence. Underline examples of structures in the Third Conditional in the article.

> **Grammar** | **Third Conditional**
>
> If the children **had been** to the library, they **would have borrowed** some books.
> **Would** she **have walked** home if it **hadn't rained**?
> We use the Third Conditional to talk about unreal situations in the *present / past*. They *happened / didn't happen*, and *will / won't* happen.
> We form it with If + *Simple past / Past Perfect* + would + have + past participle.
>
> GRAMMAR TIME ▸ PAGE 113

4 Circle the correct option.
1. If we had seen the weather forecast, (we wouldn't have gone) / wouldn't go to the beach!
2. If she *saved / had saved* more money, she would have traveled more.
3. If Matt had read the ad, he would *have applied / applied* for the job.
4. If Rachel *hadn't run / hasn't run* the marathon, she wouldn't have hurt her leg.

5 Complete the questions with the correct form of the verbs in parentheses to make the Third Conditional.
1. What other language *would you have studied* (you/study) if you *hadn't started* (not start) English classes?
2. Where _____ (you/go) to school if you _____ (not come) to this one?
3. If you _____ (come) to school today, where _____ (you/go)?
4. How _____ (you/celebrate) your last birthday if you _____ (have) an unlimited budget for the party?
5. If you _____ (go) to bed at 7 p.m. last night _____ (you/sleep)?

6 In pairs, ask and answer the questions in Activity 5.

And YOU

84 Unit 8

8.5 LISTENING and VOCABULARY — Awkward moments

I can identify specific information in dialogues and talk about awkward moments.

1 Have any of these "awkward moments" ever happened to you? In pairs, discuss what you would say or do in each situation.
- You call your teacher "mom" or "dad" by accident.
- You're playing with your pen when it flies across the classroom.
- You're at school and realize your T-shirt is inside out.

2 🔊 2.54 Listen to four dialogues. Circle the pictures that correspond to the correct answers.

1 What does the teacher want Emily to do before the test?
   A   B (circled)   C

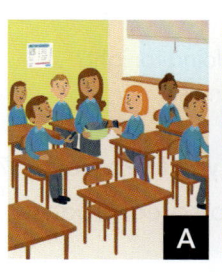

2 Where are all the other students in Max's class now?
   A   B   C

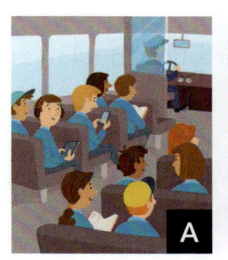

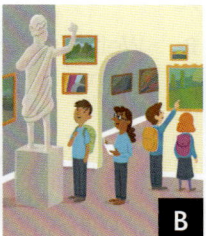

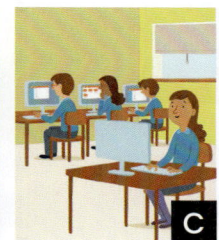

3 What happened to Ben's form?
   A   B   C

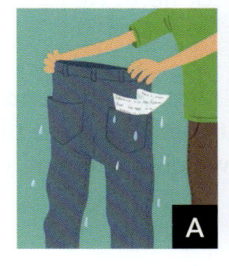

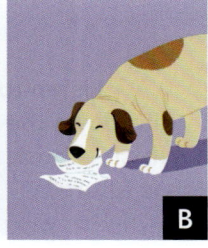

4 What were Madison and Anya doing?
   A   B   C

3 🔊 2.54 Listen again. Which situation is the most embarrassing? In pairs, discuss how you would react in each of them.

4 🔊 2.55 Study the Vocabulary box, then circle the correct options to complete the sentences. Listen and check.

Vocabulary	Phrasal verbs
calm down fill out (a form) get on	
hand in/out look over look up mess around	

1 The teacher asked us all to (hand in) / look up our homework on time.
2 Students who finish early should get on / look up with some extra reading.
3 Please don't mess around / hand out in the art class.
4 Make sure you get on / look over all your answers before you finish.
5 You can look up / look over any words you don't know in a dictionary.
6 We have to fill out / calm down this form with our name and number.
7 Calm down / Get on, Alice! Your grade in the math test was bad, but that's not the end of the world!

5 🔊 2.55 Listen again to the sentences in Activity 4. Which part of the phrasal verbs is stressed: the verb or the particle? **Speak UP!**

6 🔊 2.56 Listen to four dialogues and match the students to the "awkward moment" they went through. There is one extra moment.

1 Alex   2 Hanna   3 John   4 Robbie

☐ He/She got a bad grade in a test
☐ He/She fell asleep in class.
☐ He/She forgot to do homework.
☑ 1 His/Her essay was too short.
☐ He/She fell off a chair while messing around.

7 In your notebook, write a short paragraph about an "awkward moment" that has happened to you. Then share it in small groups. Who has the most embarrassing story? **And YOU**

Unit 8 85

8.6 SPEAKING Exchanging personal information

I can have a casual conversation and exchange personal information.

1 **CLASS VOTE** Have you ever changed schools? If so, what was it like?

2 🔊 **2.57** Listen and read. Answer the questions in your notebook.
1. How is Dan feeling?
   He's very tired.
2. Does Ed like his American college?
3. Is this Dan's first time in New York?
4. What are their plans?

HOW WAS YOUR JOURNEY?

Ed: Dan! Great to see you! Sorry I couldn't meet you at the airport.
Dan: That's all right. It was easy by taxi. It's good to be here.
Ed: How was your trip?
Dan: Tiring! I feel exhausted!
Ed: Well, let's put your bag in my locker, and then we'll get something to eat.
Dan: The college looks amazing. Do you like it here?
Ed: Yeah. I've made some good friends already. What about you? How have you been?
Dan: Everything's fine. The house is quiet without you, though.
Ed: Oh! So, do you miss me?
Dan: Not really. Well … only sometimes!
Ed: Ha! Oh, there's Miguel. Let me introduce you. Hey, Miguel! Come and meet my brother, Dan.
Miguel: Nice to meet you, Dan. Is this your first time in New York?
Dan: Yes, we lived on the west coast when we were younger. I can't wait to look around.
Miguel: So what are you guys doing tonight?
Ed: We're grabbing a bite here, and then I'm going to show Dan around. Would you like to join us?
Miguel: Sure thing. I'd love to.

3 🔊 **2.58** Study the Speaking box, then match the questions to the responses. Listen and check.

Speaking	Exchanging personal information

Past
How have you been?
How was your trip?
Is this your first time in the United States?
Present
Do you like it here?
Future
What are you guys doing tonight?
Would you like to join us?

1. **A:** *Would you like to join us?*
   B: That would be great. Thanks.
2. **A:** _____
   B: Fine. What about you?
3. **A:** _____
   B: Well, it's interesting, but I miss home.
4. **A:** _____
   B: No, it isn't. We had a vacation in Florida when I was younger.
5. **A:** _____
   B: Well, there's a great pizza restaurant near here. We're going to try it.

4 🔊 **2.59** Listen to Miguel, Dan, and Ed. Write down the three questions they ask. Which is past, which is present, and which is future?
- Question 1: past
- Question 2: present
- Question 3: future

5 Work in groups of three. Role-play one of the situations below. Students A and B are friends, and they meet Student C, who is a friend of Student A.
1. at a party
2. at the movie theater
3. in a sports club

And YOU?

8.7 WRITING — An email giving information

I can write an email giving information.

1 **CLASS VOTE** What information would you give to a school exchange student who was coming to your school?

2 Read the emails. What does Nadia want to know? Does Kyla include all the information Nadia asks for? Answer in your notebook.

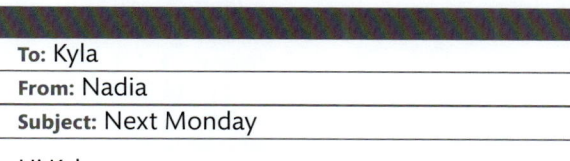

To: Kyla
From: Nadia
Subject: Next Monday

Hi Kyla,
As you know, I'm arriving next Monday evening. I'm attaching a recent picture, so you can se what I look like! Can you tell me a few things about your school? Like, is it big and do you wear uniforms? Also, are you going to meet me at the airport, or should I take a taxi?
See you soon,
Nadia

[Send]

To: Nadia
From: Kyla
Subject: Next Monday

Dear Nadia,
Thanks for your email. I'm looking forward to meeting you as well.
You asked about my school. Well, there are about a thousand students, and the teachers are friendly. We wear uniforms, but I can lend you a spare one if you like. I have basketball club after school on Fridays, so you're welcome to come along.
Of course we're going to meet you on Monday! I'll be at the airport with my parents. We'll have a big card with your name on, but our picture is attached to this email, too, just in case!
Don't worry about anything, we're going to have fun!
Best wishes,
Kyla

[Send]

---

3 Look at the phrases in purple. What do they mean? Why does Kyla use them?

4 Study the Writing box. Complete blanks a–d with sentences from Kyla's email.

Writing — An email giving information

1 Starting your email
Hi / Hello / Dear (name), …
It was good to hear from you.
a _____ Thanks for your letter. _____
It was nice to hear your news.

2 Making it clear why you're writing
You wanted to know about my school. Well, …
You asked for information about the school here.
b _____

3 Giving useful information
There are about a thousand students.
c _____

4 Making arrangements
We'll definitely meet you.
We'll be there at 7:15 p.m.
d _____

5 Before you finish
I'm really looking forward to seeing you (again).
We're going to have a great time.

6 Ending your email
Best wishes, / See you soon,

---

5 Go to page 115 and read the email. Write a reply.

Writing Time

1 ❗ **Find ideas**
In your notebook, take notes about what you will include in your email. Remember to:
- thank Jack for his email and say why you're writing.
- reply to all the questions.
- express your feelings about the visit.

2 📄 **Draft**
Write a draft of your email. Use the Writing box to help you.

3 🔗 **Share**
Share your email with another pair of students for feedback. Listen to their opinion and suggestions. Check the spelling and grammar. Make any necessary changes to your text.

4 ✓ **Check and write**
Make changes to your text. Do you use appropriate language? Write the final version of your email.

Unit 8

WORDLIST
School subjects | Learning and assessment | Describing students | Phrasal verbs

ability [n]
art [n]
average [adj]
awkward [adj]
biology [n]
board [n]
boarding school [n]
brain [n]
branch [n]
cafeteria [n]
calm down [phr v]
certificate [n]
cheat [v]
chemistry [n]
citizenship [n]
college [n]
computer science [n]
confident [adj]
cooking [n]
creative [adj]
critical thinking [n]
curriculum [n]
drama [n]
education [n]
effort [n]
enrol [v]
essay [n]
experiment [n]
fashion design [n]

fill out (a form) [phr v]
film-making [n]
gardening [n]
general knowledge [n]
geography [n]
get on [phr v]
gifted [adj]
gym [n]
hand in/out [phr v]
hard-working [adj]
health [n]
high school [n]
home economics [n]
homeroom teacher [n]
imagination [n]
improvement [n]
influence [v]
information [n]
instructor [n]
intelligence [n]
intelligent [adj]
IQ [n]
karate [n]
kindergarten [n]
lazy [adj]
learn [v]
learner [n]
library [n]
life skill [n]

literature [n]
locker [n]
look over [phr v]
look up [phr v]
math [n]
measure [v]
memorize [v]
mess around [v]
middle school [n]
miss [v]
music [n]
paper clip [n]
pass [v]
PE [n]
performance [n]
personal finance [n]
photography [n]
physics [n]
population [n]
practical test [n]
presentation [n]
principal [n]
private school [n]
problem-solving [n]
progress [n]
project [n]
public school [n]
public speaking [n]
raise money [v]

school exchange [n]
school secretary [n]
science [n]
score [n]
social studies [n]
solution [n]
speaking test [n]
spill [v]
study [v]
subject [n]
talented [adj]
teaching assistant [n]
teamwork [n]
technical [adj]
uniform [n]
written test [n]
yoga [n]

WORD FRIENDS
make changes
take a test
make sense
miss a person
take/make notes
make progress
take a look
make an improvement
make a mistake

VOCABULARY IN ACTION

1 Use the Wordlist to find and write in your notebook:
  1 four types of test or assessment
     performance, ...
  2 five adjectives to describe students
  3 three life skills

2 In pairs, use the Wordlist to discuss which subjects:
  1 are useful for you
  2 are not very useful for you
  3 are hard to understand
  4 are fun
  5 you would like to try in the future

3 Use four words from the Wordlist to describe an "ideal" student in your notebook. Compare with a classmate. Are your ideas the same?

4 Complete the sentences with the words below.

  mistake   notes   progress   sense   test

  1 My sister's taking her driving ___test___ today.
  2 It doesn't make _____ to me.
  3 Listen and take _____.
  4 My grades are improving, so I'm making _____.
  5 I didn't get an A on the test because I made a _____ on one question.

5 🔊 2.60 **PRONUNCIATION** Listen to the intonation in each question and repeat.

Do you like it here?
Would you like to join us?
Did you enjoy the movie?
Have you been here before?
Are you going to visit your family?

6 🔊 2.60 Listen again. What do the questions in Activity 5 have in common? Does the intonation rise or fall in them? In pairs, ask the questions with the correct intonation.

SELF-CHECK

1 Write the correct word for each definition.
1. great poems, novels, and other books
   l _i_ _t_ _e_ _r_ _a_ _t_ _u_ _r_ _e_
2. a piece of paper you get when you pass an exam
   c _ _ _ _ _ _ _ _ _ _
3. If you have a test tomorrow, you should do this.
   s _ _ _ _ _
4. a person who teaches you a special skill, like driving
   i _ _ _ _ _ _ _ _ _ _ _ _ _
5. a presentation using dance, music, acting, or movement
   p _ _ _ _ _ _ _ _ _ _ _ _

2 Complete the questions.
1. Do you prefer to relax and not work hard? Are you sometimes l _a_ _z_ _y_?
2. Are you shy or are you c _ _ _ _ _ _ _ _ _ _?
3. Can you work well with other people? Are you good at t _ _ _ _ _ _ _ _?
4. Do you know a lot about the world? How's your g _?
5. Can you use your imagination? Are you c _ _ _ _ _ _ _ _?
6. Do you have some natural skills, for example, in sports or music? Are you t _ _ _ _ _ _ _ _?

3 In pairs, ask and answer the questions from Activity 2.

4 Complete the text with the correct form of the verbs in parentheses.

Teachers at a school in Canada have taken unhealthy snacks out of students' lunchboxes.
If the students ¹_____ (not bring) unhealthy snacks to school, the teachers ²_____ (not take) them.

Ex-police officers are going to get students out of bed and drive them to school!
If the students ³_____ (not miss) classes before, the school ⁴_____ (not introduce) this scheme.

An angry principal makes parents pay a fine after they miss parent-teacher evening.
If the parents ⁵_____ (go) to parent-teacher evening, they ⁶_____ (not have) to pay a fine.

5 Read the answers. Complete the questions.
1. A: _____*Is it raining*_____ now?
   B: No, it isn't raining now.
2. A: Where _____?
   B: Rosie goes to school in New York.
3. A: When _____?
   B: The movie finished at eight o'clock.
4. A: Who _____?
   B: Miss Navarro teaches them Spanish.
5. A: Who _____?
   B: She called Carl.

6 Work in pairs. Imagine you are an exchange student in the United States. Go to page 115, choose a "character," and use the information to ask and answer questions. Add two more questions and extra information of your own.

A: *Angelina? That's a nice name. Where are you from?*
B: *France. I live in Paris.*
A: *Is this your first time in the United States?*

7 🔊 **2.61** Listen, then listen again and write down what you hear.

_____
_____
_____
_____
_____

SELF-ASSESSMENT Think about this unit. What did you learn? What do you need help with?

CULTURE

Do smartphones make you smarter?

How do teenagers in the UK and the USA use their cell phones?

More than ninety percent of British teenagers own a cell phone; a minority have two or more. These *screenagers* spend more than twenty-seven hours a week online. They can now connect when and where they like with smartphones and tablets. Apparently, UK teenagers avoid using smartphones to chat with friends. Instead, they choose to watch video clips, play games, share pictures, and send instant messages. As for social media, teens like keeping in touch via Twitter, Snapchat, or Instagram. They leave Facebook to their moms and dads!

Teenagers may be connected all the time, but there is one place where most teenagers can't use their digital devices: school! In the UK there is no law about cell phone use in schools, but teachers can remove devices from students if necessary. However, not all teachers agree and some even try to use smartphones in class.

A recent British report said that removing smartphones from schools will give students more time for their education. It said that smartphones are a big distraction, make students less productive, and are bad for learning.

However, in the USA some people do not agree. Recently one school in New York decided to allow students to use smartphones at school. They said that smartphones can be an excellent resource for the classroom. We carry a lot of information in our pockets and this information can be really useful. In this New York school, smartphones can definitely make you smarter!

GLOSSARY
device (n) a machine or tool
distraction (n) something that takes your attention away from what you are doing
law (n) a system or rules
minority (n) a small part of a larger group
remove (v) take away

EXPLORE

1 In pairs, ask and answer the questions.
1. What do you do with your cell phone?
2. Do you think it makes you smarter or less smart? Why?
3. Do many people have smartphones in your country?

2 In your notebook, correct the sentences about the article.
1. All UK teachers believe smartphones are bad for students.
2. A recent UK report said that using smartphones at school can be positive.
3. All schools in the USA and the UK have similar ideas about smartphone use in schools.

EXPLORE MORE

3 ▶ 01 Watch Part 1 of the video and answer the questions in your notebook.

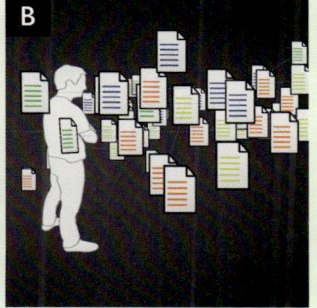

A B C D

1. Picture A (above) shows a busy street in an Asian country. Which country is it?
2. Why is this country so important in the video?
3. How similar is your country to the one in the report?

4 ▶ 01 Complete the sentences about South Korea with the numbers below. Then watch Part 1 again and check.

eight   a couple of   ~~ten~~   eighteen   four

1. You can download files ___ten___ times faster here.
2. Even _____ -year-olds spend _____ hours a week online.
3. Some teenagers use the internet for _____ hours a day.
4. Will your country be like this in _____ years from now?

5 What do you think about the issue of internet addiction in South Korea? Do you think the same thing could happen in your country in the future?

6 ▶ 02 Watch Part 2 of the video. Match pictures B–D to captions 1–3.
1. ☐ Students can interact online to solve problems.
2. ☐ B ☐ Reading online is not like reading a book.
3. ☐ This is part of a big online conversation.

7 ▶ 02 Watch Part 2 again. Circle the correct option.
1. Now we *send* / (*receive*) information via connections or hyperlinks.
2. You can watch the angry cat and then create your own *clip* / *text*.
3. South Korea is the most *addicted* / *connected* country in the world.
4. They are regularly at the *top* / *bottom* of the world's education league tables.

8 Do you think the report is in favor or against the use of the internet? Why? Discuss in pairs.

YOU EXPLORE

9 **CULTURE PROJECT** In groups, prepare for a debate based on the question: "Do smartphones make you smarter?"
1. In your notebooks, prepare a list of points to support your argument.
2. Present your argument to the class.
3. What was the most common point of view among your classmates?

CULTURE

What do the British really eat?

Popular food in the UK

Most people think that British food in Britain is all about fish and chips, chip butties (basically a French fry sandwich!), or afternoon tea, but that's not the whole story. There are so many different cultures in the UK that you have a huge choice of flavors and cuisines to choose from.

1. Indian food has been the country's favorite for years. Every town has at least one Indian restaurant. People even say that the national dish is now *chicken tikka masala*, a spicy curry usually served with rice or Indian bread called *naan*. It's delicious!

2. American food is everywhere. There's not only McDonald's now, but new gourmet burger restaurants like Five Guys. American food is popular because the recipes are very familiar to British people — hot dogs, fried chicken, pepperoni pizza, nachos, and BBQ ribs are all big favorites.

3. People have a passion for fresh and healthy food these days and that's why Japanese food is popular. It's also easy to eat as a takeaway meal. Young people now prefer to eat sushi at lunch to the traditional British sandwich, although some still have problems with chopsticks!

Do you want to try more international food? Then check out the amazing Zaza Bazaar in Bristol! It opened in 2011 and has become one of the most popular places to eat in the city. It's also the biggest restaurant; they can serve over 1,000 people and have food from everywhere — Vietnam, Italy, China, Thailand, as well as Britain's three favorites, of course!

GLOSSARY
chopsticks (n) a pair of thin sticks used for eating in China, Japan, and other Asian countries
cuisine (n) style of cooking typical of a country or region
gourmet (adj) high quality (of food)

EXPLORE

1 In pairs, ask and answer the questions.
1. What do people like eating in your country?
2. What are your favorite dishes?
3. What do you think British people really eat?

2 Read the article. Mark the sentences true (T) or false (F). Then check your answers to question 3 in Activity 1.
1. [T] People have the wrong idea about food in the UK.
2. [ ] It's easy to find an Indian restaurant in the UK.
3. [ ] American food is not very varied.
4. [ ] A lot of people eat sushi for their evening meal.
5. [ ] Zaza Bazaar doesn't serve Indian food.

3 According to the article, why is each food particularly popular? Match types of food 1–3 to adjectives a–c.
1. American [c]   a practical
2. Japanese [ ]   b tasty
3. Indian [ ]   c familiar

EXPLORE MORE

4 ▶ 03 Watch Part 1 of the video and answer the questions in your notebook.
1. Who are Anjum and Lynn?
2. What type of food are they cooking?

5 ▶ 03 Watch Part 1 again. Circle the correct option.
1. Kerala is in *northern* / (*southern*) India.
2. Anjum and Lynn go to the market to *raise money for charity* / *help the community*.
3. Keralan food is *heavy and spicy* / *light and healthy*.
4. It's *easy* / *difficult* to find the ingredients for Keralan dishes in Liverpool.

6 Check (✓) the three dishes that Anjum and Lynn are going to make.
1. [ ] coconut curry with pepper
2. [✓] coconut chicken with ginger
3. [ ] spicy salmon wraps
4. [ ] rice and salmon wraps
5. [ ] rice noodles
6. [ ] vegetable noodles

7 Which of the three dishes would you like to try? Why?
I'd like to try the first dish because I love coconut.

8 ▶ 04 Watch Part 2 of the video. Answer the questions.
1. Does Anjum like Lynn's cooking?
2. How many people visit Liverpool's farmers' market?
3. Do the people at the market buy Lynn's food immediately?
4. Do they sell all the food?

9 Have you ever cooked for a lot of people? Or have you ever helped out in the kitchen? What did you do?
I once helped my mom cook dinner for twenty relatives.

YOU EXPLORE

10 CULTURE PROJECT In groups, prepare a survey based on the question: "What do people really eat in your town?"
1. Prepare a questionnaire. Include local and international dishes (e.g., *pizza, burgers*).
2. Give the questionnaire to friends and family. Then collect the results.
3. Report your results to the class.

Can you believe this weather?

What's the weather like?

If you don't know what to talk about, there's always the weather. In the UK, people do this a lot because although the weather is quite mild, it changes a lot.

But American weather systems are very different – they have great extremes. When it's freezing cold in the Midwest, you can barely go outside. In the South East, tropical storms form in the Atlantic. They can build into tornadoes or hurricanes and bring high winds, torrential rain, floods, and devastation. The population is prepared for this and there are even storm chasers. They are people who follow tornadoes at high speed to see the damage they cause and to warn local people of the dangers.

In the UK, it seems that people are never prepared! When extreme weather comes, it's always a shock. A few years ago a freak snowstorm brought chaos to transportation in the country. British Rail canceled trains because of "the wrong kind of snow!" People in places like Canada and Russia thought this was funny - heavy snow is just part of life for them!

And can the weather affect our moods or character? Well, there is a saying in the UK: "I feel a bit under the weather." It means you don't feel very well. People who live in sunny climates seem happier. Those who live with grey skies and little light in winter can be more melancholic. But that's certainly not the whole story. Economic and social factors are more important to people's well-being than whether the sun is out or not.

GLOSSARY
devastation (n) ruin
freak (adj) very unusual
predict (v) to say that something will happen
torrential rain (n) very heavy rain

EXPLORE

1. Do you think the weather can affect you? How? Discuss in pairs.

2. Read the article. Mark the sentences true (T) or false (F).
   1. [F] Americans are less prepared for bad weather than the British.
   2. [ ] The British are less prepared than Canadians and Russians for winter.
   3. [ ] To be *under the weather* means "to be depressed."
   4. [ ] The tone of the article is quite serious.

3. Read the article again. Answer the questions in your notebook.
   1. Does the writer think that the weather can affect mood or character greatly? Do you agree with this opinion?
   2. Think about people from different parts of your country. Are their characters very different depending on the weather where they live?

EXPLORE MORE

4. ▶ 05 Watch Part 1 of the video. Match animals 1–6 from the video to pictures A–F. Which of these animals live in your country?
   1. [C] whale
   2. [ ] penguin
   3. [ ] shark
   4. [ ] seal
   5. [ ] dolphin
   6. [ ] manatee

A
B
C
D
E
F

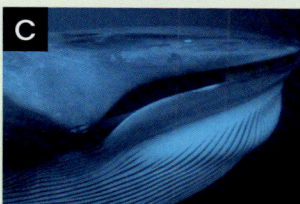

5. What does the narrator say about the Atlantic Ocean? Circle the best summary.
   1. It's very large and mysterious.
   2. It's dangerous and beautiful at the same time.
   3. It's the most famous ocean in the world.

6. ▶ 06 Watch Part 2 of the video. Circle the correct option.
   1. Here *warm* / (*hot*) winds from the Sahara Desert have made the sea turn *wild* / *crazy*.
   2. The waves are *huge* / *giant* and the conditions are *awful* / *difficult*.
   3. *Warm* / *Cool* air rises from the sea and creates *thick* / *black* clouds.
   4. *Torrential* / *Light* rain arrives on land and *frightening* / *enormous* waves and *heavy* / *strong* winds cause devastation.

7. What images do you remember of the storm? What most surprised you about it? Discuss in groups.

8. ▶ 07 Watch Part 3 of the video. Complete the sentences in your notebook.
   1. The strong hurricane destroyed … *houses, trees and businesses*
   2. The young dolphin is in danger because …
   3. The thick vegetation in the mangrove forests is good because it …
   4. The Atlantic can be a heaven or a hell, depending on …

9. Do you have examples of extreme or changeable weather in your country? Where? What kind of weather can you get there?

YOU EXPLORE

10. **CULTURE PROJECT** In groups, prepare a presentation about the weather in your country.
    1. Use the internet or other sources to research different types of weather in your country.
    2. Write a short script and think about images or videos to use in your presentation.
    3. Present it to the class.
    4. Report back: what did you learn from the other presentations?

Where do they toss the caber?

Aussie Rules

If you think the most popular sport in Australia is rugby or cricket, think again. It's a sport that you have probably never heard of, called Australian Rules Football. Commonly known as "Aussie Rules," big games attract huge crowds, especially in the large stadiums of Sydney and Melbourne.

So what is Aussie Rules? Well, it's very different from the soccer that you and I know. The game is played between two teams of eighteen players and the field is oval-shaped. Though called football, it is more similar to rugby. For example, the ball is oval and you score points by kicking it between two goalposts, just like in rugby.

However, players can be anywhere on the field and they can use any part of their bodies to move the ball. Running with the ball is fine, but you have to bounce it or touch it on the ground at the same time. Throwing the ball is not allowed. Aussie Rules includes a lot of physical contact and can be dangerous. Players can tackle each other using their hands or even their whole body!

The sport was invented in the 1850s in Melbourne, but amazingly, a national competition didn't take place until the 1980s. It is equally popular among men and women. Because it is purely Australian, it is rich in cultural history and references. Australians identify with it greatly. They are very proud to have a sport that they can call their own.

It is only really played in Australia, but it has fans worldwide. Who knows? Maybe one day it will become very popular in other countries, too.

GLOSSARY
bounce (v) (of a ball) hit the ground and go up
goalpost (n) one of the two posts of a goal in games such as soccer
league (n) a group of sports teams or players who compete against each other
oval (adj) shaped like an egg
tackle (v) to try to take the ball from another player

EXPLORE

1 In pairs, ask and answer the questions.
1. What sports do you practice? Who do you play with? Why do you play them?
2. What is the national sport in your country?
3. What role do sports have in your country?

2 Read the article and answer the questions in your notebook.
1. In what ways is Aussie Rules culturally important for Australia?
2. Do you think many sports have this cultural role? Why? / Why not?

EXPLORE MORE

3 ▶ 08 Watch Part 1 of the video with no sound. Order the actions as they appear in the video.
a ☐ men running a race
b ☐ spectators watching the sports
c ☑ 1 a man throwing a large piece of wood (the "caber")
d ☐ men playing bagpipes and drums
e ☐ a man throwing a hammer
f ☐ two men wrestling
g ☐ two girls dancing

4 ▶ 08 Watch Part 1 of the video with sound. Complete the sentences with the words below.

> Olympics   parks   ~~tradition~~
> celebration   disappeared

1. The Highland Games are a very old _tradition_.
2. They include the colors and symbols of a culture that almost _____.
3. The Highland Games are a meeting place of strength, speed, and _____.
4. Today the Games are played on sports grounds, farmers' fields, and city _____.
5. For Scottish people, the Highland Games are Scotland's _____.

5 ▶ 08 Watch Part 1 once more. Answer the questions in your notebook.
1. What do the Games capture?
2. Why are the Games in the village of Ceres important?
3. At what time of the year do they hold the Highland Games?
4. For many Scots, the Highland Games are as important as which other events?

6 ▶ 09 Watch Part 2 of the video. Check (✓) six sports you hear or see.
1 ☑ cycling
2 ☐ horseback riding
3 ☐ climbing
4 ☐ tossing the caber
5 ☐ running
6 ☐ wrestling
7 ☐ hammer throw
8 ☐ handball
9 ☐ stone shot
10 ☐ hockey

7 ▶ 09 Watch Part 2 again. Circle the correct option.
1. The Highland Games are a unique blend of sports and *fantasy* / (*culture*).
2. The Games usually include athletics and *sometimes* / *always* heavy events.
3. The caber is six meters long and weighs *fifteen* / *fifty-five* kilos.
4. There are more Highland Games celebrated *in* / *outside* Scotland.
5. The Games are about competing and making time for old *traditions* / *friends*.

8 In pairs or groups, ask and answer the questions.
1. Would you like to attend the Highland Games? Why? / Why not?
2. Which part of the Highland Games would you enjoy the most: the music and dancing, or the sports? Why?

YOU EXPLORE

9 CULTURE PROJECT In pairs or groups, prepare a presentation about a national sport in another country.
1. Write a short script and think about images or videos to use in your presentation.
2. Present it.

Where do the Brits love to go on vacation?

The Brits on vacation

It could be because their weather is so unpredictable, but British people – the Brits – love to go abroad. They even invented the concept of budget airlines. In fact, these cheap airlines have allowed more people to travel to more destinations for less money. There isn't much luxury on these flights and you have to pay for all extras, like your luggage and to choose your seats. But the Brits love them because they can go to many different countries for a weekend without spending a lot of money. So, what kind of vacation do they prefer and what activities do they like most?

Beach holidays are still their preferred option and sunbathing, their favorite occupation. After the beach, sightseeing remains very popular and city breaks are the way many Brits like to go sightseeing. Some incredible destinations are just a short flight away, so people go there for a long weekend. Some lazy Brits love a cruise vacation, while more dynamic travelers choose activity vacations which involve outdoor sports, trekking, or camping.

So, what city could combine all of these vacation types? It's easy: Barcelona, in Spain! It's unique because it combines the beach and sightseeing. And as an important port, Barcelona also attracts cruises, especially in summer. You can even have an adventure vacation in the Pyrenees mountains nearby. The city soccer team, Barça, is also a great attraction.

But it's not just Barcelona. Spain has been the Brits' clear favorite since 1994. More than twelve million Brits visit the country every year. Obviously, the weather is a key factor. Sun is guaranteed most of the year round in most places. There are large communities of British people along the coast, so speaking English is not a problem. Spanish people also have a friendly reputation and the food is popular, especially the tapas. It's a surprise that the Brits haven't taken it over completely!

GLOSSARY
abroad (adv) to a different country
budget (adj) cheap (in the context of the article)
lazy (adj) not very active
occupation (n) a way of spending your time
unpredictable (adj) changing a lot so it is impossible to know what will happen

EXPLORE

1 In pairs, ask and answer the questions.
1. What type of vacation do you prefer? Do you like to:
   - relax?
   - try something new?
   - do lots of activities?
2. What is your favorite vacation destination?
3. Would you like to go on an adventure vacation? Why? / Why not?

2 Read the article. Answer the questions in your notebook.
1. Why do the British love to go abroad?
2. Why can more people travel by plane now than in the past?
3. Why is it easy for the Brits to go sightseeing abroad?
4. Why are cruises and activity vacations opposites?
5. Why is Barcelona such a popular city with tourists?

EXPLORE MORE

3 ▶ 10 Watch Part 1 of the video. Mark the sentences true (T) or false (F). Correct the false sentences.
1. [T] The Maldives is a luxury vacation destination.
2. [ ] Kirstie really wants to do jet skiing from the beginning.
3. [ ] Going jet skiing is very cheap.

4 ▶ 11 Watch Part 2 of the video. Circle the correct option.
1. To go snowmobiling in Iceland, you need special protective (clothing) / vehicles.
2. You should follow your guide's advice because the sport can be *difficult* / *dangerous*.
3. Icelandic landscapes look like the surface of *Mars* / *the Moon*.

5 ▶ 12 Watch Part 3 of the video. Complete the sentences with one word in each blank.
1. The hot-air ballooning option is a much more _relaxing_ choice.
2. The great thing about this sport is the total _____ when you're up there.
3. You see the landscapes below from such a different _____ .

6 ▶ 10-12 Watch the three parts of the video again. Match activities a–c to sentences 1–9 used to describe them.
a. jet skiing (the Maldives)
b. snowmobiling (Iceland)
c. hot-air ballooning (Morocco)

1. [a] You can also practice other less energetic activities there.
2. [ ] A vehicle is specially prepared for this activity.
3. [ ] The landscapes are unique there.
4. [ ] You can do this activity with many other people.
5. [ ] Some people get annoyed by this activity.
6. [ ] You can only do this at a certain time of day.
7. [ ] You have to hold on tight when you do this activity.
8. [ ] The views are particularly special.
9. [ ] It's the best possible way to relax.

7 Which of the activities would you most like to do? What rules and regulations do you think you have to follow to do each one? Discuss in pairs.

YOU EXPLORE

8 **CULTURE PROJECT** In groups, prepare a presentation about an adventure sport.
1. Use the internet or other sources to research an adventure sport.
2. Write a short script and think about images or videos to use in your presentation.
3. Present it to the class.

BBC CULTURE: Is moving good for you?

Mobile homes in the USA

Some people say that moving is the most stressful thing in the world. That's why Americans only move once a decade on average. However, some people are on the move the whole time!

In the United States, there are 8.5 million mobile homes. In South Carolina almost twenty percent of all homes are mobile and many people live in trailer parks. These parks, which have a bit of an image problem in the country, are often home to people who can't afford a house. But that is not always the case.

In states like Florida, there are trailer parks full of retired couples. They often have a great community spirit. Mobile housing expert John O'Reilly explains why: "People in these parks put up with a little discomfort to feel part of a group and have a sense of identity. The atmosphere is great, people hang out with each other and get along really well. They're like one big happy family."

Some people stay in the same trailer park for years, but others travel around. For Michael Branston, who has just bought a new trailer with his family in Alabama, choosing a mobile home was all about freedom. "Even if I could, I wouldn't change my mobile home for a fixed one. Trailer parks are usually quiet, clean, and safe, and there are no parking problems! We would rather buy our own mobile home than rent an apartment in the city. At least you have a place you can call your own and you're free to move when and where you like. Moving is great because you see many places and it broadens your horizons. Go ahead and try it!"

GLOSSARY
can't afford (v) don't have enough money to buy/pay something
discomfort (n) a feeling of being uncomfortable
expert (n) someone with special knowledge
retired (adj) a retired person has stopped working, usually because of his/her age
trailer park (n) a place where trailers are parked and used as people's homes

EXPLORE

1 How would you feel if you had to move to another house?

2 Read the article. Mark the sentences true (T) or false (F). Correct the false sentences in your notebook.
1. [T] Trailer parks have a negative image in the United States.
2. [ ] Trailer parks are always home to poor people.
3. [ ] Some people like living in mobile homes in Florida because they want to live alone.
4. [ ] Some people prefer to live in mobile homes because they don't like to stay in one place.
5. [ ] According to the article, trailer parks are often dangerous places to live.

3 Read the article again. Answer the questions in your notebook. Give reasons for your answers.
1. Does the article present mobile homes in a positive or negative way?
2. Does the article present moving house in the same way?

EXPLORE MORE

4 ▶ 13 Watch the video with no sound. Order the actions as they appear in the video.
a. [ ] a family eating together
b. [ ] a child standing in a big coat
c. [ ] a man throwing a rope over a reindeer
d. [1] white dogs sitting in the snow
e. [ ] people moving house with reindeer
f. [ ] a man cutting ice with a knife
g. [ ] a man putting frozen fish in a sack
h. [ ] people collecting wood
i. [ ] a man cutting raw fish

5 In pairs, ask and answer the questions.
1. Where do you think the people in the video live?
2. Is it an easy or a difficult life? Why?
3. Why do you think they move?
4. How long do you think they take to move?

6 ▶ 13 Watch the video with sound. Check your answers to Activity 5.

7 Were you surprised by the answers? Discuss in pairs.

8 ▶ 13 Watch the video again. Circle the correct option.
1. The village in the video is home to (two) / a few extended families.
2. Temperatures in the *fall* / *winter* are as low as -40°C.
3. The Dolgan people use reindeer fur *only for clothes* / *for clothes and their homes*.
4. Their favorite food is *raw fish* / *reindeer meat*.
5. Over a year, the Dolgan people travel *hundreds* / *thousands* of miles.
6. The Dolgan people first came to the Arctic because of the *fishing* / *reindeer*.

9 Would you like to live like the Dolgan people in the Arctic? Why? / Why not? Do you know of any other kinds of nomadic people in the world?

YOU EXPLORE

10 **CULTURE PROJECT** In groups, prepare a presentation about nomadic people.
1. Use the internet or other sources to research nomadic people in the world.
2. Write a short script and think about images or videos to use in your presentation.
3. Present it to the class.
4. Report back: what did you learn from the other presentations?

Is chewing gum a crime?

Crime facts from around the world

Countries pass different laws because they often have different attitudes to certain crimes. Punishments vary greatly, too. Here are a few facts about laws from some of the safest countries in the world:

- Did you know that in Singapore it is illegal to chew gum because it damages the city's pavements and gets stuck in subway doors? You can get a fine or even go to prison for a petty crime like that!

- Hong Kong has some of the strictest laws in the world. For example, it is illegal to play music on the streets. If you are a busker, it's certainly not the place for you!

- In Finland, fines for certain crimes are based on your income. If you are rich, you pay more! A few years ago the director of a cell phone company, Nokia, was caught speeding and got a fine of over €100,000! Do you think that's fair?

- In Iceland, thefts and robberies almost never happen. House burglaries are unknown. People leave the front door to their houses open or their bicycles unlocked on the street. The police are largely invisible.

- In the USA, it's illegal to cross the street when the traffic light is green. This can be strange for some tourists!

- Of course, street crime exists in Britain, and there are more CCTV cameras per person there than anywhere else in the world. If you have your bag stolen, there is a good chance that the police will catch the criminal. For that reason, British people feel very protected. Edinburgh in Scotland is considered to be the country's safest city and it's also a beautiful place to visit!

GLOSSARY
attitude (n) what you think and feel about something
busker (n) someone who plays music on the streets to earn money
income (n) the money you earn
petty crime (n) a crime that is not very serious
vary (v) if things vary they are all different from each other

EXPLORE

1 In pairs, ask and answer the questions.
1. What countries do you think are the safest and the most dangerous in the world?
2. Is there much crime where you live?
3. What kinds of crimes happen, if any? Are they serious or not?
4. Do you think the laws where you live are fair? Why? / Why not?

2 Read the article. Mark the sentences true (T) or false (F). Correct the false sentences.
1. [F] You cannot chew gum in Singapore because it's bad for you.
2. [ ] The writer thinks that chewing gum is a serious crime.
3. [ ] In Hong Kong there are some unusual laws.
4. [ ] In Finland the punishment varies depending on the money you earn.
5. [ ] The police have a lot to do in Iceland.

EXPLORE MORE

3 Read the article again. Answer the questions in your notebook.
1. Does the article say that safe countries have similar or different kinds of laws?
2. Do you think CCTV cameras are a good way to make a place safer? Why? / Why not?
3. Which of the countries' laws mentioned in the text do you agree/disagree with? Why?

4 ▶ 14 Watch Part 1 of the video. Answer the questions in your notebook.
1. When did the robbery happen?
2. Where did it take place?
3. Why is it described as a robbery from a movie?

5 ▶ 14 Watch Part 1 again. Answer the questions in your notebook.
1. How did the robbers get from the building to the vault?
2. What was the robbers' biggest challenge?
3. How thick was the concrete wall?
4. How long did it take the specialists to drill the same holes as the robbers?

6 Match words 1–4 to pictures A–D.

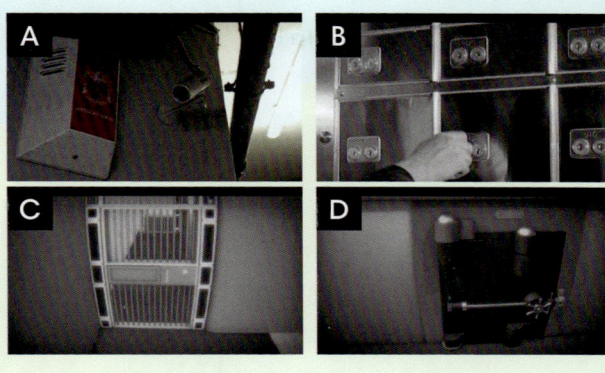

1. [B] security boxes
2. [ ] vault
3. [ ] CCTV camera
4. [ ] security door

7 In pairs, retell the story of how the robbers got to the diamonds. Use the words from Activity 6 and the pictures to help you.

First, they turned off all the CCTV cameras, except one. Then they climbed down the elevator …

8 ▶ 15 Watch Part 2 of the video. Circle the correct option.
1. According to the video, it's (easy) / difficult to open the boxes.
2. The police only discovered the crime *a day / two days* after the robbery.
3. We *know / don't know* exactly how much loot the robbers escaped with.
4. The police *caught / didn't catch* the robbers in the end.
5. The police were *faster / more intelligent* than the robbers with technology.

9 In pairs or groups, ask and answer the questions.
1. Do you think robberies like this still happen in your country? Why? / Why not?
2. What kinds of crimes are committed digitally?

YOU EXPLORE

10 CULTURE PROJECT In groups, present a famous movie about a robbery.
1. Find out about a movie you like.
2. Write notes about what happens in the movie.
3. Tell the story to the class.

BBC Culture 7 103

Can school be fun?

Another way to learn: A day in the life of a student at an alternative school

Adam
"I go to a Steiner school. It's very different from the traditional schools that my friends go to. First of all, our learning is far more creative and interactive. We don't sit in class and memorize facts; we get up and do practical stuff, which I think is really alternative.

For example, today we had a biology class. As we were learning all about the body, the teacher asked us to make clay models and draw pictures of different body parts. It was much more fun than just reading information in a book. Also, we did this in a group, so we learned from each other. Then we took turns to give presentations about a subject of our choice. I gave a talk about modern-day allergies. I researched this topic because I think it's really interesting.

Anyway, it's great that we have the freedom to do that. And the other positive thing is that there are no tests – we just study the material in our own time!

We also usually only have one academic subject per week. It's just two or three hours in the morning, then the rest of the day we do gardening, arts, and crafts. Today we did singing and dancing – my favorites! One thing that they discourage at my school is the use of computers. We aren't allowed to sit in front of a screen for a long time. I don't like this, but I understand the reasons – we can do that at home.

Here the teachers are very different, too – they are our friends. They don't just instruct us; they help us achieve our potential. I love that. I actually look forward to going to school!"

GLOSSARY
achieve (v) to succeed in doing something
clay (n) a type of material that is used to make pots
discourage (v) to try to make someone want to do something less often
take turns (phrase) when people take turns to do something, they do it one after the other

EXPLORE

1 In pairs, ask and answer the questions.
1. Describe something you have learned recently that was fun or interesting. Why was it a good learning experience?
2. What makes a class interesting or boring for you? Give examples.

2 Read the article. Mark the sentences true (T) or false (F). Correct the false sentences.
1. [T] Adam knows that his school is alternative.
2. [ ] He would like to read more in class.
3. [ ] He chose a subject he liked for his presentation.
4. [ ] The students study academic subjects at the same time.
5. [ ] Adam would like to spend more time on the computer.
6. [ ] He thinks that the teachers are similar to those in traditional schools.

3 Read the article again. In pairs, ask and answer the questions.
1. What information in the text surprises you about this alternative school?
2. How does the "day in the life" compare to daily life at your school? Which do you prefer? Why?

EXPLORE MORE

4 ▶ 16 Watch Part 1 of the video. Which school would you prefer to go to? Why? Discuss in pairs.

5 ▶ 16 Watch Part 1 again. Circle the correct option.
1. At King's School order and *creativity* / *(discipline)* is important.
2. Today's class is a *math* / *leadership* class.
3. The girl interviewed wants to be a *teacher* / *banker*.
4. The Steiner school is more *formal* / *informal* than King's.
5. At the Steiner school, academic studies start at *six* / *seven* years old.

6 ▶ 17 Watch Part 2 of the video. Complete the text with the words below. There are two extra words.

> memory   movements   ~~fourteen~~   words
> alternative   English   forty   colours

In the UK, there are ¹ _fourteen_ schools which specialize in teaching children with dyslexia. Dyslexia affects reading and spelling, and your short-term ² _____. So, the students learn new ³ _____ with shapes and ⁴ _____. Kara attends an ⁵ _____ class. In the class the students spell out words with physical ⁶ _____.

7 What's your opinion about the different schools from the video? Discuss in pairs.

I think the school that specializes in helping children with dyslexia is great.

YOU EXPLORE

8 **CULTURE PROJECT** In groups, prepare a presentation based on the question: "What would your ideal school be like?"
1. Use these notes to help you:
   - practical tasks/academic tasks: what's the right balance?
   - use of computers: a lot or a little?
   - how much freedom of choice?
   - discipline: how important?
2. Write a short script to describe your ideas. Think about images or videos to use in your presentation.
3. Present it to the class. Whose ideal school is the best? Why?

GRAMMAR TIME

1.2 Simple Present, Present Continuous, and state verbs

Simple Present
We use the Simple Present for facts, permanent situations, and routines.
They sing in a band.
She doesn't use her tablet every day.

Time expressions
every day/week/month/year
once/twice/three times a month
on Mondays/weekdays/vacation
always/usually/often/sometimes/rarely/never

Present Continuous
We use the Present Continuous for actions that are happening at or around the time of speaking.
They're playing a video game right now.
I'm recording songs this week.

Time expressions
now, at the moment, this morning/afternoon, this year, these days

State verbs
State verbs express opinions, preferences, mental states, and perception.
love, like, hate, prefer, want, need, understand, think, feel, hear, see
They don't normally have a continuous form, even if they refer to the time of speaking.
I want to see your new cell phone.

1 Complete the text with the correct form of the verbs below.

> (not) like   dance   go   make   prefer
> show   ~~think~~   wear

I ¹ _think_ one of the favorite free-time activities for my generation is watching music videos online. My favorite is the one by Ylvis called "What does the fox say?" Do you want to watch it?

Look, there's a costume party and all the people ² _____ animal costumes. They ³ _____ in the forest and ⁴ _____ crazy animal sounds! It's amazing, although a little old now! My sister ⁵ _____ music videos – she ⁶ _____ videos about shopping where people ⁷ _____ shopping for clothes or cosmetics and then ⁸ _____ the viewers what's in their shopping bags … Not my kind of thing, really.

2 In your notebook, write a similar text about the types of videos you like to watch and describe your favorite one.

1.4 Verb + -ing/verb + to-infinitive

Verbs followed by the -ing form:
avoid, can't stand, enjoy, finish, (not) mind, miss, practice, stop
I avoid using flash in my camera.
The -ing form is also used after prepositions.
I'm looking forward to seeing my grandpa.

Verbs followed by the to-infinitive:
agree, allow, ask, choose, decide, forget, hope, learn, offer, plan, try, want, would like/love
I hope to become a good photographer in the future.

Some verbs can be followed by either the to-infinitive, or the -ing form:
like, love, hate, prefer, start
I love taking pictures of cats.
I love to take pictures of cats.

1 Complete the sentences with the correct form of the verbs in parentheses.

1. Martha's parents often allow her _to stay up_ (stay up) late at night.
2. I would love _____ (buy) a new camera.
3. My boyfriend is crazy about _____ (watch) old silent movies.
4. Why don't you practice _____ (play) this song again?
5. Please, try _____ (stay) calm.
6. Would you mind _____ (help) me with this poster?

2 Circle the correct option.

A: What are you planning ¹(to do)/ doing on the weekend, Josh?
B: I don't know. I want ²to write / writing the essay for the French class. Finish ³to write / writing it, in fact.
A: Doesn't sound very exciting!
B: Well, no, it doesn't. I can't stand ⁴to learn / studying on the weekend. What about you, Jessica?
A: Well, I'm trying ⁵to earn / earning some money for a new cell phone. My old one is broken. I can help my aunt in her backyard. She is offering ⁶to pay / paying me five dollars an hour. Actually, she wants me ⁷to bring / bringing a friend, too … There's enough work for two people with planting apple trees.
B: That's great! I need some cash. And I'm really good at ⁸to plant / planting!
A: Really? That's new!

GRAMMAR TIME

2.2 Present Perfect with *ever*, *never*, *just*, *already*, and *yet*

For the Present Perfect, we use *have/has* and the past participle form of the main verb. For regular verbs, the past participle is the same as the past form. Many past participles are irregular (see page 116).

We use the Present Perfect to talk about:

- life experience up to now with *ever* (in questions) and *never* (in negatives).
  Have you **ever eaten** pizza with bananas?
  I've **never been** to this restaurant.
- actions that finished a short time ago with *just*.
  I'm not hungry. I've **just had** a sandwich.
- actions that are (or are expected to be) completed by now with *already* (in affirmative sentences) and *yet* (in negatives and questions).
  I've **already cooked** lunch.
  I **haven't cooked** lunch **yet**.
  Have you **cooked** lunch **yet**?

1 Complete the sentences with the correct form of the words in parentheses.

1. We can eat pizza now! The takeout _____has just arrived_____ (just / arrive).
2. Joshua _____ (already / wash) the dishes, so we can relax.
3. A: _____ (the kids / have lunch / yet)?
   B: No, they _____ .
4. A: _____ (you / do the shopping / yet)?
   B: Yes, I _____ (just / return) from the mall.
5. These almond cookies are absolutely amazing! I _____ (never / eat) better!
6. We are still working on a cooking project for school and we _____ (not finish / yet).

2 In your notebook, write questions about the activities in the chart. Use *ever*. Then ask and answer the questions in pairs.

	YOU	YOUR CLASSMATE
1 try snails		
2 watch a horror movie		
3 bake a cake		
4 cook a family dinner		

Have you ever tried snails? Yes, I have.

2.4 Present Perfect with *for* and *since*; Present Perfect and Simple Past

Present Perfect with *for* and *since*
We use the Present Perfect with *for* and *since* to describe an unfinished action that started in the past and still continues.
Use *for* with:
a week/a month/a year/ages, etc.
They **have owned** this restaurant **for** two years.
Use *since* with:
2012/March/last Tuesday/the day we met, etc.
I've **had** this game console **since** February.

Present Perfect and Simple Past
Use the Simple Past in sentences with a reference to a specific time in the past.
I **went** to this pizzeria **last Sunday**.

Use the Present Perfect to talk about life experiences up to now.
I've **been** to this pizzeria. It's really nice.

We use the Present Perfect with times and dates when we want to say how long something has lasted (*for* how long or *since* when).
I've **known** my best friend **for** ten years.

1 Complete the sentences with *since* or *for*.

1. I've lived in this house __since__ I was born.
2. I've known him _____ ten years.
3. I've had this furniture _____ two months.
4. I haven't seen him _____ yesterday.

2 Write sentences from the prompts. Use the Simple Past or the Present Perfect.

1. Maria / have / her cell phone / since Christmas.
   Maria has had a cell phone since Christmas.
2. She / win / her skiis in a skiing competition / last year.
   _____
3. She / make / her sweater herself / last winter.
   _____
4. She / meet / a famous actor in a park.
   _____
5. She / study / French / for three years
   _____
6. Her parents / teach / her how to cook / two years ago.
   _____

Grammar Time 107

GRAMMAR TIME

3.2 Past Perfect

For the Past Perfect, we use *had/hadn't* and the past participle form of the main verb. For regular verbs, the past participle is the same as the past form. Many past participles are irregular (see page 116).
We use the Past Perfect to talk about actions and situations that took place before specific points in the past.
Paula **hadn't been** abroad before her trip to Spain last week.
Richard **hadn't** already **seen** the movie.
Had you **eaten** breakfast before lunch?
Yes, I **had**. / No, I **hadn't**.

1 Complete the sentences with the correct form of the verbs in parentheses.
1. I had ____*visited*____ (visit) my aunt before her illness.
2. I _____ (never/see) a rainbow before yesterday's rain.
3. It _____ (rain) heavily before their arrival.
4. My camera broke, but I _____ (take) a lot of pictures on our vacation.
5. I _____ (not spend) a lot of time on the project before the school break.
6. I _____ (have) fried eggs for breakfast.

2 In your notebook, write questions from the prompts below.
Before you started at this school, …
1. you / study English?
2. you / be abroad?
3. your parents / visit the school?
4. you / meet the teachers?
5. what / school subjects / you study?
6. you / travel / by plane?

3 In pairs, ask and answer the questions in Activity 2.
A: *Before you started at this school, had you studied English?*
B: *No, I hadn't.*

3.4 Simple Past and Past Perfect

Simple Past
We use the Simple Past to talk about actions and situations that finished in the past. We often mention when these actions/situations happened.
We **saw** a storm **yesterday**.
We **didn't see** the storm.
Did you **see** the storm?
Some verbs in English have regular past forms: *happen–happened, move–moved, study–studied*
Many past forms are irregular. (See page 116.)

Time expressions
yesterday
two hours/days/weeks/years ago
last week/year/night
in 2001

Past Perfect and Simple Past
The Past Perfect is used to show how an event in the past is related to another past event. We use the Past Perfect for the earlier event and the Simple Past for the later event. The events can be connected with time conjunctions (*when, after, before*, etc)
I **had been** in the forest for an hour **when** I suddenly **got** lost.
Anne **called** after she had **arrived** at home.

1 Complete the sentences with the Simple Past or the Past Perfect form of the verbs in parentheses.
1. Mark *had already taken* (already/take) a shower when Larissa _____ (call) to cancel the party.
2. I _____ (not study) enough, so I _____ (not get) a good grade on the test.
3. Becky _____ (never/play) that video game before, but she still _____ (get) to the top level!
4. _____ (Mom/give) you money when you _____ (ask) Dad for more?
5. We _____ (not want) to go to that restaurant because we _____ (eat) there before. The food wasn't good!

GRAMMAR TIME

4.2 The future: will / going to / Present Continuous / Simple Present

We use **will/won't** to talk about predictions or decisions made at the moment of speaking.
I don't think he'll win the competition.
Wait, I'll help you.

We use **be going to** to talk about intentions and plans, or to make predictions based on things we know now.
I'm going to take up kayaking next summer.
Look at the sky: it's going to rain.

We use the **Present Continuous** to talk about fixed arrangements.
We're having a competition next month.

We use the **Simple Present** to talk about timetables and schedules.
Basketball practice starts in October.

1 Circle the correct option.
1 (I'm going to buy) / I'll buy some new sneakers, so I'm looking for some offers on eBay.
2 No, I'm sorry. I can't visit you on Tuesday evening. *I'm having / I'll have* guests.
3 In our school, all extra-curricular classes *are going to start / start* in October.
4 Look at Susan! She looks really pale. She *isn't going to finish / doesn't finish* the race.
5 Bob, I've arranged an interview with *Teen Magazine*. They *are coming / are going to come* tomorrow at 6:30.
6 A I'm starving.
   B *I'm going to make / I'll make* you a sandwich.

2 Complete the questions with the words below.

having   going (x2)   meeting   ~~will~~ (x2)

1 What do think the weather __will__ be like tomorrow?
2 Are you __going__ to get a job during the summer vacation?
3 Are you _____ any extra-curricular classes tomorrow?
4 Are you _____ your friends tonight?
5 Do you think people _____ read printed books in the future?
6 Are you _____ to organize a birthday party for Emma?

4.4 First Conditional

We use the **First Conditional** (If + Simple Present, will + verb) to talk about things that will (or won't) happen in the future under certain conditions.
If you like gymnastics, you'll love slacklining.
You'll love slacklining if you like gymnastics.
Will you try slacklining if you have a chance?
We can use the *if*-clause a the beginning or end of a sentence. When it comes first, we use a comma (,) to separate it from the other clause.

if not/unless
If the condition is negative, use *if not* or *unless*.
You won't be good at slacklining **if** you don't practice.
You won't be good at slacklining **unless** you practice.

time clauses with *when*
Notice the difference between a First Conditional sentence and a time clause with *when*.
I'll tell Jack about the competition **if** he comes. (Jack may or may not come.)
I'll tell Jack about the competition **when** he comes. (Jack will come and then I will tell him.)

1 Complete the sentences with the correct form of the verbs in parentheses.
1 We __'ll/will go__ (go) skiing if it __snows__ (snow).
2 I _____ (show) her some skateboarding tricks when she _____ (come) over.
3 Your team _____ (lose) the volleyball game if they _____ (not change) a few players.
4 If the train _____ (not be) late, the soccer players _____ (arrive) in Madrid at 5 p.m.
5 The practice _____ (not start) if the coach _____ (be) sick.
6 I _____ (take up) jogging when the weather _____ (get) better.

2 Circle the correct answers. In pairs, ask and answer the questions.
1 Will you do your English homework _____ home?
   a if you return
   (b) when you return
2 Will you buy a new soccer shirt _____ some money for Christmas?
   a if you get
   b when you'll get
3 Will you ride your bike on the weekend _____ nice?
   a when the weather will be
   b if the weather is

GRAMMAR TIME

5.2 Modal verbs for obligation, prohibition, and advice: *must, have to, ought to, should*

Obligation and prohibition
To express obligation, we use *must* and *have to*.
Students **must** arrive on time.
We **have to** wear uniforms.

To express lack of obligation, we use *don't have to*.
She **doesn't have to** work in July.

Must not expresses prohibition.
You **must not** smoke during the flight.

Advice
Use *should/shouldn't* and *ought to* to give advice.
The use of *ought to* is less common than *should* and in negatives, it is more common to use *shouldn't*.
You **should/shouldn't** take the train.
You **ought to** pack your luggage now.

Must, should, and *ought to* are modal verbs. They have the same form in all persons singular and plural. Questions are formed with inversion.
She **must/should/ought to** leave now.
Must/Should she leave now?
Ought she **to** leave now?

Questions and negatives with *have to* are formed with auxiliaries.
She **has to** go now.
She **doesn't have to** work hard.
Does she **have to** pack now?

1 Complete the second sentence so that it means the same as the first sentence. Use the verbs in parentheses.

1. Wearing suits and white shirts is obligatory in Joanna's school.
   Joanna **has to wear suits and white shirts** at school. (have)
2. Is it a good idea for us to check out before breakfast?
   _____ before breakfast? (should)
3. Don't take your passport. It's not necessary.
   You _____ passport. (have)
4. You should buy new sunglasses.
   You _____. (ought to)
5. Smoking is forbidden at the airport.
   People _____ at the airport. (must not)
6. Is it necessary for Sue to take a sleeping bag?
   _____ a sleeping bag? (must)

5.4 Modal verbs for speculation: *must, could, might/may, can't*

We use a modal verb + infinitive to speculate about the present.

We use *must* + infinitive when we strongly believe that something is true.
She **must feel** exhausted after the trip. (= I'm sure she feels exhausted.)

We use *might, may,* or *could* + infinitive when we think something is possibly true.
It **might/may/could be** cold at night in the mountains. (= It's probably cold.)

We use *can't* + infinitive if we believe something is not true.
This rucksack **can't weigh** more than 20 kilos. It's so small! (= I'm sure it doesn't weigh more than 20 kilos.)

1 Complete the dialogues with the words below.

1

might   can't   ~~must~~

A: Look at him! He [1] **must** be exhausted!
B: Oh, yes! He [2] _____ be an experienced cyclist! Look at his backpack! It's weird!
A: Yeah. He [3] _____ be an artist or something.

2

can't   must   could

A: The water [4] _____ be freezing! Look, nobody's swimming.
B: No, it [5] _____ be freezing, not with this sunny weather. The water is always quite warm here.
A: I'm not going in, anyway. It [6] _____ be dirty or full of seaweed … Brr …

2 Complete the text with one word in each blank.

Hi Mark,
I'm writing about the cruise. I've analyzed all the pros and cons and I finally think it [1] **m ight** not be the best idea because a cruise in the Caribbean [2] **m**_____ cost a fortune! Looking at the sea [3] **c**_____ be a little boring. Also, you usually get to the port in the evening. It [4] **c**_____ be frustrating because it's too late to go sightseeing. Let's go sailing instead. I think it's more exciting and it [5] **m**_____ be cheaper, too!
Let me know what you think.
Love,
Mary-Jane

GRAMMAR TIME

6.2 Second Conditional

We use the **Second Conditional** (*If* + Simple Past, *would* + verb) to talk about imaginary situations in the present and future.
If I **had** a brother, I'**d share** my room with him.
(= I don't have a brother, so I don't share my room.)
If I **had** some money, I **would buy** my sister a new cell phone.
I **would buy** my sister a new cell phone **if** I **had** some money.

Notice the difference between First and Second Conditionals:
I'**d be** very happy **if** my grandma **visited** me in the summer.
(= she isn't going to visit me)
I'**ll be** very happy **if** my grandma **visits** me in the summer.
(= there's a chance she's going to visit me)

In the if-clause, we can use was or were with *I*, *he*, *she*, and *it*.
If I **was/were** taller, I'**d** become a professional basketball player.

1 Order the words to make Second Conditional sentences.
  1 behave / if / how / you / were / me / would / you / ?
    How *would you behave if you were me?*
  2 if / laugh / feel / at him / Chris / wouldn't / so bad / his friends / didn't
    Chris _____
  3 if / your aunt / would / your family / do / didn't / help / you / what / ?
    What _____
  4 get along well / would / do / if / with your mom / what / you / didn't / you / ?
    What _____
  5 I / were / with your sister / you / I / fight / wouldn't / all the time / if
    If _____

2 Complete the Second Conditional sentences with the correct form of the verbs in parentheses.

A good friend:
  1 *would help* (help) me if I *were* (be) in trouble.
  2 _____ (give) me some money if I _____ (not have) any.
  3 _____ (buy) me some medicine if I _____ (be) sick.
  4 _____ (not get) angry with me if I _____ (do) something wrong.
  5 _____ (not complain) if I _____ (not be) in a good mood.

6.4 Defining and non-defining relative clauses

We use relative clauses to give information about people, things, and places. We use *who* to refer to people, *which* to refer to things, and *where* to refer to places.

We use **defining relative clauses** to give essential information about people, things, and places.
I've just seen a man who lives on my street. (this piece of information is essential to identify the man)

Non-defining relative clauses are used to give additional information.
I've just seen Frank Jones, who lives in my street. (information not essential to identify who I'm talking about)

In defining relative clauses *who* and *which* can be replaced with *that*:
This is the woman **that** asked about you.

In non-defining relative clauses we use commas. We can't use *that* to replace *who* and *which*.
This is Maria Kennel**,** who is going to work with us.

1 Complete the questions with *who*, *which*, or *where*.
  1 That's the hospital *where* I was born.
  2 What's the name of the teacher _____ taught you in first grade?
  3 What's the title of the movie _____ you went to see at the movie theater?
  4 What is the address of the park _____ the picnic is going to take place?

2 In your notebook, combine the sentences using relative clauses with *who*, *which*, or *where*. Add commas where necessary. In which sentences could you use *that*?
  1 During my brother's wedding, I met an elderly lady. She used to know my great-grandmother.
    During my brother's wedding, I met an elderly lady who used to know my great-grandmother.
  2 She told me a lot of things. I had no idea about them.
  3 My great-grandmother lived in a village near Edinburgh. Edinburgh is the capital of Scotland.
  4 The lady told me about a house. My great-grandmother lived there.

Grammar Time

GRAMMAR TIME

7.2 The passive (Simple Present and Simple Past)

In the passive, we use a form of the verb *to be* and the past participle.
We use the passive when we think *what* happens is more important than *who* does it, or when we don't know who does it.
To say who performed an action, use *by*.
The book **was published by** Puffin.
Who **was** the book **published by**?

Simple Present
I **am** often **punished** at school for my bad behavior.
The performance **is based** on Agatha Christie's novel.
The tickets for the performance **aren't sold** online.
Are shoplifters always **caught by the police**?

Simple Past
The witness **was interviewed** yesterday.
The criminals **were arrested** on Monday.
He **wasn't found** guilty.
Who **were** the robbers **punished** by?

1 Complete the second sentence so that it means the same as the first sentence.

1 Someone damaged the school gate last night.
   The school gate ___was damaged last night___.
2 Nobody uses CCTV cameras just for fun.
   CCTV cameras _____.
3 Nobody saw the suspect in Central Park on Sunday.
   The suspect _____.
4 Did the police chase the robbers?
   Were _____?
5 Do people find fingerprints on food as well?
   Are _____?
6 Someone stole my aunt's purse.
   My aunt's purse _____.

2 Complete the text with the words below.

| is based   wasn't completed   were published |
| was published   is sold   ~~were written~~   wasn't written |

The Millenium is a series of best-selling Swedish crime novels. They ¹ ___were written___ by Stieg Larsson, who created two fantastic characters, Lisbeth Salander and Mikael Blomkvist. Because of Larsson's sudden death in 2004, the series ² _____. Only three books of the series ³ _____ out of ten planned. The first book, *The Girl with the Dragon Tattoo* ⁴ _____ in 2005, after Larsson's death. The series ⁵ _____ in over fifty countries. In 2015, a new book in the series appeared. It ⁶ _____ by Larsson, but by David Lagercrantz, a Swedish author and crime journalist. The book ⁷ _____ on Larsson's characters and ideas in his novels.

7.4 have/get something done

We use *have/get something done* to talk about things that we don't do ourselves and that somebody else (usually a professional) does for us.
I **made** my costume. (= I made it myself.)
I **had** my costume **made**. (= Somebody else made it for me.)
Get is more informal and is used more often in spoken English.

1 Complete the questions with the correct form of the words in parentheses.

1 How often do you ___have your hair cut___?
   (have / your hair / cut)
2 Have you ever _____?
   (have / your bike / repair)
3 Do you sometimes _____
   (have / your pictures / print) or do you only keep them in your computer?
4 Would you ever _____
   (have / your hair / color) blue or green?

2 Complete the text with the words below.

| my hair cut   some pictures taken |
| ~~my dress made~~   my nails painted |
| them repaired   it styled |

Hi Jessie,
How are you? How are the preparations going for the end-of-year party? I've already had ¹ ___my dress made___. The dress is red and it has little red roses at the front. I'm going to wear my red shoes. They are the same color as the dress, and I had ² _____ last week. Anyway, I don't want to have ³ _____ although it's a bit long now … I'm only going to have ⁴ _____ before the party. And I'm not going to have ⁵ _____. I'll paint them myself.
By the way, remember we're having ⁶ _____ on Monday for the year book. Do you know what we should wear then?
Best,
Liz

GRAMMAR TIME

8.2 Word order in questions

When the question word (*what*, *when*, *who*, etc.) is the object in questions and in *Yes/No* questions, we use a verb or an auxiliary verb before the subject.

- With the Simple Present or the Simple Past of the verb *to be*, invert the verb and the subject.
  He was talented. → Was he talented?

- With verb structures formed by an auxiliary verb and the main verb, e.g., Present and Past Continuous, Present Perfect, *be going to*, Simple Future, modal verbs, we use the auxiliary verb before the subject of the sentence.
  They have failed the test. → Have they failed the test?
  What have they failed?
  She will succeed next time. → Will she succeed next time? When will she succeed?
  She studies abroad. → Does she study abroad?
  Where does she study?
  They passed the test → Did they pass the test?
  What did they pass?

When *who* or *what* is the subject of a question, we use the same word order as in the affirmative sentence. Don't use inversion or auxiliary verbs to form subject questions.
Cristina often helps Sue in science. → Who often helps Sue in science?
PE makes me tired. → What makes you tired?

1 Order the words to write questions in your *notebook*.
1. do / most useful / what subjects / you / find / ?
   What subjects do you find most useful?
2. you / how many / take / tests / did / ?
3. doing / at 5 p.m. / yesterday / what / you / were / ?
4. cheated / in a test / you / have / ever / ?

2 In your notebook, write one subject question and one object question using the words in parentheses.
1. My dad has bought me a new English dictionary. (Who …? What …?)
   Who has bought you a new English dictionary?
   What has your dad bought you?
2. Jessica is going to take a French test tomorrow. (Who …? When …?)
3. Mark wants to study in Belgium. (Who …? Where …?)
4. The accident happened in the science lab. (What …? Where …?)
5. A giant spider bit the biology teacher. (What …? Who …?)
6. The teachers were absent because of the strike. (Who …? Why …?)

8.4 Third Conditional

We use the Third Conditional (*If* + *had* + past participle, *would* + *have* + past participle) to talk about imaginary situations in the past.
If I had studied more, I'd have passed the test.
(= I didn't study more, so I didn't pass the test.)
If I hadn't spent all my money, I would have eaten lunch at the snack bar.
I would have eaten lunch at the snack bar if I hadn't spent all my money.

Both the Second and the Third Conditional are used to talk about hypothetical situations, but notice the difference in the time they refer to:
If I traveled to Spain this summer, I would learn some Spanish. (= I'm not going to travel, so I'm not going to learn.)
If I had traveled to Spain last summer, I would have learned some Spanish. (= I didn't travel last summer, so I didn't learn.)

1 Complete the Third Conditional sentences with the correct form of the verbs in parentheses.
1. If I _____*had gone*_____ (go) to Japan, I _____ (eat) with chopsticks.
2. Matt _____ (not find) out about his bad tooth if he _____ (not go) to the dentist.
3. The team _____ (win) the game if they _____ (play) better.
4. If Sam _____ (not copy) his friend's essay, he _____ (not call) to the principal's office.
5. _____ (the train/arrive) on time if it _____ (not snow) so much?

Grammar Time 113

STUDENT ACTIVITIES

Unit 1   Lesson 1.5, Activity 2

ANSWER KEY

Mostly As: You're obviously busy with other things in life, and that's great. Have fun and enjoy real time with your friends!

Mostly Bs: You know it's there when you need it, but technology isn't the most important thing in your life.

Mostly Cs: You're internet crazy! You love going online and checking messages from friends. Make sure you take time to do other things, too.

Unit 2   Self-check, Activity 7

MENU

Food
Pizza with cheese and tomato
Chicken salad
Fresh sandwiches with tuna or cheese
Ice cream — any flavor!

Drinks
Fruit juice   Smoothies
Coffee   Tea   Water

Unit 6   Lesson 6.1, Activity 5

ANSWER KEY

Mostly As: You don't like big crowds and are probably happy on your own. You know how to be a good friend to a few special people.

Mostly Bs: You love having lots of friends. You give your opinion honestly, and you don't mind if other people agree. You are happiest when you're busy and in a crowd.

Mostly Cs: You know how to get a balance. You can have fun when you want, but you're not afraid to do things on your own.

Unit 6   Lesson 6.6, Activity 4

Student Activities

STUDENT ACTIVITIES

| Unit 7 | Self-Check, Activity 6 |

A: Your parents want you to stay with your cousins for the summer. You don't want to.

B: Your teacher says you must study more for your tests, but you want to do more sports.

| Unit 8 | Lesson 8.7, Activity 6 |

Hi Bryan,
As you know, I'm arriving next week by train. What are the plans for meeting me? Should I call you from the station, or take a taxi?
Should I bring anything special with me (e.g. warm clothes, sports equipment, hiking boots, etc.)? I'm not sure about the weather, and your plans for the weekend. Please let me know.
Jack

Send

| Unit 8 | Self-check, Activity 6 |

Personal details: Selma, 14
From: Mexico
First time in the USA? Yes.
Interests: soccer, art, food
While in the USA, would like to … go to MoMA in New York and to a baseball game!

Personal details: Tomek, 16
From: Poland
First time in the USA? No, had been here before.
Interests: nature and animals, handball
While in the USA, would like to … go to the zoo and eat lots of pizza

Personal details: Angelina, 15
From: France
First time in the USA? No, had been here three times.
Interests: photography, old movies, acting
While in the USA, would like to … see some musicals and improve my accent

Personal details: Selim, 15
From: Turkey
First time in the USA? Yes.
Interests: American football, history, architecture
While in the USA, would like to … visit Ground Zero and go to an NFL game

Student Activities

IRREGULAR VERBS LIST

INFINITIVE	SIMPLE PAST	PAST PARTICIPLE
be	was/were	been
become	became	become
begin	began	begun
break	broke	broken
bring	brought	brought
build	built	built
burn	burned/burnt	burned/burnt
buy	bought	bought
can	could	been able to
catch	caught	caught
choose	chose	chosen
come	came	come
cost	cost	cost
cut	cut	cut
do	did	done
draw	drew	drawn
dream	dreamed/dreamt	dreamed/dreamt
drink	drank	drunk
drive	drove	driven
eat	ate	eaten
fall	fell	fallen
feed	fed	fed
feel	felt	felt
fight	fought	fought
find	found	found
fly	flew	flown
forget	forgot	forgotten
forgive	forgave	forgiven
get	got	got
give	gave	given
go	went	gone
grow	grew	grown
hang	hung	hung
have	had	had
hear	heard	heard
hide	hid	hidden
hit	hit	hit
hold	held	held
hurt	hurt	hurt
keep	kept	kept

INFINITIVE	SIMPLE PAST	PAST PARTICIPLE
know	knew	known
learn	learned/learnt	learned/learnt
leave	left	left
lend	lent	lent
let	let	let
lie	lay	lain
lose	lost	lost
make	made	made
meet	met	met
pay	paid	paid
put	put	put
read	read	read
ride	rode	ridden
ring	rang	rung
run	ran	run
say	said	said
see	saw	seen
sell	sold	sold
send	sent	sent
set	set	set
shine	shone	shone
sing	sang	sung
sit	sat	sat
sleep	slept	slept
speak	spoke	spoken
spell	spelled/spelt	spelled/spelt
spend	spent	spent
stand	stood	stood
steal	stole	stolen
sweep	swept	swept
swim	swam	swum
take	took	taken
teach	taught	taught
tell	told	told
think	thought	thought
understand	understood	understood
wake	woke	woken
wear	wore	worn
win	won	won
write	wrote	written

Irregular verbs list

WORKBOOK

WELCOME TO WOODLEY BRIDGE

1 Match 1–5 to a–e to make sentences.

1 [c] I don't like doing
2 [ ] We love going
3 [ ] Do you like listening
4 [ ] I don't like reading
5 [ ] My dad likes taking

a books.
b to the movies.
c ~~nothing! It's boring!~~
d pictures, especially family pictures.
e to music?

2 Complete the sentences with the words below. There are two extra words.

| can can't doesn't don't
| likes ~~love~~ stand

1 I _love_ going shopping with my friends, especially when I have money to spend.
2 Jake _____ watching movies at home, but I prefer going to the movies.
3 I can't _____ waiting for people. It really annoys me!
4 My dad _____ mind giving me money. He's really kind!
5 My brother _____ stand walking to school. He always gets the bus.

3 Write the correct home and furniture word for each definition.

1 You stay under this to wash yourself. s _h o w e r_
2 You lie on this to sleep. b __ __
3 This is made of glass, so you can see through it. w __ __ __ __ __ __
4 You eat meals in this room. d __ __ __ __ __ __ r __ __ __ __
5 You can see yourself if you look in this. m __ __ __ __ __ __

4 Circle the correct option.

1 (There's) / There are a big table in the dining room.
2 There's / There are lots of clothes on the floor in my bedroom.
3 There are some / any lovely flowers in the yard.
4 There aren't some / any towels in the bathroom.
5 There isn't / aren't a mirror in the kitchen.

5 Complete the second sentence so that it means the same as the first sentence. Use possessive adjectives or the possessive 's.

1 These shoes belong to Jack.
   These are ___Jack's___ shoes.
2 This car belongs to my parents.
   This is _____ car.
3 Does this backpack belong to you?
   Is this _____ backpack?
4 This yard belongs to us.
   This is _____ yard.
5 That jacket belongs to Laura's dad.
   That is _____ jacket.

6 Look at the pictures. Order the letters below and write the words for clothes and accessories.

| ~~cakjte~~ inrreags llsabeab pac tcahw T-hitsr

1 _jacket_   2 _____
3 _____   4 _____
5 _____

Welcome!

7 How is each person feeling? Circle the correct answers.

> It's the first day of my vacation! The weather's beautiful and I want to do lots of different things.

1   a sad   (b) excited   c nervous

> All my friends are away this weekend. It's raining outside and there's nothing to do!

2   a bored   b shocked   c excited

> I don't like it when my sister wears my clothes. She never asks me first!

3   a worried   b relaxed   c annoyed

> I have a science test tomorrow. The tests are always really difficult, so I never do very well.

4   a nervous   b tired   c relaxed

> I always go to bed late, so I never get much sleep. I want to sleep now!

5   a excited   b shocked   c tired

> It's Saturday morning and I don't have any homework this weekend! I wonder what's on TV.

6   a relaxed   b frightened   c annoyed

8 Complete the sentences with words for countries and languages.

1 Jacek is from _New Zealand_, so he speaks English.
2 My cousins live in Italy, so they can speak _____.
3 Ana is from _____, so she speaks Italian.
4 I want to visit China, so I'm learning to speak _____.
5 My aunt lives in Paris, in _____, so she can speak French.
6 Maria is from Portugal, so she speaks _____.
7 In Egypt, people speak _____.
8 We often go to Spain on vacation, so we're learning to speak _____.

9 Circle the correct answers.

1 _____ lots of people at the party last night – more than fifty!
   a Were   (b) There were
   c There was
2 Jamie _____ at school yesterday.
   a wasn't   b were
   c weren't
3 Our classes _____ very difficult last semester.
   a was   b there weren't
   c were
4 _____ the weather good for your vacation?
   a Were   b Was there
   c Was
5 _____ many people in the restaurant last night.
   a There wasn't   b There weren't
   c Weren't
6 _____ a good movie on TV last night?
   a Was there   b There wasn't
   c Were there

10 Complete the sentences with the Simple Past form of the verbs below.

live   ~~not enjoy~~   not play   not rain   study   want

1 I _didn't enjoy_ the concert last weekend – it was awful!
2 My parents _____ in New York when they were younger.
3 Alex _____ soccer yesterday because he was sick.
4 My mom _____ French at college.
5 My uncle _____ to be a pop singer when he was younger.
6 We were lucky because it _____ when we were on vacation.

11 Write questions and short answers in the Simple Past.

1 you / like / your gifts? ✓
   A: _Did you like your gifts?_
   B: _Yes, I did._
2 your parents / help / you / with your homework? ✗
   A: _____
   B: _____
3 she / invite / all her friends / to the party? ✓
   A: _____
   B: _____

Welcome! 119

1 THAT'S MY WORLD!

1 Look at the pictures and complete the words.

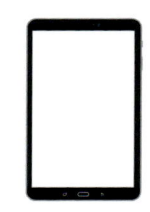

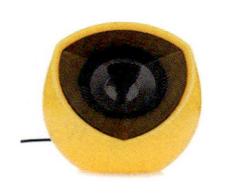

1 t <u>a</u> <u>b</u> <u>l</u> <u>e</u> <u>t</u>
2 b _ _ _ _ _ _ _
3 e _ _ _ _ _ _ _ _
4 s _ _ _ _ _ _ _
5 p _ _ _
6 s _ _ _ _ _ _ _ _ _
  s _ _ _ _ _
7 c _ _ _ _ _
8 c _ _ _ _ _ _ _

2 Write the correct word for each definition. Use the words in Activity 1.

1 It's a small computer you can hold in your hands.
   <u>tablet</u>
2 You put this inside a camera or other piece of technology to make it work. _____
3 It's a piece of wire to join things. _____
4 You use this to take a picture of yourself. _____
5 You use these to listen to music so that no one else can hear. _____
6 You push this into the wall to connect to the power supply. _____
7 You use this to put more power into your phone. _____
8 This is a device that reproduces sound. _____

3 Complete the sentences with the words below. There is one extra word.

> chat   download   games   listen   make
> messages   ~~online~~   read   send   share
> text   videos

1 I usually go <u>online</u> after dinner and _____ with my friends.
2 When I find a song that I like, I buy and _____ it, and then _____ to it on my music player.
3 On vacation, I usually _____ e-books or play _____ on my tablet.
4 I use my cell phone to _____ my friends or send _____ to them.
5 I take a lot of pictures, then I _____ them with my friends.
6 I love music, so I watch a lot of music _____. I'd like to _____ a video some day!

4 Circle the adjective that does NOT fit in each sentence.

1 I don't like that movie. I think it's ____.
   a awful   (b) exciting
   c boring
2 E-books on tablets are ____ because they're light and easy to carry.
   a brilliant   b perfect
   c noisy
3 My old cell phone is ____, but I'd like to get a new one.
   a disgusting   b OK
   c all right
4 Thank you for the gift. What a ____ surprise!
   a nice   b disgusting
   c lovely
5 I love your new tablet. It's ____!
   a awful   b amazing
   c awesome
6 I like Sara, but I don't know why she wears such ____ clothes.
   a weird   b noisy
   c old-fashioned

Unit 1

5 Complete the text with one word in each blank.

I'm really ¹___into___ technology. I always have my tablet with me, so I can ²_____ online whenever I want. It's brilliant for listening ³_____ music. I can ⁴_____ songs that I like, and I've just bought some new ⁵_____, so I can listen to them on the bus on my way to school. My tablet also has a really good camera. I often take pictures and ⁶_____ them with my friends online. I don't have a ⁷_____ stick, though – I don't often take pictures of myself. I send a lot of text ⁸_____ to my friends and I sometimes ⁹_____ games, but not very often. My brother loves games, but he only likes really modern ones, not ¹⁰old-_____ ones.

6 Circle the correct option. Then mark the sentences SP (Simple Present) or PC (Present Continuous).

1. Joe's *do* / *doing* some tricks on his bike at the moment. __PC__
2. We *aren't* / *don't* often go to the movies. ____
3. Sara *doesn't* / *isn't* wearing her helmet today. ____
4. My dad never *travels* / *traveling* by bus. ____
5. *Are* / *Do* you usually do your homework after dinner? ____
6. What *do* / *are* you doing here? ____

7 Match questions 1–6 to answers a–f.

1. [c] Are you enjoying the movie?
2. [ ] Does your uncle live in Miami?
3. [ ] Do you go online every day?
4. [ ] Are they making a movie?
5. [ ] Is Jack practicing on his skateboard?
6. [ ] Do your friends play in a band?

a. Yes, I do. I chat with friends online every evening.
b. No, they aren't. They're just taking some pictures.
c. ~~Yes, I am. It's great!~~
d. Yes, they do, and they're awesome!
e. No, he isn't. He's playing tennis.
f. No, he doesn't. He lives in Orlando.

8 Read the dialogues. Circle the correct option.

A
A: Hi. What ¹*are you doing* / *do you do*?
B: ²*I try* / *I'm trying* to take a selfie while I'm on my skateboard, but ³*I think* / *I'm thinking* it's impossible! ⁴*I fall off* / *I'm falling off* every time I try!

B
A: ⁵*Do you like* / *Are you liking* the new James Bond game?
B: Yes, I ⁶*am* / *do*. But ⁷*I don't spend* / *I'm not spending* much time on video games at the moment because ⁸*I study* / *I'm studying* hard for my tests.

C
A: Hi! Are those your new earphones? What ⁹*do you listen* / *are you listening* to?
B: That new band, The Fun. ¹⁰*Do you know* / *Are you knowing* them?

9 Complete the email with the Simple Present or Present Continuous form of the verbs in parentheses.

Hi Jen,

How are you? I ¹___'m staying___ (stay) with my uncle in Toronto this weekend because there's a big video games fair here. My uncle ²_____ (come) to this event every year. You ³_____ (know) I ⁴_____ (love) games and I ⁵_____ (play) them every day at home, so this is a great place for me. At the moment, I ⁶_____ (sit) in a big hall with lots of other games fans.
We ⁷_____ (try) a new game – it's awesome! The only problem is it's a difficult game and I ⁸_____ (not do) very well! We're on a break at the moment. OK, I know you ⁹_____ (not like) video games because you ¹⁰_____ (think) they're boring, but maybe you should try this one. What ¹¹_____ (you/do) this weekend? Write and tell me.

Paul

1 THAT'S MY WORLD!

10 Read the text. Match gadgets 1–3 to pictures A–C.

1 ☐ EnSoles   2 ☐ UE Boom 2   3 ☐ Nixie

Gadget World

Read about our three top gadgets this month.

The **UE Boom 2** is a small speaker with a really big sound! It's about the size of a can of soda, so you can carry it with you easily. It's round, so the sound comes out in all directions. It's powerful enough to fill a large room with music, so you can have a party wherever you are! It's made of strong plastic, so it's OK if you drop it, and it's also waterproof, so you can use it at the beach or in the shower. And the battery lasts for fifteen hours.

Do you sometimes forget to charge your phone? Well, why not buy some **EnSoles**? They look like normal insoles, but they use the power that you create when you're walking to charge your phone. Just put the Ensoles in your shoes, plug your phone cable to them and you can chat or text while you walk. They're really cool, and a very useful gadget.

Taking selfies is fun, but sometimes you'd like your selfie stick to be just a little bit longer. Well, **Nixie** is the perfect gadget for you! It's a camera that flies! You wear it on your arm like a watch, so it's easy to carry. When you're ready to take a picture, you let it go and it flies up into the air. It knows where you are and it can follow you to take some awesome pictures. It then comes back down, you catch it and put it back on your arm. Simple! Nixie isn't available to buy yet, but you can put your name on the list to get one as soon as it's on sale.

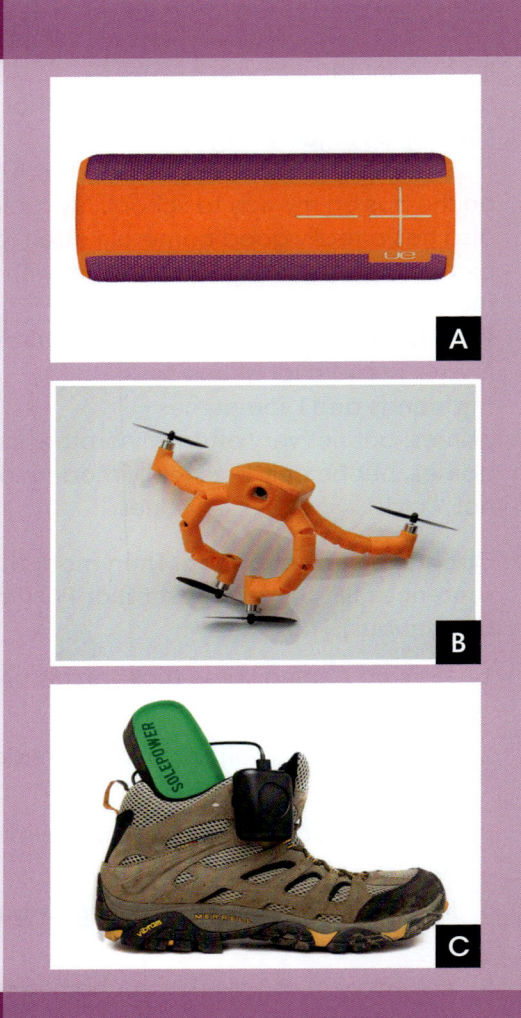

11 Read the text again. Circle the correct answer.

1 You can only use the UE Boom 2 speaker inside a room.
   a True   **(b) False**   c Doesn't say
2 The UE Boom 2 speaker doesn't break easily.
   a True   b False   c Doesn't say
3 The EnSoles are expensive.
   a True   b False   c Doesn't say
4 The EnSoles use power from the sun to charge your phone.
   a True   b False   c Doesn't say
5 The Nixie camera is comfortable to wear.
   a True   b False   c Doesn't say
6 You can't buy a Nixie at the moment.
   a True   b False   c Doesn't say

12 Match 1–6 to a–f to make sentences.

1 [c] I'm looking forward
2 ☐ Sonia can't
3 ☐ I don't
4 ☐ I would like
5 ☐ Dan is very good
6 ☐ Please stop

a mind helping with the party.
b making so much noise!
c ~~to seeing you.~~
d at playing the guitar.
e to go to New York.
f stand cooking.

13 Complete the sentences with the correct form of the verbs in parentheses.

1. My grandma wants _to learn_ (learn) how to download apps.
2. Why don't you come to my house when you finish _____ (do) your homework?
3. We're planning _____ (go) to France in the summer vacation.
4. Are you interested in _____ (see) the new superhero movie?
5. Mark never offers _____ (do) the dishes!
6. My sister sometimes asks me _____ (help) her with her homework.

14 Find and correct the mistakes in the sentences. One sentence is correct.

1. My brother often chooses watching movies on his tablet.
   My brother often chooses to watch movies on his tablet.
2. I can't stand to listen to that awful music!
   _____
3. Hurry up – I hate being late!
   _____
4. I hope my dad agrees paying for our tickets.
   _____
5. I'm really looking forward to read that book.
   _____

15 Complete the text with the correct form of the verbs below.

> be   choose   download   ~~make~~   get   make
> practice   ride   see   visit

I love ¹ _making_ videos of me and my friends. We all enjoy ² _____ our BMX bikes, and some of the tricks we can do look great when you film them. I always try ³ _____ interesting places for the videos – next month we're planning ⁴ _____ a big park in San Francisco to make a movie there. I've asked all my friends ⁵ _____ their tricks, so they can do them really well. I'm really looking forward to ⁶ _____ the results. My friends all tell me I'm quite good at ⁷ _____ videos. I wouldn't mind ⁸ _____ a job with a movie company when I'm older. I'd love ⁹ _____ a famous movie director one day! Click here if you want ¹⁰ _____ some of my videos and watch them. I hope you enjoy them!

16 Circle the correct option.

1. I get up for school at 7 **a.m.** / p.m.
2. There are sixty seconds in *a minute* / *an hour*.
3. I often see my friends *in* / *on* weekends.
4. I usually text my grandma *once* / *once time* a week.
5. My brother usually gets up late *at* / *on* Sundays.
6. I sometimes watch TV *in* / *on* the evening.

17 How often do you do these things? Write sentences. Use a different time expression for each sentence.

1. text friends
   I text my friends every day.
2. chat with friends
   _____
3. find information online
   _____
4. download apps
   _____
5. listen to the radio
   _____
6. watch TV shows online
   _____
7. upload videos
   _____
8. print pictures
   _____

1 THAT'S MY WORLD!

18 Complete the replies in the dialogues with the words below.

> cool ~~great~~ rather sure why

1. A: Why don't you add some music to the video?
   B: Yes, _great_ idea.
2. A: You could buy a better camera.
   B: I'd _____ not. They're very expensive!
3. A: Why don't you use your brother's video camera?
   B: I'm not _____. He doesn't like people using his things.
4. A: Let's make a video about soccer.
   B: Yes, _____ not?
5. A: Do you want to go to the park?
   B: OK, _____.

19 Write the responses from Activity 18 in the correct column.

Accepting a suggestion	Rejecting a suggestion
Yes, great idea.	

20 Match suggestions 1–4 to responses a–d.

1. [c] Let's make a video of our band.
2. [ ] You could use the camera on your cell phone.
3. [ ] Why don't you ask someone to help you?
4. [ ] Do you want to meet at six o'clock?

a. I'm not sure. It doesn't take very good pictures.
b. I'd rather not. I want to do it myself.
c. ~~Great idea! We might get famous online!~~
d. OK, cool. See you then.

21 Complete Matt's article for his school magazine with the words below.

> evening has ~~home~~ usually view weekdays

My unusual lifestyle
by Matt Thompson

Most people live in a house or flat, but my ¹ _home_ is in a boat. I always have a ² _____ of water! It ³ _____ three bedrooms and a small living area. There's a kitchen and a bathroom, too. Although it's small, it's warm and comfortable. We don't have much technology. However, I have a tablet in case I want to go online to chat with friends or watch movies in the ⁴ _____.
I live with my parents and my sister. We ⁵ _____ stay in one place during school time. I get up early on ⁶ _____ because I help look after the boat. On school vacations, we travel around. I like this lifestyle because I visit interesting places. Also, I meet lots of different people – as well as my school friends. I have friends all over the country!

22 Read the text again. Mark the sentences true (T) or false (F).

1. [F] Matt can't use the internet on his boat.
2. [ ] Four people live on Matt's boat.
3. [ ] Matt and his family never stay in one place for more than a few weeks.
4. [ ] Matt enjoys his lifestyle.

23 Circle the correct option.

1. My home isn't very big. *Although / (However)*, I enjoy living in it.
2. I meet lots of interesting people, *so / because* I never get bored.
3. There's an extra bed *as well as / in case* we want to invite friends to stay.
4. There's a living area inside the boat and there's space outside, *as well as / too*.

Unit 1

SELF-ASSESSMENT

Vocabulary

1 Complete the words in the sentences.

0 My phone has no power – I need to find my
   c h a r g e r .
1 This s _ _ _ _ _ _ _ s _ _ _ _ _ _ is great for taking pictures of yourself.
2 Do you usually s _ _ _ _ _ pictures with your friends online?
3 I love games, so I d _ _ _ _ _ _ _ _ a lot of apps for my cell phone.
4 I hate that TV show – it's a _ _ _ _ _ _ !
5 It's really hot and sunny today – it's a p _ _ _ _ _ _ day to go to the beach!

/5

2 Complete the sentences with the words below. There is one extra word.

> evening   made   recess   ~~twice~~   ugly
> useful   weekend

0 I go swimming **twice** a week, on Wednesdays and Fridays.
1 This is a very _____ gadget. I'd really like one.
2 I don't like this bag – it is _____ .
3 Is that bag _____ of plastic?
4 At eleven o'clock our classes stop because it's _____ .
5 I often listen to music in the _____ .

/5

Grammar

3 Complete the sentences with the Simple Present or the Present Continuous form of the verbs in parentheses.

0 Can you wait a minute? I **am chatting** (chat) with my friends at the moment.
1 I _____ (not often/watch) movies on my tablet – I prefer a bigger screen.
2 My uncle _____ (live) near the beach.
3 I _____ (not like) her music. I think it's boring!
4 It _____ (not rain) now, so we can go out.
5 Jake _____ (not want) to come to the party.

/5

4 Complete the questions with the Simple Present or the Present Continuous form of the verbs in parentheses. Then complete the short answers.

1 A: 0 **Do you often read** (you/often/read) e-books?
2 B: No, I 1_____ . I prefer printed books.
3 A: 2_____ (Jamie/listen) to music at the moment?
4 B: Yes, he 3_____ . He's upstairs in his room.
5 A: 4_____ (you/think) it's a good movie?
6 B: Yes, I 5_____ . It's brilliant!

/5

5 Circle the correct option.

0 Hurry up – I can't stand to be /(being) late!
1 George never offers to pay / paying for anything.
2 Please be quiet – I'm trying to listen / listening to music.
3 My parents allow me to stay up / staying up late on the weekend.
4 It's OK – I don't mind to wait / waiting for you.
5 Mike is hoping to go / going to art school.

/5

Speaking language practice

6 Complete the dialogue with one word in each blank.

A: Why 0 **don't** we organize something for Alana's birthday?
B: Yes, great 1_____ . We 2_____ have a party.
A: I'm not 3_____ . A party's quite expensive. 4_____ don't we go out for a pizza?
B: I'd rather 5_____ . I don't really like pizza.

/5

Vocabulary	/15
Grammar	/10
Speaking language practice	/5
Your total score	/30

Unit 1 125

2 THE TASTE TEST

1 Find seven more food and drink words in the word search and write them below.

H	O	N	E	Y	N	G	A	P	L
W	M	Z	A	X	G	S	N	E	E
A	C	H	I	P	S	S	U	D	M
S	R	B	I	E	A	O	T	F	O
O	E	O	S	A	B	K	S	E	N
M	A	R	N	C	R	L	C	C	A
E	M	I	C	H	O	L	H	T	D
F	A	Y	O	G	U	R	T	G	E
L	E	T	T	U	C	E	O	E	H
A	A	E	V	N	O	I	C	L	N

1 h _o_ _n_ _e_ y
2 p o t a t o c _ _ _ _ s
3 y _ _ _ _ _ t
4 l _ _ _ _ _ _ e
5 c _ _ _ _ m
6 p _ _ _ _ h
7 n _ _ _ s
8 l _ _ _ _ _ _ _ e

2 Circle the correct answers.

1 Which one is NOT a fruit?
   a garlic   b pear   c pineapple
2 Which one is a kind of meat?
   a flour   b beef   c cheese
3 Which one is NOT a drink?
   a ice cream   b smoothie   c lemonade
4 Which one is a dairy food?
   a honey   b tuna   c cheese
5 Which one is NOT a vegetable?
   a lettuce   b cucumber   c grapes
6 Which one is NOT sweet?
   a honey   b potato chips   c chewing gum
7 Which one makes you feel hot?
   a chili   b bread   c cream

3 Match descriptions 1–7 to foods a–g.

1 [c] It's a vegetable you use in salads.
2 [ ] It's a drink made with fruit.
3 [ ] It's a large fruit.
4 [ ] It's a kind of fish.
5 [ ] You eat them as a snack.
6 [ ] You use it to make bread.
7 [ ] It's a cold, sweet food.

a flour
b tuna
c ~~cucumber~~
d ice cream
e smoothie
f potato chips
g pineapple

4 Order the letters and complete the words in the sentences.

What's your favorite ice cream flavor?

1 I like fruit flavors like ___melon___ (emoln) and _____ (wabesrtrry).

2 My favorite ice cream flavors are _____ (lacohotec) and _____ (laivlna). Mmm!

3 I love _____ (mtni) because it's a lovely cool flavor.

4 I like _____ (menlo) because it isn't sweet.

5 _____ (nccootu) is definitely my favorite! I like _____ (foecef) as a drink, but I hate it as an ice cream flavor.

Unit 2

5 Complete what the people say about food and drink with the words below.

> ~~bread roll~~   fruit juice   lettuce
> potato chips   strawberry   yogurt

I usually eat a ¹ _bread roll_ with butter and jam for breakfast, and drink a glass of ² _____ – apple is my favorite. For lunch, I often have a salad with ³ _____ and cucumber or maybe a sandwich. I don't eat many snacks like ⁴ _____ because they aren't good for you. If I'm hungry, I often have a fruit ⁵ _____ – my favorite flavor is ⁶ _____ !

> beef   nuts   pineapple   smoothie
> tuna   vanilla

I'm a vegetarian, so I don't eat meat such as ⁷ _____. I eat fish, though, especially ⁸ _____ ! I try to eat a lot of fruit because it's good for you – my favorite fruit is ⁹ _____. Sometimes I use lots of different kinds of fruit to make a ¹⁰ _____ – it's my favorite drink. I usually try to eat healthy snacks, like ¹¹ _____, but I also love ¹² _____ ice cream!

6 Complete the sentences with the Present Perfect form of the verbs in parentheses.

1. I _'ve invited_ (invite) all my friends to the party.
2. Sam _____ (not decide) what to do yet.
3. _____ (you/try) mint ice cream?
4. We _____ (not have) lunch yet.
5. Sasha _____ (eat) noodles with chili!
6. _____ (your dad/order) the pizzas yet?
7. I _____ (hear) his music before – it's really good.

7 Make sentences in the Present Perfect. Use the words in parentheses.

1. you / meet / a famous chef / ? (ever)
   Have you ever met a famous chef?
2. the movie / start (already)
   _____
3. your email / not arrive (yet)
   _____
4. you / make / Sara's birthday cake / ? (yet)
   _____
5. Mike / cook / a meal (never)
   _____
6. we / order / our food (just)
   _____

8 Circle the correct option.

1. Have you (ever)/ yet eaten chili ice cream?
2. I've never / already seen that movie, so I don't want to see it again.
3. Have you made the pizza yet / ever?
4. Jo isn't here – she's just / yet left.
5. I've ever / never tried Chinese food.
6. I haven't finished my homework yet / already.

9 Complete the dialogues. Use the Present Perfect.

A
A: ¹ _Have you finished your homework yet?_ (you/finish/your homework/yet) ?
B: No, I ² _____ . But Tara ³ _____ (do/already) all the math activities, so she can help me!

B
A: ⁴ _____ (you/try/ever) a vegetable smoothie?
B: Yes, I ⁵ _____ . I have a smoothie maker, and I ⁶ _____ (make/just) a carrot and tomato smoothie – delicious!

C
A: ⁷ _____ (you/watch) that new cooking show on TV?
B: No, I ⁸ _____ (hear) people talking about it a lot, but I ⁹ _____ (never/see) it. Is it good?
A: Yes, it's great. I ¹⁰ _____ (learn/already) a lot just from watching the first two shows.

Unit 2

2 THE TASTE TEST

10 Complete the sentences with the correct form of *make* or *do*.

1. Sam _makes_ a lot of cakes.
2. _____ your homework now.
3. Have you _____ your decision yet?
4. Please don't _____ a mess in here!
5. You didn't win the competition, but you _____ your best, so well done!

11 Read the article. Choose the correct answers.

1. Why did Dean first start making chocolates?
   a. He wanted to earn some money.
   b. He wanted a special gift for a relative.
   c. He was looking for a new hobby.
   d. He wanted to win a competition.

2. What happened when he first tried to sell his chocolates?
   a. Only his family and friends bought his chocolates.
   b. He made too many chocolates and couldn't sell them all.
   c. Family members had to help him make more chocolates quickly.
   d. His prices were too high.

3. Why is his honey and chili chocolate his favorite?
   a. It makes the most money.
   b. It is the most popular with his customers.
   c. It's his most unusual flavor.
   d. It was his own idea.

4. What are Dean's plans for the summer?
   a. to work on some new chocolates to sell
   b. to work for a chocolate-maker in his town
   c. to visit France with his family
   d. to go on vacation with friends

A passion for chocolate

Dean Pollard is seventeen and he runs a successful business, making delicious chocolates.

Dean has made chocolates since he was ten years old, but he didn't plan to make money from them at first. He just wanted to give his grandma something special for her birthday. He found that he enjoyed making chocolates and he soon started winning competitions. His parents were just pleased that his hobby didn't have a bad effect on his studies.

In the beginning, Dean just made chocolates for family and friends and he never asked for any money. But at the age of fifteen he decided to turn his passion into a business, so he set up a website. He kept his prices quite low, and the first weekend the website came online he was so busy that his parents had to help out so there were enough chocolates for all the customers! He soon decided to put his prices up!

Dean makes a huge range of chocolates with different flavors and he's especially proud of his more unusual flavors, like his lemon coconut creams. Mint and strawberry are the most popular flavors with customers, but Dean is particularly proud of his honey and chili chocolate, not because it makes a lot of money for him, but because it was the first flavor that he developed himself.

So, what are Dean's plans for the summer? A local chocolate-maker in his town has offered him the chance to work for them during the summer vacation, but Dean isn't interested in the job. He really wants to spend the summer working on some exciting new flavors for his chocolates. "My friends have invited me to go to France with them, but I'm just too busy," he says. "Maybe next year!"

Unit 2

12 Write the words below in the correct column.

> ~~a few weeks~~   an hour   last Tuesday
> my birthday   November   Saturday
> ten years   three days   two months   2012

For – a period of time
a few weeks

Since – a point in time

13 Complete the sentences with *for* or *since*.
1. We've been here ____for____ nearly an hour, and the train hasn't arrived yet!
2. There has been a movie theater here _____ 2002.
3. We haven't had any homework _____ Monday.
4. Mr. Thomas has worked at this school _____ over twenty years.
5. Tom has been at college _____ a few months now and he loves it.
6. I've had this cell phone _____ last summer.

14 Choose the correct option.
1. I (went) / have been to New York two years ago.
2. This restaurant *opened* / *has opened* in 2015.
3. We *lived* / *have lived* in this house for two months now, so it's beginning to feel like home.
4. I *knew* / *have known* Paul since I was five years old – he's my best friend.
5. *Did you see* / *Have you seen* Emily yesterday?
6. *Did you ever go* / *Have you ever been* to Paris?

15 Complete the texts with the Present Perfect or the Simple Past form of the verbs in parentheses.

I ¹ ____went____ (go) to the Chinese restaurant on Dalton Street last night. ² _____ (you/eat) there? The food's really nice. I ³ _____ (have) some tuna, which ⁴ _____ (be) very tasty!

I ⁵ _____ (try) that restaurant. I ⁶ _____ (not like) it at all, and we ⁷ _____ (wait) for ages for our food! But that ⁸ _____ (be) about six months ago.

I think the food ⁹ _____ (improve) since last year. A lot of people I know ¹⁰ _____ (enjoy) the food there. Two of my friends ¹¹ _____ (eat) there last Saturday and they ¹² _____ (not have) any complaints.

16 Complete the words for describing food.
1. sw _e_ _e_ t
2. b l _ _ d
3. b _ t t _ r
4. f _ _ _ h
5. s _ _ r
6. s p _ _ y
7. r _ _ h
8. d _ y
9. d _ l _ c _ _ _ s
10. s t _ _ e
11. t _ _ _ y

17 Choose the correct option.
1. I made this cake six days ago, so it's probably a bit (stale) / *spicy* now.
2. I love this icing – it's *bland* / *delicious*!
3. It's a nice sauce, but it's quite *rich* / *tasty*, so I can't eat very much.
4. Don't add too much sugar – I don't like food that's too *bland* / *sweet*.
5. These grapes are nice and *fresh* / *dry*!
6. Lemon juice is too *spicy* / *sour* to drink.

2 THE TASTE TEST

18 Write the phrases below in the correct column.

> ~~Are you ready to order?~~
> Can I get you something?
> Excuse me, can I have ...?
> Here you are.
> I'd like a ...
> I'll have ...
> Just ... for me, please.
> Not for me, thanks.
> What would you like to drink?
> Take a seat and I'll get you the menu.
> Would you like anything to eat?

The customer says
The server says
Are you ready to order?

19 Circle the correct responses.

1 Would you like anything to eat?
 a Here you are.
 ⓑ Not for me, thanks.
 c I'll get it.

2 Excuse me, can I have a strawberry smoothie, please?
 a Thanks.
 b Are you ready to order?
 c Of course.

3 Can I get you something?
 a Nearly.
 b Just a sandwich for me, please.
 c Take a seat.

4 I'd like a slice of lemon cake.
 a I'll give you the menu.
 b Me too.
 c Sorry I'm late.

20 Order the letters and write the verbs in the sentences.

1 You need a knife to ____chop____ (hcpo) the onions and carrots.
2 _____ (ryf) the fish in a bit of butter.
3 I usually _____ (lobi) eggs for about four minutes.
4 Add the cheese and _____ (xmi) everything together.
5 _____ (liesc) the tomato and put it on top of the pizza.

21 Write the sentences in the correct group.

> ~~Bye for now.~~   Great to hear from you.   See you soon.
> I can't wait to hear more about it.   I'm making a pizza.
> I'm writing to ask if you'd like to come.   How are things?
> We've just finished our final tests.

Starting your email	Thanks for getting in touch.
Responding to news	It was great to hear about your vacation.
Giving your news	We've decided to organize a class lunch.
Explaining why you're writing	By the way, I was wondering if you'd like to come.
Ending your email	Let me know if you can make it. *Bye for now.*

SELF-ASSESSMENT

Vocabulary

1 Circle the odd one out.

0	(garlic)	grapes	pear
1	smoothie	cream	lemonade
2	beef	tuna	nuts
3	cheese	potato chips	ice cream
4	cucumber	honey	lettuce
5	coconut	mint	flour

☐ /5

2 Choose the correct option.

0 Our school is in a modern *build* / (*building*).
1 Jenny Sharp is the best *contestant* / *competition* on the show.
2 Who will *win* / *winner* the prize?
3 I don't know what to do – I can't *make* / *do* a decision.
4 Don't worry about winning – just *make* / *do* your best.
5 Oh, I love this vanilla ice cream – it's *delicious* / *bland*!

☐ /5

Grammar

3 Complete the sentences with the Present Perfect form of the verbs in parentheses.

0 Don't worry, the movie ___hasn't started yet___ (not start/yet).
1 _____ (you/try/ever) chili chocolate?
2 Come in – we _____ (finish/just) eating.
3 I _____ (see/never) Tim so angry before!
4 _____ (it/stop/raining/yet)?
5 _____ (already/read) that book.

☐ /5

4 Circle the correct answers.

0 I've ___ been to New York, but I'd love to go there one day.
  a just   b already   (c) never

1 Yeah! Jim's ___ won the competition!
  a since   b just   c ever
2 I haven't finished my homework ___.
  a yet   b already   c just
3 Don't worry. I've ___ invited him.
  a ever   b yet   c already
4 My uncle has lived in Spain ___ two years.
  a for   b since   c already
5 Poor Sara has been ill ___ last Saturday.
  a since   b yet   c for

☐ /5

5 Complete the sentences with the Present Perfect or the Simple Past form of the verbs in parentheses.

0 I ___have visited___ (visit) Paris a few times. It's a beautiful city.
1 We _____ (not go) away on vacation last year.
2 I _____ (write) an email to Max three days ago, but he _____ (not reply) yet.
3 I _____ (never/have) a chocolate smoothie, but I _____ (try) a coconut smoothie last summer.

☐ /5

Speaking language practice

6 Complete the dialogues with the phrases below.

| could I have | excuse me | almost | of course |
| thank you | would you like | | |

0 A: Are you ready to order?
  B: ___Almost___. We'll be ready in a minute.
1 A: Can I get you something to drink?
  B: _____ a lemonade, please?
2 A: Excuse me, can I have some water, please?
  B: _____.
3 A: _____ anything to eat?
  B: Could I have a toasted sandwich, please?
4 A: Here you are.
  B: _____.
5 A: _____.
  B: Yes?

☐ /5

Vocabulary ☐ /10
Grammar ☐ /15
Speaking language practice ☐ /5
Your total score ☐ /30

Unit 2

3 WILD NATURE

1 Complete the weather words.

Noun	Adjective
snow	¹ s n o w y
² s __ __	sunny
fog	³ f __ __ __ __
⁴ c __ __ __ __	cloudy
wind	⁵ w __ __ __ __
⁶ i __ __	icy
storm	⁷ s __ __ __ __ __

2 Circle the correct answers.

1. We don't want to drive because it's _____ today, so you can't see very well.
   a ice   b icy
   c fog   **d foggy**
2. We can't go out in our boat because it's _____ and the sea is rough.
   a sun   b sunny
   c storm   d stormy
3. It's very cold here in winter and there's often _____ on the ground.
   a snow   b snowy
   c rain   d rainy
4. Look, it's a lovely _____ day. Let's go swimming in the sea!
   a sun   b sunny
   c wind   d windy
5. You should drive slowly when there's _____ on the roads.
   a storm   b stormy
   c ice   d icy
6. There's a beautiful blue sky today – it isn't _____ at all.
   a sun   b sunny
   c cloud   d cloudy
7. Sometimes things blow away when it's very _____ .
   a wind   b windy
   c ice   d icy
8. Everything in the yard gets wet when it's _____ .
   a cloud   b cloudy
   c rain   d rainy

3 Find and correct the mistakes in the sentences. One sentence is correct.

1. It very foggy today.
   It's very foggy today.
2. Oh, no! It getting cloud!
   _____
3. Look, it's snowy. Let's build a snowman!
   _____
4. It's getting a little storm now.
   _____

4 Circle the correct answers.

1. Which word do we use for "-" in -10?
   ⓐ minus   b less   c lower
2. Which word does NOT mean "hot"?
   a warm   b boiling   c chilly
3. Which word does NOT mean "cold"?
   a mild   b cool   c freezing
4. Which word do we use to say "°" in 35°?
   a hot   b degrees   c temperature

5 Circle the correct option.

1. Put your coat on – it's *freezing* / mild outside!
2. It's a nice chilly / warm day, so we can sit outside.
3. It's often hot boiling / boiling hot here in the summer.
4. The water's a bit cool / mild, but it's not too cold.
5. It's lower / minus fifteen here, so it's very cold!
6. Sometimes the temperature reaches forty points / degrees in the summer.

6 Complete the crossword.

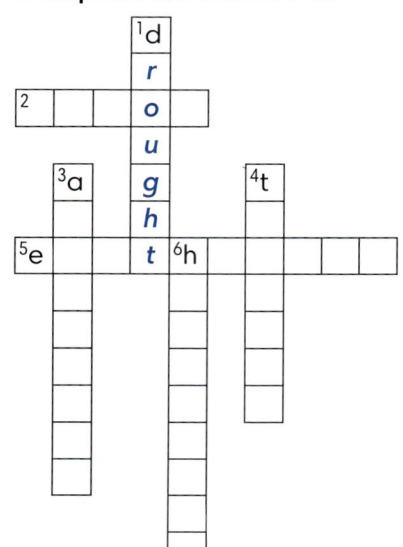

```
        ¹d
        r
    ²□ □ o □
        u
    ³a  g    ⁴t
        h    □
    ⁵e □ t ⁶h □ □
             □
             □
             □
```

Across
2 when a lot of water covers the land
5 when the ground shakes

Down
1 when there is no rain for a long time and the ground becomes very dry
3 when a lot of snow falls from a mountain
4 when a very big wave comes from the ocean onto the land
6 when there is a very strong wind

7 Read what four people say about the weather in their area. Circle the correct option.

It's a horrible wet, ¹(rainy)/ sunny day here in New Orleans, so you need your umbrella. It's also pretty ²chilly / boiling, so you definitely need your coat.

Sometimes we have ³earthquakes / floods here in Hawaii and our house shakes. It's very scary. I live near the sea, so when this happens, we always worry that there might be ⁴an avalanche / a tsunami, too.

Winters are usually ⁵boiling / freezing cold in Alaska and we often have lots of ⁶ snow / snowy. It's great because we can build snowmen, but the roads are dangerous because they're often ⁷cloudy / icy.

Usually the summers are warm and ⁸sun / sunny in Miami, but this year it's really ⁹cool / mild. It's also very rainy, so we're worried there might be a ¹⁰ flood / hurricane.

8 Complete the sentences with the Past Perfect form of the verbs in parentheses.
1 We ___had done___ (do) all of the work. Ralph _____ (not help) us.
2 I _____ (not hear) that song before.
3 _____ (you/seen) the weather forecast?
4 She _____ (study) with the teacher before.
5 We _____ (already/ask) him for help.
6 Sara _____ (not look) very happy.

9 Match infinitives 1–8 to their past participle forms a–h.
1 [c] become   a met
2 [ ] see   b thought
3 [ ] feel   c become
4 [ ] think   d known
5 [ ] take   e seen
6 [ ] meet   f gone
7 [ ] go   g felt
8 [ ] know   h taken

10 Use the prompts to write questions in the Past Perfect.
Before you arrived at school today ...
1 you / brush your teeth
   had you brushed your teeth?
2 your mom or dad / make breakfast
   _____
3 you / use your cell phone
   _____
4 you / do your homework
   _____
5 it / rain
   _____
6 your neighbors / play loud music
   _____

11 Answer the questions in Activity 10 about you.
1 *Yes, I had. / No, I hadn't.*
2 _____
3 _____
4 _____
5 _____
6 _____

12 **WORD FRIENDS** Circle the word that does NOT fit in each sentence.
1 You look _____ ridiculous in that hat!
   (a) very   b completely
   c absolutely
2 My brother is _____ crazy!
   a absolutely   b completely
   c very
3 Samia is _____ good at English.
   a very   b really
   c totally
4 That class was _____ interesting.
   a completely   b very
   c really
5 This place is _____ amazing!
   a very   b absolutely
   c totally
6 It's usually _____ cold here in winter.
   a really   b pretty
   c totally

Unit 3 133

3 WILD NATURE

13 Read the forum posts. Match headings 1–4 to posts A–D.
1. [C] Extreme heat
2. [ ] On top of the world
3. [ ] River adventure
4. [ ] A wild place close to home

WILD PLACES
There are hundreds of amazing places to visit in the world. Tell us about your experiences!

A Last summer I went to Tibet with my family. We were in a very wild area high up in the Himalayas. It was a walking trip, so we walked and climbed every day – sometimes up to over 4,000 meters! It's really beautiful in the summer, but in the winter it's very dangerous because there's a lot of snow and there's always a possibility of avalanches. The local people believe that human-like creatures called yetis live in the mountains, but we didn't see any! *Max*

B I live in the town of Moteuka in New Zealand, near the Abel Tasman National Park. The park is named after Abel Tasman, one of the first Europeans to reach New Zealand. It's an amazing wild place. There are forests where you can walk and camp, and some absolutely stunning beaches. I swam in the sea last week and it was really warm. Winter is pretty mild and summer isn't too hot. There are a lot of earthquakes in New Zealand, but they aren't usually very bad in this area. *Emma*

C In July I traveled to Death Valley in the USA. It's a very dry place, with almost no rain for most of the year, so there aren't many plants. It's absolutely boiling in summer, with temperatures over 50°C! We learned about what life was like here in the past – that was absolutely fascinating. The first Europeans who arrived called it Death Valley because without water, you can't live there for very long! *Sara*

D My uncle went on an adventure vacation to South America last year. He travelled by boat through the rainforest of Brazil. He went in July - the weather was hot, as usual, but there was less rain – he was pleased about that! He saw some really colorful birds and monkeys, too. He didn't see any dangerous animals, though. The pictures he took are absolutely amazing! Some people still live a traditional life in the forest. Scientists are trying to learn from them how to use all the plants in the forest as medicines. I'd love to go there one day! *Paul*

14 Read the texts again. Match people 1–5 to phrases a–f to make true sentences. There is one extra phrase.
1. [ ] Max
2. [ ] Emma
3. [ ] Sara
4. [ ] Paul's uncle
5. [ ] Paul

a. lives in a place where there are sometimes natural disasters.
b. was happy with the weather during a trip.
c. enjoyed a very active vacation.
d. had a problem while on a trip.
e. wants to travel to a place that a relative visited.
f. enjoyed learning about the history of a place.

15 Complete the sentences with the Simple Past form of the verbs in parenthesis.
1. He ___found___ (find) unusual plants in Mexico.
2. They _____ (not listen) when the guide explained the dangers of eating wild plants.
3. What _____ (you/do) when you saw the avalanche?
4. They _____ (swim) in the ocean on vacation.
5. _____ (it/rain) when you were in Greece?
6. Someone _____ (steal) my camera at the beach!

Unit 3

16 Circle the correct option.
1. The train had left when I *had gotten /(got)* to the station.
2. Jack had fallen asleep before the movie *had ended / ended*.
3. The mail carrier *had left / left* by the time I opened the door.
4. When the firefighters *had arrived / arrived*, Max had already rescued the cat.
5. Local authorities had rung the bell before the avalanche *started / had started*.
6. Nobody *had known / knew* about the tsunami when it hit the coast.

17 Complete the sentences with the Simple Past or Past Perfect form of the verbs in parentheses.
1. Everyone was happy that the drought ____was____ (be) over. Nothing ____had grown____ (grow) for a long time.
2. By the time the police _____ (arrive), the criminal _____ (disappear).
3. We _____ (not check) the weather forecast before we _____ (book) the vacation.
4. The plane _____ (take) off before we _____ (arrive) at the gate.
5. The dress I wanted _____ (already sell) out when I _____ (get) to the store.

18 Look at the pictures and complete the words.
1. w_a_t_e_r_f_a_l_l_ 
2. s_____
3. s_____ 
4. l_____ 
5. b___ 
6. b___ 

19 Complete the sentences with the words below. There is one extra word.

| path ~~cave~~ bat stars wildlife sky |

1. It was very dark at the back of the __cave__.
2. At night you can see the _____ shining.
3. There is a lot of interesting _____ in the forest.
4. We followed the _____ until we came to a river.
5. There were only a few clouds in the _____.

20 **WORD FRIENDS** Match 1-6 to a-f to make sentences.
1. [d] It was raining, so we made
2. [ ] It was cold, so we made
3. [ ] I really want to learn
4. [ ] It's too cold to sleep
5. [ ] Last year scientists discovered
6. [ ] We looked

a. about the wildlife in the forest.
b. some interesting plants here.
c. a fire to keep warm.
d. a shelter to keep us dry.
e. for wild animals, but didn't find any.
f. outside.

21 Complete the sentences with the words below.

| mean wanted careful realize ~~thinking~~ |

1. What were you __thinking__?
2. I didn't _____ to.
3. Just be more _____ next time.
4. I really _____ to make you laugh.
5. I'm sorry, I didn't _____.

22 Order the words to make sentences.
1. for / do / what / you / that / did / ?
   What did you do that for?
2. thought / I / asleep / you / were
   _____
3. do / why / you / that / did / ?
   _____
4. hurt / didn't / you / mean / I / to
   _____
5. wanted / really / to / help / I
   _____

Unit 3

3 WILD NATURE

23 Write the phrases below in the correct column.

> I didn't mean to …
> ~~I really wanted to …~~
> Just be more careful next time.
> What did you do that for?
> What were you thinking of?
> Why did you do that?
> I didn't realize.
> I thought you were …

Criticizing

Explaining
I really wanted to …

24 Circle the correct responses.

1. You lost my cell phone! Why did you do that?
   a I thought it was your cell phone.
   (b) I didn't mean to lose it.
   c Just be more careful next time.

2. Surprise! Look at this big spider!
   a I didn't mean to scare you.
   b Oh, I'm sorry. I didn't realize.
   c Why did you do that? You know I hate spiders!

3. I'm sorry my ball broke your window.
   a Well, just be more careful next time.
   b What did you do that for?
   c Oh, I didn't realize.

4. You used my bike without asking me! What were you thinking of?
   a Why did you do that?
   b I'm sorry. I thought it was OK to use it.
   c Just be more careful next time.

25 Complete the text with the phrases below.

> did you know that   In conclusion   In my opinion   It is a fact that   ~~The purpose of this campaign is to~~

SAVE THE TREES AT GREEN PARK
ONLINE PETITION

¹ *The purpose of this campaign is to* convince people in Greenville to sign the petition to save the trees in Green Park. The local authorities are planning to cut the trees to build a racetrack for people that go running at Green Park.
² _____, this is absolutely ridiculous! There are several areas where people can go jogging in our city already – ³ _____ we actually have a path for runners among the trees at Green Park? And that lots of people use it?
⁴ _____ a famous sports brand wants to build this racetrack and then put lots of billboards and posters advertising their products along it. This is the real reason why the local authorities want to cut the trees!
⁵ _____, I believe that we should all do our part and sign this petition NOW! Saving the trees at Green Park is just one click away!
Click here to sign the online petition.

SELF-ASSESSMENT

Vocabulary

1 Complete the words in the sentences.

0 We couldn't see very well because it was **f o g g y**.
1 It's pretty **m _ _ _** today, so you don't need a coat.
2 Shut the door! It's **f _ _ _ _ _ _ _** cold outside!
3 The temperature is twenty-seven **d _ _ _ _ _ _ _** today.
4 It rained for five days and there was a **f _ _ _ _** in our town.
5 Our school building shook during the **e _ _ _ _ _ _ _ _ _ _**.

/5

2 Circle the correct option.

0 The *stars* / *(leaves)* fall off in fall.
1 We found a small *path* / *sky* going through the forest.
2 We tried to *have* / *make* a shelter, but it was too difficult.
3 Scientists *watched* / *discovered* some unusual plants near the river.
4 This book is *completely* / *really* interesting.
5 You won the game? That's *totally* / *very* awesome!

/5

Grammar

3 Complete the sentences with the Simple Past form of the verbs below.

go   have   not see   not want   stay   take

0 I _stayed_ at the camp for three days.
1 We spent three weeks in Iceland, but we _____ the Northern Lights.
2 I _____ swimming every day when I was on vacation.
3 His first concert _____ place in London last week.
4 She _____ to touch the spider.
5 _____ you _____ a good time on the Survival Weekend?

/5

4 Complete the sentences with the Past Perfect form of the verbs in parentheses.

0 I knew that my dad _hadn't watched_ (not watch) the whole movie because he was asleep.
1 Lia didn't go to PE class because she _____ (hurt) her knee.
2 They _____ (not meet) before now.
3 _____ (the weather be) good before that?
4 _____ (the children/clean) their bedrooms?
5 It _____ (not rain) all vacation.

/5

5 Circle the correct option.

1 I ⁰*saw* / *(had seen)* a really big spider so I ¹*screamed* / *had screamed*.
2 We ²*watched* / *had watched* the sunset before we ³*returned* / *had returned* home from Scotland.
3 The hurricane ⁴*didn't finish* / *hadn't finished* when we ⁵*opened* / *had opened* the door.

/5

Speaking language practice

6 Complete the dialogues with the phrases below.

be more careful   I didn't mean to   I didn't realize
I really wanted   I thought you were   ~~why did you do that~~

1
A: Where's my bike?
B: I said that Jo could use it today.
A: ⁰ _Why did you do that_ ? I need it today.
B: Sorry, ¹_____ you needed it.

2
A: Oh look – the pizzas are burned!
B: Sorry, ²_____ burn them. ³_____ to help, so I put them in the oven. ⁴_____ going to be late.
A: Well, just ⁵_____ next time.

/5

Vocabulary /15
Grammar /10
Communication /5
Your total score /30

Unit 3

4 THE BIG GAME!

1 Look at the pictures and complete the words.

1 b _a d m i n t o n_

2 i _ _ - s _ _ _ _ _ _

3 g _ _ _ _ _ _ _ _ _

4 d _ _ _ _ _ _

5 s _ _ _ _ _ _ _ _ _

6 v _ _ _ _ _ _ _ _

7 h _ _ _ _ _ _ _ _

8 s _ _ _ _ _ _ _

2 Read the descriptions. Write the sports.

1 It's a really exciting sport. You use a paddle to move through the water.
kayaking

2 This is a very relaxing sport. You move your body slowly into different positions. It's good for stretching your muscles.
_____

3 I play this sport for my school team. You can throw the ball to other people or you can run and bounce the ball on the ground. You score points by throwing the ball through a hoop.
_____

4 You need to be strong to do this sport. You use your arms to pull yourself up the side of a mountain.
_____

5 The ball you use for this sport is very small. You hit it across a table.
_____

6 I love animals, so this is my favorite sport. You have to wear a special hat to protect your head if you fall off.
_____

3 WORD FRIENDS Match 1–5 to a–e to make sentences.

1. [d] I sometimes go
2. [ ] I've decided to take
3. [ ] My brother does
4. [ ] I have skiing
5. [ ] I sometimes play

a karate – he loves martial arts!
b volleyball at school.
c up gymnastics.
d ~~walking with my friends.~~
e classes in the winter.

4 Circle the correct words to complete the sentences.

1. Would you like to *play* / (*do*) yoga?
2. I want to *take* / *get* up a new sport this year.
3. A lot of my friends *go* / *play* skiing in the winter.
4. Do you *have* / *do* tennis practice every week?
5. I sometimes *go* / *play* handball with my friends.
6. You need to be very fit to *do* / *play* gymnastics.

5 Complete the words in the sentences.

1. We get changed in the **l o c k e r r o o m s** before the game.
2. Our team wears a blue and white **u _ _ _ _ _ _ _**.
3. I'd love to be a team **m _ _ _ _ t** and walk onto the game with the players.
4. There were over 50,000 people in the **s _ _ _ _ m** for the big game.
5. Our **s _ _ _ s** were right at the front, so we could see the players really well.
6. At the end of the game, the **s _ _ _ _ b _ _ _ d** said 12–8 for my team!

6 Complete the dialogue with the words below. There is one extra word.

| fans   goal   seats   ~~game~~   field   score   team |

A: Wow! That was a really exciting soccer ¹ *game*! I'm glad our ² _____ won in the end.
B: Yes. I was a bit worried at half time when the ³ _____ was 1-0 for the other team, but then Juan Fernandez scored that amazing ⁴ _____!
A: Yes. That gave our players a lot of confidence. And the ⁵ _____ all got really excited when he scored another one!
B: Yeah. A few people tried to run onto the ⁶ _____ to celebrate, but of course, you aren't allowed to do that!

7 Match the verbs in bold in sentences 1–6 to functions a–f.

1. [c] Off you go. I'm sure you**'ll have** fun.
2. [ ] Don't worry, I**'ll do** the dishes.
3. [ ] I**'m meeting** Sam this afternoon.
4. [ ] I**'m going to get** fit this year!
5. [ ] Look – it**'s going to rain**.
6. [ ] The movie **starts** at 7:30.

a an arrangement
b a schedule
c ~~a prediction made at the moment of speaking~~
d a prediction based on what we know now
e a decision made at the moment of speaking
f a plan

8 Read the dialogue. Circle the correct answers to complete the blanks.

A: Hi, James. What are your plans for the weekend?
B: Well, I ¹_____ soccer on Saturday afternoon.
A: Really? What time ²_____ the game start?
B: At three o'clock.
A: Cool! ³_____ and watch.
B: Great! I think it ⁴_____ an exciting game.
A: Good. What about later? Do you have any plans?
B: Yes, Ali ⁵_____ me after the game. He wants to go to the movies in the evening. Do you want to come with us?
A: Sorry, I can't. ⁶_____ dinner with my grandparents at eight o'clock. Maybe next week.

1. a I play (b) I'm playing c I going to play
2. a will b is c does
3. a I'll come b I come c I'm coming
4. a is b will be c is being
5. a calls b is going to call c won't call
6. a I'm having b I'll have c I have

Unit 4

4 THE BIG GAME!

9 Complete the second sentence so that it means the same as the first. Use up to three words.

1. Nick's plan is to get a part-time job.
   Nick ___is going to___ get part-time job.
2. What's the closing time at the gym?
   What time _____ close?
3. What's your prediction for the final score?
   What do you think the final score _____?
4. What time is your meeting with the principal?
   What time are _____ the principal?

10 Circle the correct option.

MESSAGES

Hi. Mia ¹*comes* / (*is coming*) to my house this evening to watch a movie. Do you want to come?

What movie ²*will you* / *are you going* to watch?

The new Avengers movie. I think you ³*enjoy* / *'ll enjoy* it.

OK. My tennis class ⁴*finishes* / *will finish* at 5:30, so I can come after that.

Great! Mia ⁵*is going to order* / *orders* some pizzas, too – well, that's the plan. I need to remind her!

Cool! And ⁶*I'm going to bring* / *I'll bring* some snacks with me.

Great! See you later.

11 Circle the correct option.
1. We were trying to get to Los Angeles, but we (*ended up*) / *set up* in San Diego!
2. Will you help me *pick up* / *clean up* the kitchen?
3. Jeremy had to *give up* / *end up* basketball when he hurt his knee.
4. I'd love to *take up* / *set up* a gymnastics club at school.
5. My uncle offered to *pick me up* / *set me up* from the airport.
6. I wanted to get fit, so I decided to *pick up* / *take up* running.

12 Read the article. Complete the form.

Name: George Samson   **Age:** 16
Start date of the event: ¹ May 14
No. of days attending the event:
²_____

- Access allowed to sports halls and ³_____
- Pictures allowed, but no ⁴_____
- Interview rooms available from 10 a.m. until ⁵_____
- Lunch available in the ⁶_____

My name's George Samson and I'm sixteen. I often write articles for the school magazine because I want to be a journalist when I leave school. Next week I'm going on my first trip as an official press reporter. I'm attending a sports event for teenagers with disabilities and I'm really looking forward to it.
The event starts on Friday, May 14, and goes on for four days. I only have a pass for the Saturday and Sunday, but I'm sure there will be lots to see. I don't want to miss out on any of the excitement! As a young journalist, I can go into all the sports halls and also the swimming pool. I'm going to take my camera, of course, and I'm allowed to take as many pictures as I like – I'll probably take a lot! Videos aren't allowed, though. There are special interview rooms where I can talk to some of the competitors. They're only open from ten in the morning until two in the afternoon, so I'll have to be well-organized! There's also a special food tent where all the journalists can get free food at lunch time, so I'll be able to hang out with some professional journalists!
If you love sports, why don't you come along to the event? You can help out as a volunteer if you want. Check out the website for more details and look out for my report in next month's magazine!

13 Read the article again. Mark the sentences true (T) or false (F).
1. [F] George writes articles for a local newspaper.
2. [ ] He has not worked as an official press reporter before.
3. [ ] The sports event lasts for three days.
4. [ ] George isn't going to take many pictures.
5. [ ] He won't have to pay for food at the event.
6. [ ] You can find details of the event in the school magazine.

Unit 4

14 Circle the correct option.

1 *You enjoy* / (*You'll enjoy*) gymnastics if (*you try*) / *you'll try* it.
2 If *you have* / *you'll have* some skiing classes, *you be* / *you'll be* a very good skier.
3 We *don't go* / *won't go* walking unless the weather *is* / *will be* good.
4 *You get* / *You'll get* fitter if *you join* / *you'll join* a gym.
5 *I call* / *I'll call* you when *I get* / *I'll get* home.
6 You *don't improve* / *won't improve* unless *you practice* / *you'll practice*.

15 Complete the sentences with *if* or *unless*.

1 We'll go to the game ___unless___ the tickets are too expensive.
2 He won't lose weight _____ he doesn't do any exercise.
3 You won't get into the team _____ you're very good.
4 We'll stop playing _____ it starts to rain.
5 They won't cancel the game _____ the weather is so bad that they can't play.
6 They won't let you in _____ you don't have a ticket.

16 Complete the dialogue with the correct form of the verbs in parentheses.

A: Do you want to go ice-skating with me on Saturday?
B: But I don't have any skates!
A: I'm sure Jenna ¹ ___will lend___ (lend) you hers if you ² _____ (ask) her.
B: But I'm worried I ³ _____ (hurt) myself if I ⁴ _____ (fall) over.
A: Don't worry. You ⁵ _____ (not get) injured if you ⁶ _____ (be) careful.
B: But sometimes there are lots of people there.
A: Well, if it ⁷ _____ (be) very busy when we get there, we ⁸ _____ (wait) until it's quieter. We ⁹ _____ (not go) on the ice unless you ¹⁰ _____ (feel) it's safe.
B: OK. Why not? I'll give it a go!

17 Read the text. Circle the correct answers to complete the blanks.

So, my climbing adventure starts today! I have my first class at the climbing center in my town. I'm feeling a bit nervous, but I know that the instructors will help me ¹_____ have any problems. I'll start on the junior climbing wall and I'll have a rope on, so I won't get hurt ²_____ fall. There are three higher walls, but the instructors probably won't allow me to go on them ³_____ think I'm able to cope with them. My uncle does lots of climbing and he says that ⁴_____ enjoy it, he'll take me climbing with him in the mountains. I won't go with him ⁵_____ feel really confident, though. Climbing can be a dangerous sport!

Well, I have to go now. My class starts at two and I'll be late ⁶_____ leave soon!

1 a if I'll (b) if I
  c unless I   d if I don't
2 a if I   b if I'll
  c unless I   d if I won't
3 a unless they'll   b unless they
  c if they   d if they won't
4 a unless I   b if I'll
  c if I won't   d if I
5 a if I won't   b unless I'll
  c if I'll   d unless I
6 a if I   b if I won't
  c unless I   d unless I'll

18 WORD BUILDING Complete the chart.

Verb	Noun (action)	Noun (person)
¹ ___train___	training	² _____
run	³ _____	runner
play	–	⁴ _____
⁵ _____	practice	–
coach	–	⁶ _____
⁷ _____	race	racer
score	⁸ _____	scorer
⁹ _____	kick	–

Unit 4 141

4 THE BIG GAME!

19 Complete the sentences with a word formed from the word in parentheses.

1 They do three hours of _training_ (train) every week.
2 Rob _____ (practice) his volleyball skills every day.
3 Stella is a really good tennis _____ (play).
4 All the _____ (run) looked exhausted at the end of the race.
5 My uncle works as a sports _____ (train).
6 Who _____ (score) the winning goal in last week's game?

20 Match 1–6 to a–f to make sentences.

1 [c] What are you up
2 [ ] I don't have
3 [ ] Do you have any
4 [ ] I'm visiting my
5 [ ] What are you
6 [ ] I'm going to

a doing tonight?
b grandparents on Sunday.
c ~~to on Saturday?~~
d the movies on Friday.
e any plans yet.
f plans for the weekend?

21 Complete the dialogue with the words below.

about   after   ~~first~~   know   then   what

A: What are you doing on the weekend, Laura?
B: ¹ _First_ of all, I'm going shopping on Saturday morning. ²_____ that I'm meeting some friends for lunch. What ³_____ you? What are you doing?
A: I don't ⁴_____ what I'm doing yet. What about you, Sam? ⁵_____ are your plans?
C: I'm going swimming in the morning. ⁶_____ I'm going to a soccer game.

22 Complete the requests with the phrases below.

could you please look   if it's OK with you
let me know   would it be possible   ~~would you mind~~

1 _Would you mind_ sending me Cara's address?
2 We could meet at my house. _____ if that's OK.
3 _____ to meet at seven o'clock?
4 _____, could we go on Saturday morning?
5 _____ in your car to see if my cell phone's there?

23 Write the phrases below in the correct group.

~~See you!~~   Could you please send me the pictures?
Hi, there   Hey   I had a great time skiing.
I loved snowboarding.   Let me know if that's OK.
See you later.   Thanks for your message.

Greeting	Hi Hiya
Thanking the other person	Thanks for inviting me. Just a quick note to thank you for …
Introducing the topic	I really enjoyed taking part in the race.
Making a request	Would you mind keeping my jacket for me? Would it be possible to send me Tim's email address?
Ending	All the best. Bye! _See you!_

Unit 4

SELF-ASSESSMENT

Vocabulary

1 Complete the sentences with the words below.

> basketball   climbing   diving   ice-skating
> snowboarding   yoga

0 Ali loves team sports. He plays for the school __basketball__ team.
1 I don't like going underwater, so I hate _____!
2 I love winter sports – _____ is my favorite because I love coming down the mountain really fast!
3 In a _____ class, you move your body gently into different positions.
4 My sister's a good dancer, so she'd be good at _____, too.
5 You need very strong arms to go _____ because you have to lift your body up the side of a mountain.

/5

2 Circle the correct option.

0 We couldn't play soccer because the (field) / game was too wet.
1 The Brazilian team wears a yellow and blue *mascot / uniform*.
2 The *fans / seats* all cheered when she scored.
3 The final *scoreboard / score* was 4–2.
4 Lisa is a really good soccer *play / player*.
5 I love water sports – I want to *take up / set up* kayaking in the summer.

/5

Grammar

3 Complete the sentences with the verbs below.

> 'll pay   'll win   'm going to take up   'm meeting
> opens   's going to score

0 The library __opens__ at nine o'clock tomorrow morning.
1 Don't worry – I'm sure you _____ the game tomorrow.
2 Look, Ronaldo has the ball – he _____! Yes!
3 I _____ tennis next summer.
4 The movie starts at eight. I _____ Tina at 7:30.
5 No, don't give me any money. I _____ for the tickets.

/5

4 Complete the sentences with the correct form of the verbs in parentheses.

1 I⁰ __'ll get__ fitter if I¹ _____ running. (get, take up)
2 If you² _____ regularly, you ³_____ into the team. (not practice, not get)
3 You⁴ _____ the race unless you ⁵_____ fast. (not win, run)
4 If it⁶ _____, we⁷ _____ table tennis indoors. (rain, play)

/7

5 Decide if the sentences in each pair have the same meaning (S) or a different meaning (D).

0 [S] a I won't call you unless I'm sick.
     b I'll only call you if I'm sick.
1 [ ] a We'll go swimming unless it's cold.
     b If it's cold, we'll go swimming.
2 [ ] a If Dan doesn't invite me to the party, I won't be upset.
     b I'll be upset unless Dan invites me to the party.
3 [ ] a I'll play in the game unless I'm sick.
     b I won't play in the game if I'm sick.

/3

Speaking language practice

6 Complete the dialogues with the words and phrases below.

> don't know   first   have any plans   not much
> up to   what about

A: What are you ⁰ __up to__ on the weekend?
B: ¹_____. Just watch TV, probably. ²_____ you?
A: I ³_____ yet. But Eddie wants to get together. Do you want to join us?
B: Yeah, cool!
A: Do you ⁴_____ for Saturday?
B: Yeah. ⁵_____, I'm going into town to buy some new sneakers. Then ...

/5

Vocabulary /15
Grammar /10
Communication /5
Your total score /30

Unit 4   143

5 SEE THE WORLD!

1 Order the words to make traveling phrases.

1. how / excuse / airport / do / get / me, / I / the / to / ?
   Excuse me, how do I get to the airport?
2. train / I'd / to / buy / like / a / to / London / ticket
3. me, / excuse / is / bus / a / near / there / here / station / ?
4. time / the / train / what / leave / does / ?
5. platform / what / arrive / train / does / at / the / ?

2 Complete responses a–e with the words below. Then match the responses to sentences 1–5 in Activity 1.

~~end~~   platform   p.m.   return   service

a. [3] Yes, it's at the ___end___ of the road.
b. [ ] At 3:45 _____
c. [ ] Single or _____ ?
d. [ ] _____ 10.
e. [ ] There's a bus _____ every twenty minutes.

3 Complete the words for types of vacation.

1. cr _u_ _i_ _s_ e
2. a _ t _ v _ _ _ y c _ _ p
3. b _ _ _ h v _ c _ _ _ _ on
4. c _ _ y b _ _ _ _ k
5. c _ _ p _ _ g t _ _ p
6. s _ _ _ _ t s _ _ _ _ g v _ c _ _ _ _ on
7. b _ _ _ p _ _ _ i _ g v _ c _ _ _ _ on

4 Read the comments and write the type of vacation each person wants.

1. I'd love to visit some of the monuments in ancient Egypt. *sightseeing vacation*
2. I'd like to go to Paris for a weekend. _____
3. My dream vacation would be to spend two weeks on a ship, visiting different places. _____
4. I just want to lie in the sun and swim in the sea! _____
5. I enjoy sleeping in a tent and cooking outdoors. _____

5 Complete the review with the words below.

check out   facilities   floor   guests
pool   ~~reception~~   reservation
single   view

REVIEWS ★★★★

This is a great hotel and good value for money. The staff at the ¹ _reception_ desk was really friendly. I made my ² _____ online. I was traveling on my own, so I had a ³ _____ room. Ask for a room at the front of the hotel and on the top ⁴ _____ – they're a bit more expensive, but worth it for the ⁵ _____ of the beach. There's a ⁶ _____ where you can swim, but there are 300 ⁷ _____ in the hotel, so it's often quite busy. Other ⁸ _____ include a gym and a spa. Be careful: on the day you leave, you have to ⁹ _____ by ten o'clock. If you're late, they'll charge you for another day!

6 Look at the pictures and complete the words.

1. b _a_ _c_ _k_ p _a_ _c_ _k_
2. t _ _  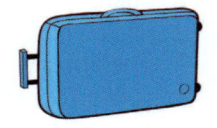
3. s _ _ _ _ _ _ _
4. g _ _ _ _ _ _ _ _ _  
5. m _ _

Unit 5

7 Complete the definitions with the words below.

> ~~flashlight~~ passport sleeping bag
> sunglasses sunscreen

1 You use this to help you see at night: _flashlight_
2 You put this on your skin so you don't burn in the sun: _____
3 This is like a large bag that you can sleep in: _____
4 You wear these to protect your eyes from the sun: _____
5 You show this to officials when you enter a country: _____

8 Match 1–5 to a–e to make sentences.

1 [c] If you're tired, you
2 [ ] My sister's 12 now, so she
3 [ ] There's a bus service, so we
4 [ ] Your cousins live in Sydney, so you
5 [ ] Weigh your suitcase – it

a must not weigh more than 23 kilos.
b ought to visit them while you're there.
c ~~should have a sleep.~~
d has to pay the full price for tickets.
e don't have to drive to the airport.

9 Complete the sentences with the verb structures below. There is one extra structure.

> don't have to pay   must go   must not pay
> ~~must not worry~~   should drink
> shouldn't spend   will have to ask

1 You _must not worry_ about anything – everything will be fine!
2 We've already paid for the hotel, so we _____ for anything when we get there.
3 Madrid is a beautiful city – you really _____ there.
4 You _____ plenty of water when you're out in the sun all day.
5 I know I _____ so much money on vacation, but I just love shopping!
6 I'd love to go on a camping trip with you, but I _____ my parents first.

10 Circle the correct modal verbs to complete the text.

> *Top tips for backpackers*
>
> Traveling abroad is great fun, but there are a few simple rules you ¹_____ follow. First, you ²_____ make sure you have all the documents you need – that's really important. You ³_____ take a few simple first aid products like painkillers and plasters. And you ⁴_____ forget your cell phone! Remember to keep in touch with your family while you're away – you ⁵_____ call them every day, but you ⁶_____ to call or email at least once a week, or they'll get worried. Look after your money and documents carefully while you're away. You ⁷_____ keep your passport safe – you can face a lot of problems if you lose it. And remember the date and time of your flight home. If you miss your flight, you ⁸_____ pay for another one, and it will probably be expensive!

1 a must not   b don't have to
   c won't have to   (d) have to
2 a shouldn't   b must
   c don't have to   d must not
3 a should   b shouldn't
   c don't have to   d ought
4 a must   b must not
   c ought to   d don't have to
5 a have to   b must
   c don't have to   d should
6 a must not   b should
   c don't have to   d ought
7 a ought   b must not
   c must   d don't have to
8 a should   b don't have to
   c have to   d will have to

11 WORD FRIENDS Complete the sentences with the correct form of the verbs below.

> explore go learn meet ~~plan~~ share

1 We're _planning_ a trip to Australia next year.
2 Should we go and _____ the old part of the city?
3 I'd love to _____ Chinese, but I guess it's a very difficult language!
4 We usually _____ on vacation in August.
5 It's fun to make videos and _____ them with your friends online.
6 A backpacking vacation is a great way to _____ people.

Unit 5 145

5 SEE THE WORLD!

12 Read the article. Complete the sentences with one word in each blank.
1. Gina decided to go to _the USA_ as an exchange student.
2. She chose not to live in a big _____ for her exchange year.
3. Most high schools in the USA have large _____.
4. Gina was surprised that the _____ was nice.
5. She enjoyed having _____ in the summer.
6. She was a _____ at her high school once.

An exchange student

We all love traveling to other countries, but how much do we really learn about the places we visit? We admire the view from our hotel room, we consult our guidebook and visit the popular tourist spots, then we return home with happy memories and 200 pictures! But what's it like to live and study in another country?

Gina Rossi decided to spend a year in the USA as an exchange student. She knew the language would be difficult at first and she knew she would miss her friends back home, but she wanted to experience a year abroad.

Gina stayed with a family in Mead, Colorado. "I didn't want to go to a big city," she says. Mead is a small town, so it was ideal for her. What was the first thing that she noticed in the USA?

"Everything was bigger," she says. "The houses, the schools, the stores." Gina found school life difficult at first. The classes in most high schools are very large and you have to be quite independent. And of course, everything was in English. But the teachers were excellent and the students were all really friendly. "They soon made me feel at home," she says. Did anything surprise her? "I was expecting the food to be awful," she says. "But the family I stayed with enjoyed cooking, so in fact, it was really nice. In the summer, when the weather was hot, we had a lot of barbecues – I liked those."

Gina now says that living in a place, rather than visiting as a tourist, is the only way to experience the culture of another country. And her advice for others? "If you decide to go on an exchange program, you should join in with everything, to make the most of the experience." Gina even stood in as a cheerleader for a high school football game – but only once!

13 Read the text again. Mark the sentences true (T) or false (F).
1. [F] Gina didn't expect to have any problems with the language.
2. [ ] Mead is a small town in Colorado.
3. [ ] At first, Gina didn't find it easy being at an American school.
4. [ ] Not all the students at her high school were friendly.
5. [ ] Gina believes you can learn about other countries as a tourist as well as when you live there.
6. [ ] Her advice to other exchange students is to take part in lots of activities.

14 Complete the sentences with *must* or *can't*.
1. That tent's tiny! It _can't_ be big enough for eight people!
2. Look, that _____ be our hotel over there – I recognize it from the website.
3. The boat trips are very popular, so they _____ be good!
4. Everyone's swimming in the sea, so the water _____ be too cold.
5. The food in that restaurant looks amazing, so it _____ be expensive!
6. That _____ be our bus – our bus isn't due until 10:30, and it's only ten o'clock.

15 Circle the correct conclusion for each sentence.

1 Tom's gone home early.
   (a) He might be sick.
   b He can't be sick.
2 I'm not sure where my cell phone is.
   a It must be in my backpack.
   b It may be in my backpack.
3 Carrie's shoes are black, but these ones are brown.
   a These could be Carrie's shoes.
   b These can't be Carrie's shoes.
4 I don't know where the museum is.
   a It might be near the station.
   b It can't be near the station.
5 Everyone's wearing T-shirts.
   a It must be hot.
   b It can't be hot.
6 I don't know what the museum's like. The guidebook doesn't mention it.
   a It might be interesting.
   b It must be interesting.

16 Circle the correct words to complete the sentences.

1 Look, that boy's standing up in the pool – it _____ be very deep.
   a may   (b) can't   c must
2 I guess this _____ be Jack's umbrella, but I'm not sure.
   a must   b can't   c could
3 There are hundreds of deckchairs on the beach. It _____ be a very popular beach!
   a must   b might   c can't
4 I'm not sure if the gym is open now – it _____ be closed.
   a can't   b may   c must
5 Camping _____ be fun in the rain – I guess everything gets horrible and wet!
   a must   b can't   c could
6 I don't know where he's from. I guess he _____ be French. Or maybe Spanish.
   a might   b must   c can't

17 Complete the dialogue. Circle the correct option from the pairs of phrases below.

can't be expensive / must be expensive
~~can't be fun~~ / (might be fun)
can't be lonely / could be lonely
can't be right / may be right
might be interested / must be interested

A: Have you seen this brochure for an activity camp?
B: Yeah, it looks good. It ¹ _might be fun_ to go on a vacation like this next summer. What do you think?
A: I agree. Do you think it costs a lot?
B: No, it ² _____ because it's for young people and they don't have much money.
A: That's true. What activities can you do?
B: Well, there's climbing. I don't know if I want to do that. I think it ³ _____ being up so high.
A: Yes, you ⁴ _____ about that, but the other activities look really fun.
B: Yeah, I love canoeing. Do you think Abbie ⁵ _____ in coming too? Should we ask her?
A: That's a good idea.

18 Circle the correct words to complete the sentences.

1 I think it's a good idea to _____ while you're still young.
   a trip   b journey   (c) travel
2 The hotel organizes _____ to interesting tourist places.
   a excursions   b travels   c journeys
3 I enjoyed the day out, but the _____ back home took four hours!
   a travel   b journey   c excursion
4 We're planning a three-day _____ to New York next summer.
   a travel   b trip   c journey
5 Would you like to work in the _____ industry?
   a trip   b voyage   c travel
6 We were all tired after the long sea _____.
   a voyage   b travel   c journey

Unit 5   147

5 SEE THE WORLD!

19 Order the sentences to make dialogues.

A
a ☐ What was that?
b ☐ I was just saying, there's a good movie on tonight.
c [1] Hey, Matt, there's a good movie on tonight.

B
a ☐ I said that Sam's busy, so he can't come to the party.
b ☐ Maria can come to the party, but Sam's busy.
c ☐ Sorry, I didn't get the last part.

C
a ☐ I just wanted to ask you about Friday.
b ☐ Sorry, can you say that again?
c ☐ Hi, Lily. What time are we meeting on Friday?

20 Write the phrases below in the correct part of the chart.

~~Can you speak louder?~~   What was that?
Sorry, I didn't catch that.   I said that …
I was just saying …   What I asked was …
Sorry, can you say that again?
Sorry, I didn't get the first part.
I just wanted to ask you about …

Asking for clarification	Clarifying
Can you speak louder?	

21 Complete the words in the sentences with *un-*, *dis-*, *im-*, *in-*, *il-*, and *ir-*.

1 I give up! It's simply _i_ _m_ possible to buy a plane ticket on this traveling website!
2 Did you know that it's __ __ legal to sell chewing gum in Singapore?
3 Mark traveled abroad with his school and didn't call his parents. I think he was very __ __ responsible.
4 I like Emily a lot, but I think her attitude during the sightseeing tour was really __ __ __ honest.
5 The guest exhibited __ __ usual behavior, so the hotel staff decided to call the police.
6 Kelly couldn't book a room using the travel app because her account was __ __ active.

22 Use the phrases below to complete the report.

At approximately 10 p.m.   I would also recommend   ~~The aim of this report is to~~   the hotel room was open   The objects were not in the room safe   we should consider

---

POLICE REPORT

Case No: 587   Date: October 19, 2019
Reporting Officer: Lt. Wesley Kayes
Incident: burglary

¹ *The aim of this report is to* make a record of an illegal incident at Grand Hotel on September 22, 2019.
² _____, the hotel manager, John Fernandez, called 911 to report a break-in at Room 232.
When we arrived at the crime scene, ³ _____.
The guest was a young woman from Canada, Catherine Ono. She was waiting for us outside the room with Mr. Fernandez. A bag, a pair of earrings and Ms. Ono's passport were missing.
⁴ _____.
No other items were reported missing. Ms. Ono answered all the questions and will request a new passport from the Canadian embassy.
During investigation, ⁵ _____ looking at CCTV recordings to find any unusual activity.
⁶ _____ that we interview hotel employees and other guests on the floor.

SELF-ASSESSMENT

Vocabulary

1 Complete the sentences with the words below. There are two extra words.

> backpacking   break   camp
> cruise   ~~platform~~   return
> ticket   trip

0 What ___platform___ does the train leave from?
1 I'd like a train _____ to London, please.
2 We're planning a camping _____ this summer.
3 We went on a three-week _____ and really loved being on the ship.
4 She's just been on a city _____ to Paris for the weekend.
5 You can do lots of different sports at the activity _____.

☐ /5

2 Circle the correct option.

0 Wow! There's a beautiful *pool* / *(view)* from this window!
1 There are two of us, so we need a *single* / *double* room, please.
2 I wear *sunglasses* / *sunscreen* to protect my eyes from the bright sun.
3 You can find details about the museum in the *guidebook* / *suitcase*.
4 It's a three-day *journey* / *travel* to reach this village in the mountains.
5 I'd love to *trip* / *travel* around India.

☐ /5

Grammar

3 Match the sentences to the conclusions.

0 [d] I'm not sure whose coat this is.
1 [ ] It's only eight o'clock, but Tania's gone to bed!
2 [ ] I don't know when Max gets back from vacation.
3 [ ] You've just had a very big lunch.
4 [ ] I don't know where my passport is.
5 [ ] No one's in the ocean today.

a It could be tomorrow.
b You can't be hungry!
c It may be in my bedroom.
d It might be John's.
e It must be too cold.
f She must be tired.

☐ /5

4 Complete the chart with the correct negative adjective.

Asking for clarification	Clarifying
fair	0 *unfair*
responsible	1 _____
patient	2 _____
satisfied	3 _____
logical	4 _____
correct	5 _____

☐ /5

Speaking language practice

5 Complete the dialogues with the phrases below.

> ~~didn't catch~~   first part   I said that
> just saying   say that again   what I asked

1 A: Have you printed your plane ticket?
   B: Sorry, I ⁰ ___didn't catch___ that.
   A: ¹ _____ was if you've printed your plane ticket.
2 A: Sara's picking us up and Tom's meeting us at the airport.
   B: Sorry, I didn't get the ² _____.
   A: ³ _____ Sara's picking us up.
3 A: There's a special offer on cruises.
   B: Sorry, can you ⁴ _____?
   A: Yes, I was ⁵ _____ there's a special offer on cruises.

☐ /5

Vocabulary ☐ /15
Grammar ☐ /10
Communication ☐ /5
Your total score ☐ /30

Unit 5 149

6 GETTING TO KNOW YOU

1 Circle the correct answer.

1 Who shares one parent with you, but not two parents?
   a your stepson
   (b) your half-brother

2 Who is your mother's mother?
   a your great-grandmother
   b your grandmother

3 If your mother marries again, who is the man?
   a your grandfather
   b your stepfather

4 Who is your father's grandfather?
   a your great-grandfather
   b your great-great-grandfather

5 If your father marries again and his new wife already has two daughters, who are they?
   a your half-sisters
   b your stepsisters

2 Read the comments and write the family words.

1 Tom's the same age as me and I really like him. His mom's married to my dad now, but I'm only related to him by marriage, not by blood. He's my ___stepbrother___.

2 Elsie is my dad's mother, so she's my _____. She's nearly seventy and she's still very active!

3 Lucy's the youngest in my family and she's my _____. We have the same mom, but we have different dads.

4 My mom died when I was quite young. My dad has a new wife now, called Sara. I really like her, and I call her Mom, even though she isn't my real mother. She's my _____.

5 The oldest person in my family is Albert. He's eighty-nine and he's my mom's grandfather, so he's my _____.

3 Circle the correct option.

1 I *go* / *get* along really well with my cousin Jack – he's great!
2 You should talk to someone if you have a problem – don't just deal *for* / *with* it on your own.
3 I really enjoy *hanging* / *holding* out with my friends.
4 If you're feeling lonely, you should go *out* / *over* and meet some new people.
5 I *got* / *fell* out with Tania last week, but we soon sorted things out and we're friends again now.
6 I share a bedroom with my sister, but I can't *put* / *get* up with all her mess. I want my own room!

4 Complete the sentences with the correct form of the phrasal verbs below.

> deal with   fall out with   ~~get along with~~
> go out   hang out with   put up with

1 I don't ___get along with___ my sister at all – we're completely different and she just annoys me!
2 It's very difficult to _____ problems such as bullying on your own. It's much easier if you ask a teacher for help.
3 When I moved to a new school, I _____ a lot because I wanted to make new friends.
4 I can't _____ noise when I'm trying to study. I need silence.
5 I prefer to _____ just a small group of friends. I don't like big crowds.
6 I _____ Dale because he kept asking me to do his homework for him and it really annoyed me!

5 Complete the text with one word in each blank.

Your problems – Emma's here to help!

My mom and dad got divorced two years ago and my dad has just remarried. I really don't ¹*get* along with his wife, my new ² _____. She also has two daughters already, so I have two ³ _____. I know I should be happy for my dad, but his wife really gets ⁴ _____ my nerves and I don't ⁵ _____ any interests with her kids!
I just stay in my bedroom all the time now because I don't know how to ⁶ _____ with this situation. Help!

Emma says: It can be difficult when a parent remarries, especially when there are also new children to add to your family. It will take time for you to ⁷ _____ to know your dad's new wife, so just be patient. But hopefully, if you make the effort and ⁸ _____ some time with her daughters, you will find that things improve.

Have your say! 2 comments

Amelia24 This happened to me two years ago when my mom remarried. I ⁹ _____ a lot of arguments with my new stepdad and I even ended up shouting at my mom and ¹⁰ _____ out with her, which was awful. You have to give the new relationships time.

SaraG Don't spend too much time at home if you find it stressful. ¹¹ _____ out when you can and hang ¹² _____ with your friends on weekends, rather than spending time ¹³ _____ your own at home. The others are right – it takes time, but I'm sure that if you make the effort with your new family members, in time you will all enjoy ¹⁴ _____ other's company.

6 Circle the correct option.
1. I *will be* / *would be* really happy if my dad *would get* / *got* married again.
2. What *would* / *will* you do if your best friend *was* / *would be* upset with you?
3. If I *had* / *would have* a lot of money, I *will take* / *would take* all my friends out for a meal.
4. Lottie *will be* / *would be* more popular if she *wasn't* / *wouldn't be* so moody!
5. If I *were* / *would be* you, I *don't worry* / *wouldn't worry* about what other people think of you.
6. If Max *wouldn't talk* / *didn't talk* so much in class, his teachers *don't get* / *wouldn't get* so angry with him.

7 Complete the second sentence so that it means the same as the first. Use the Second Conditional.
1. I have a lot of tests this year, so I'm really stressed.
   I *wouldn't be* so stressed if I *didn't have* a lot of tests this year.
2. Carrie is unfit because she doesn't do any exercise.
   If Carrie _____ some exercise, she _____ fitter.
3. Jack's parents always get worried because he never tells them where he's going.
   Jack's parents _____ worried if he _____ them where he was going.
4. I'm not old enough to watch that movie.
   I _____ that movie if I _____ older.
5. I don't have a big house, so I won't invite many people to the party.
   I _____ more people to the party if I _____ a bigger house.
6. You shouldn't spend all your money on clothes.
   If I _____ you, I _____ all my money on clothes.

Unit 6

6 GETTING TO KNOW YOU

8 Complete the text messages with the correct form of the verbs below. Use the Second Conditional.

> be (x2)   buy   ~~have~~   know   like
> not remember   not worry

Hi, Jenna! Help! I need some advice. It's Abi's birthday next Saturday and I don't know what to give her. If I ¹ _had_ plenty of money, I ² _____ her something nice to wear because I know she ³ _____ that. But I only have a few dollars. What can I do?

If I ⁴ _____ you, I ⁵ _____ about buying expensive gifts. That's not what friendship is about. Sure, Abi ⁶ _____ upset if you ⁷ _____ her birthday, but I'm sure she'd feel bad if she ⁸ _____ you were so worried. Just relax! Buy her some flowers and give her a big birthday hug!

9 Complete the article with one word in each blank.

Money or friends?

What ¹ _would_ you do if you won $10 million? ² _____ you had that amount of money, you ³ _____ need to work when you grew up! Just imagine that! If you ⁴ _____ have to work, you ⁵ _____ be able to spend your life traveling or relaxing – doing exactly what you wanted. Does that sound good to you?

Most people imagine that if they ⁶ _____ rich, they would ⁷ _____ happier. They think that if money ⁸ _____ a problem for them, they ⁹ _____ have any worries in the world. But in reality, it seems this isn't true. Psychologists have found that what really makes us happy is our family and friends, and money can't buy those. So, if you ¹⁰ _____ choose between money and friends, which ¹¹ _____ you go for?

10 Complete the words in the sentences.
1. Your c _l a s s_ m _a t e s_ s are the friends you have in your class at school.
2. Your b ___ t friends are the ones you like the most.
3. Someone who doesn't like you and tries to hurt you is your e ___ ___ y.
4. Jodie h ___ a lot of friends.
5. Marie wants to b ___ friends with me.

Would you rent a friend?

We all know it can be difficult to make new friends when you move to a new place, but would you ever consider paying someone to be your friend? This is the service that a rent-a-friend website offers. The idea is simple: you look through the online profiles and select someone you think you would get along with, then you get in touch with them. For a small fee, the person will meet you and spend time with you, doing whatever you want to do - working out at the park, watching a movie or just playing computer games.

The biggest rent-a-friend websites are in the USA, where the idea has really become popular especially in big cities such as New York. But the idea originated in Japan, where people study or work so hard that they have little time for socializing and forming genuine friendships. There are also now websites available in the UK and several other countries.

We asked our readers what they thought and some of you were in favor of the idea. Lia, from North London, thought it could be a good way to meet new people. She moved to London when she was sixteen and had to leave all her close friends behind in Australia. "It was quite hard at first," she says, "and I was a bit lonely for a while." She now has a big circle of friends, but she says that if she moved again, she would consider the idea of renting a friend. "Sometimes when you're new to a place, you just want to get out and do something, but it isn't much fun going to the movies on your own. I think it would be fun to meet someone in this way - you might even come across your new best friend!"

Tom, who lives in Canada, doesn't agree. He believes that friends are a really important part of our life and we shouldn't devalue the idea of friendship by making it into something that you can buy and sell instantly. "If I moved to a new city," he says, "I'd put the effort into getting to know my new classmates and form friendships with them. It might take a bit longer, but it's better than buying fake friends."

Have your say! Comment below.

11 Read the article. Mark the sentences true (T) or false (F).

1. [F] You pay a rent-a-friend website to choose a friend for you.
2. [ ] The first rent-a-friend websites were in the United States.
3. [ ] People in Japan are often too busy to spend time with friends.
4. [ ] Lia hasn't made many new friends in London.
5. [ ] Lia thinks you could make real friends by using a rent-a-friend website.
6. [ ] Tom thinks it takes time to make real friends, but it is worth waiting in order to have genuine friends.

12 Complete the sentences with clauses a–f.

1. The house _e_ has a big yard.
2. The men ___ both had dark hair.
3. The car ___ is quite old.
4. There's a small café on the beach ___.
5. My new bike, ___, is amazing!
6. Mrs. Perks, ___, is a dance teacher.

a where they sell really nice ice cream
b that my mom drives
c who lives on my street
d that I saw near the bank
e ~~that my parents want to buy~~
f which I bought at BikeCentral

13 Read the article. Circle the correct answers to complete it.

Real friends?

Do you think of all the people ¹_____ you know online as your friends? It seems that a lot of the people ²_____ use social media sites such as Facebook have over 200 online friends, compared to around fifty "real" friends, ³_____ they actually meet in real life. Facebook, ⁴_____ was started in 2004, now has over 1.5 billion users worldwide, and a lot of people see it as a place ⁵_____ they can meet new friends as well as keep in touch with old ones. Studies ⁶_____ have looked at how people behave on social media sites have found that people are sometimes more honest and open online than they are in real life. But psychologists say it is our ten or twelve closest relationships ⁷_____ are the most important to us. So maybe it's still better to meet your friends in the local park or mall, ⁸_____ you can talk face-to-face.

1. a which   (b) who   c where   d what
2. a that   b where   c what   d which
3. a which   b that   c who   d where
4. a what   b which   c who   d that
5. a which   b that   c who   d where
6. a that   b who   c where   d what
7. a who   b where   c which   d what
8. a which   b who   c that   d where

14 Find and correct the mistakes in the sentences. Remember to check the use of commas.

1. That's the café which we sometimes have lunch.
   That's the café where we sometimes have lunch.
2. Sophie who is French can speak French and English.
   _____
3. Their car, that is over ten years old, looks pretty new.
   _____
4. I lent the book to Dan, which loves sci-fi stories.
   _____

Unit 6 153

6 GETTING TO KNOW YOU

15 Combine the sentences using relative clauses. Use *who*, *which*, or *where*. Add commas where necessary.

1. My cousin is very good at soccer. He's three years older than me.
   My cousin, *who is three years older than me, is* very good at soccer.
2. Edinburgh is about 600 kilometers from London. It's the capital of Scotland.
   Edinburgh _____ about 600 kilometers from London.
3. Jo showed me the house. She lived there when she was younger.
   Jo showed me _____ when she was younger.
4. We met a man. He grows vegetables for the market.
   We met a man _____ for the market.
5. Portland is on the coast. My grandparents live there.
   Portland _____ on the coast.
6. The movie was very good. We saw it last week.
   The movie _____ very good.

16 **WORD FRIENDS** What does *get* mean in each sentence? Circle the correct option.

1. We didn't get home until after midnight!
   become / (arrive) / leave
2. I get bored quite quickly if I have nothing to do.
   make / bring / become
3. I got an email from my uncle yesterday.
   received / arrived / wrote
4. I need to get some new jeans.
   make / change / buy
5. My brother is trying to get a job.
   pay / find / leave
6. May I get you a drink?
   take / drink / bring

17 Complete the words in the definitions of people at a wedding.

1. The b _r_ _i_ _d_ e is the woman who is getting married.
2. The b ___ ___ g ___ ___ m is the man who is getting married.
3. A b ___ ___ ___ m ___ d is a good friend who helps the woman who is getting married.
4. A p ___ ___ b ___ y is a young boy who helps the woman who is getting married.
5. The g ___ ___ ___ s are the people who come to watch the wedding.

18 Match 1–6 to a–f to make questions.

1. [f] Who's the boy on
2. [ ] Who's the girl that is
3. [ ] Who's that guy next
4. [ ] Which one
5. [ ] Who's the woman at
6. [ ] Who's the young child in

a. wearing a blue dress?
b. do you mean?
c. the front, by the door?
d. the middle?
e. to your grandmother?
f. ~~the left?~~

19 Complete the sentences with the time words below.

| afterwards   just   ~~last~~   that |

1. _Last_ week it was my birthday.
2. _____ then, I noticed a girl who was standing on her own.
3. _____ day I made a new friend.
4. _____, she invited me to her house.

20 Rewrite the direct speech with the correct punctuation.

1. I'm having a party next weekend I said
   "I'm having a party next weekend," I said.
2. Would you like to come to my party I asked
3. I'd love to come to the party he said but I can't
4. I think that's a great idea she said

Unit 6

SELF-ASSESSMENT

Vocabulary

1 Match words 1-8 to definitions a-i.

0 _b_ grandfather
1 ☐ great-grandmother
2 ☐ half-sister
3 ☐ stepbrother
4 ☐ stepmother
5 ☐ stepson
6 ☐ aunt
7 ☐ neighbor
8 ☐ parent

a a woman who is married to your father, who is not your real mother
b the father of your mother or father
c a girl who shares one parent with you, but not both parents
d a boy who is the child of the woman a man is married to, but not his child
e the son of your stepfather, who is related to you by marriage, not by blood
f the mother of your grandmother or grandfather
g either your father or your mother
h someone who lives next to you
i your cousin's mother

/8

2 Circle the correct option.

0 Who do you *hold* / (*hang*) out with after school?
1 His teachers said they wouldn't *put* / *keep* up with his bad behavior any longer.
2 Dan and I have the same *feeling* / *sense* of humor.
3 Sara and I have a lot *in* / *for* common.
4 Peggy *went* / *got* a bit upset when I told her about the accident.
5 Kitty *has* / *keeps* loads of friends!
6 Dan's mother and my father work together at the Bank. They have been *classmates* / *co-workers* for a long time.
7 Are you good at *holding* / *making* new friends?

/7

Grammar

3 Complete the Second Conditional sentences with the correct form of the verbs in parentheses.

1 If you 0 __spent__ more time studying, you 1 _____ better grades! (spend, get)
2 We 2 _____ to the beach every day if it 3 _____ sunny. (go, be)
3 If I 4 _____ lots of money, I 5 _____ to Europe. (have, travel)

/5

4 Circle the correct option.

0 The boy (*who*) / *which* sits next to me in class is called Max.
1 That's the park *which* / *where* we sometimes hang out after school.
2 There's a new boy in my class, *that* / *who* comes from Puerto Rico.
3 Their house, *who* / *which* is downtown, is quite big.
4 Is that the bike *who* / *that* you got last week?
5 There's a lake in the park, *which* / *where* you can hire boats.

/5

Speaking language practice

5 Complete the dialogues with the phrases below.

| a laugh   at the back   do you mean |
| she's wearing   tall one   ~~up to~~   who's that boy |

A
A: Hi, Lizzy. What are you 0 __up to__?
B: I'm just showing Katie the pictures from my sister's wedding. Do you want to see them?
A: Sure. It'll be 1 _____.

B
A: 2 _____ on the left?
B: Which one 3 _____?
A: The 4 _____ with dark hair, on the right.

C
A: That's my Auntie Lucy there, 5 _____.
B: Oh yes. 6 _____ a really nice dress!

/5

Vocabulary	/15
Grammar	/10
Speaking language practice	/5
Your total score	/30

Unit 6 155

7 NO TIME FOR CRIME

1 Complete the words in the definitions.

1 A t _h_ _i_ _e_ f takes things that belong to other people.
2 A v _ _ _ _ _ _ l breaks things in public places.
3 A p _ _ _ _ p _ _ _ _ _ t takes small things from your pocket.
4 A s _ _ _ l _ _ _ _ _ r takes things from stores without paying.
5 A b _ _ _ _ _ _ _ r goes into people's homes and takes things.
6 A r _ _ _ _ _ _ r takes money from a bank or business.

2 **WORD FRIENDS** Look at pictures A–D and complete sentences 1–5 with the words below.

| ~~breaking into~~ committing damaging robbing stealing |

1 The man in picture A is _breaking into_ someone's house.
2 The woman in picture B is _____ some jewelry.
3 The men in picture C are _____ a bank.
4 The man in picture D is _____ a car.
5 The people in the pictures are all _____ crimes.

3 **WORD BUILDING** Circle the correct option.

1 The police finally caught the (burglars) / burglaries.
2 We're lucky because there isn't much vandals / vandalism in the city.
3 The bank robbers / robberies got away with over $500,000.
4 They accused her of shoplifters / shoplifting, but she said she was only trying the coat on.
5 A pickpocket / pickpocketing stole my phone.
6 She is very upset about the thief / theft of her jewels.

4 Match 1–6 to a–f to make sentences.

1 [c] She had to pay a $300
2 [ ] The bank has offered a
3 [ ] I want to go
4 [ ] The judge didn't send him to
5 [ ] What would be a suitable
6 [ ] You will need a good

a reward of $10,000 for information about the crime.
b punishment for this crime?
c ~~fine for shoplifting~~.
d lawyer to persuade the judge you are innocent.
e prison because he was under 18.
f to Law School.

5 Complete the sentences with the words below. There is one extra word.

| court ~~jail~~ judge law lawyer punishment reward |

1 Matt spent fifteen years in _jail_ for his crimes.
2 Everyone in the _____ was shocked by the details of this terrible crime.
3 He can expect to receive a harsh _____ for this crime.
4 The _____ listens to the evidence and decides how long someone should spend in prison.
5 If you break the _____, you will be punished.
6 Jen got a _____ of $50 for taking the missing bag to the police department.

Unit 7

6 Read the texts. Circle the correct answers.

The Westbury Times

They need to learn a lesson!
Two teenagers were arrested for ¹_____ their school building yesterday. The two boys broke windows in the building and sprayed paint over it. The police said the community would not put up with ²_____ of this kind. The teenagers are too young to go to ³_____, but the police hope the ⁴_____ they receive will be serious enough to teach them a lesson.

Information needed
The police are asking for help from the public after ⁵_____ got away with two valuable paintings. The criminals ⁶_____ into the town's art gallery and ⁷_____ the two paintings last night. The alarm sounded in the gallery and the police arrived, but the criminals managed to ⁸_____ through a back door. The art gallery is offering a ⁹_____ of $10,000 for the safe return of the two paintings.

Brave grandmother catches a criminal
Seventy-two-year-old grandmother Beryl Bridges was shocked when she saw a ¹⁰_____ stealing someone's wallet near the station on Saturday. She ¹¹_____ after the man and caught him when he ¹²_____ and fell. "It makes me really angry when people ¹³_____ crimes," Beryl said. "They shouldn't get away with it!" The man will appear in ¹⁴_____ tomorrow.

1	a robbing	(b) damaging	c stealing	d committing
2	a burglar	b burglary	c vandal	d vandalism
3	a jail	b fine	c reward	d judge
4	a law	b punishment	c court	d reward
5	a shoplifters	b vandals	c thieves	d pickpockets
6	a put	b broke	c sent	d escaped
7	a robbed	b committed	c stole	d put
8	a escape	b chase	c pull	d catch
9	a fine	b reward	c punishment	d law
10	a shoplifter	b vandal	c pickpocket	d burglar
11	a fell	b pulled	c pushed	d chased
12	a escaped	b tripped	c pulled	d pushed
13	a commit	b do	c have	d get
14	a judge	b law	c fine	d court

7 Complete the chart. Then circle the four verbs that are regular.

Verb	Past Participle
ask	¹ _asked_
catch	caught
chase	² _____
hide	hidden
know	³ _____
make	made
read	⁴ _____
see	seen
sell	⁵ _____
use	used
watch	⁶ _____
write	written

8 Circle the correct option.
1. The two robbers *was* / (*were*) caught as they were leaving the bank.
2. A lot of science *is* / *are* used to solve crimes nowadays.
3. A secret microphone *was* / *were* hidden under her clothes.
4. Sometimes ordinary people *is* / *are* asked to help the police with information.
5. CCTV cameras *isn't* / *aren't* used in the shopping mall.
6. The thieves *wasn't* / *weren't* seen by anyone.

7 NO TIME FOR CRIME

9 Order the words to make sentences.
1. my / stolen / wallet / pickpocket / was / a / by
   My wallet was stolen by a pickpocket.
2. every year / a lot of / cell phones / stolen / are
3. asked / she / a lot of questions / the police / by / was
4. some / reported / aren't / to / the police / crimes
5. your / car / when / stolen / was / ?
6. CCTV cameras / are / here / used / ?

10 Complete the second sentence so that it means the same as the first sentence. Use no more than three words.
1. They hide the paintings in the back of their van.
   The paintings *were hidden in* the back of their van.
2. People don't use guns in all robberies.
   Guns _____ in all robberies.
3. A sales clerk caught the shoplifter.
   The shoplifter _____ a sales clerk.
4. Millions of people watch crime dramas on TV.
   Crime dramas _____ millions of people on TV.
5. Did they send the thief to prison?
   Was _____ to prison?
6. People steal a lot of jewelry from this store.
   A lot of jewellery _____ this store.
7. They didn't find the missing money.
   The missing money _____ .

11 Complete the words in the sentences.
1. The police is interviewing a w _i_ _t_ _n_ _e_ _s_ s who saw the robbery take place.
2. It will take a very smart d __ __ __ t __ __ e to catch this criminal!
3. The police questioned the s __ __ p __ __ t, but he didn't admit that he was guilty.
4. This is a very difficult c __ __ e because there is very little evidence.
5. The police found Morton's f __ __ __ __ __ p __ __ __ __ s on the murder weapon.
6. The thieves were seen on the C __ __ V c __ __ __ __ __ s in the store.

12 Read the article on page 159. Circle the correct answer.
1. What does the writer say about the first CSI shows?
   a They attracted a lot of criticism.
   b They were less popular than CSI New York.
   (c) They were popular immediately.
   d Everything about them was new.
2. What do we learn about the work of CSIs in the series?
   a They work closely with the police.
   b Their jobs seem to be very exciting.
   c They develop new scientific techniques to solve crimes.
   d They usually solve crimes through science alone.
3. How is real life different, according to the writer?
   a In real life the police only use old-fashioned ways of solving crimes.
   b CSIs never leave their laboratories in real life.
   c The job of a real CSI is very boring.
   d CSIs in real life don't catch criminals.
4. What is the writer's main aim in the text?
   a to describe the TV series in detail
   b to explain how real CSIs catch criminals
   c to discuss how realistic the series is
   d to encourage people to learn more about the work of CSIs

13 Order the words to make sentences.
1. last summer / had / I / painted / my / bedroom
   I had my bedroom painted last summer.
2. get / teeth / you / your / should / regularly / checked
3. often / how / cleaned / the / you / do / get / windows / ?
4. stolen / his / wallet / last week / he / had
5. getting / dress / a / she's / for her wedding / made

14 Complete the second sentence so that it means the same as the first sentence, using the verbs in parentheses. Use no more than four words.

1. We could ask someone to deliver a pizza if you like. (get)
   We could _get a pizza delivered_ if you like.
2. I want someone to pierce my ears. (have)
   I want to _____.
3. An expert designed their house. (had)
   They _____ by an expert.
4. You should ask a doctor to check that injury. (get)
   You should _____ by a doctor.

15 Complete the text with the correct form of the verbs below.

> get/check   get/install   get/put up
> have/connect   ~~have/make~~   have/replace

Can you burglar-proof your house?

Maybe not completely, but security experts think it is worth ¹ _having_ a few changes _made_ to your home to make it safer. A lot of people think ² _____ a sign _____ saying "Beware of the dog" is a good idea, but according to the experts, most criminals know that family pets aren't usually dangerous. Locks are important, though. You should ³ _____ any old locks _____ with more modern ones. Modern locks are harder for criminals to open. It's also a good idea to ⁴ _____ an alarm _____. You can ⁵ _____ the alarm _____ to the local police department, so the police is alerted immediately. If you're uncertain about what changes to make to your home, you should think about ⁶ _____ your home _____ by a security expert.

CSI: fact or fiction?

When the American crime series *CSI (Crime Scene Investigation)* was first shown on TV in 2000, it was an immediate hit and soon led on to more shows such as *CSI New York* and *CSI Miami*. The series took the traditional idea of a detective story, but showed for the first time how modern scientific methods are used to study things such as fingerprints, hair and blood samples in order to solve crimes. The series has become very popular and is watched by millions of people around the world.

In the series, the investigators are shown as having quite glamorous lives. They are usually the first people to arrive at the scene of a crime. Working as a team, they eventually manage to catch the bad guys using both high-tech science and traditional police detective work. The real police seem to be irrelevant, as the Crime Scene Investigators interview witnesses, question suspects and often catch the criminals after dramatic chase scenes.

Of course, this isn't quite the same as the real world. In real life, it's the police who question suspects and solve crimes. Although science can help the police, old-fashioned ways of investigating crimes are still very important. It's true that real CSIs visit crime scenes, but the majority of their work after that takes place in the laboratory. They are scientists, trying to make sense of the samples they have collected. This doesn't mean their work is boring, but it isn't as exciting as in the TV series and they certainly don't get involved in arresting criminals.

Unit 7

7 NO TIME FOR CRIME

16 WORD FRIENDS Complete the text with the words below.

~~area~~   clues   crime   criminal   fingerprints   witnesses

When you get to a crime scene, it's important to search the ¹ _area_ first and look for ² _____. Then you should interview all the ³ _____ and take ⁴ _____ of any suspects. When you are sure who is guilty, you can arrest the ⁵ _____ and solve the ⁶ _____!

17 Write the phrases below in the correct column.

~~Come on!~~   Don't worry!   I don't know.
I know you can do it.   I suppose I can do it.
It's OK.   Just try it.   OK, I'll try.   Please!

Persuading someone	Come on!
Reassuring someone	
Responding	

18 Circle the correct response.

1 I feel really nervous!
   a Please!
   (b) You'll be fine.
   c I don't know.

2 I don't know if I'll enjoy acting.
   a OK, I'll try.
   b I don't know.
   c Why don't you try?

3 Of course you can do it!
   a OK, I'll try.
   b Come on!
   c Please!

4 What if I make a mistake?
   a I suppose I can do it.
   b Don't worry!
   c Please!

19 Read the article. Circle the correct answer.

THE ART OF POLICE WORK

Everyone would agree that being a police officer is a very ¹ _____ job, and it is important to catch people who behave in ² _____ ways. But it isn't always easy to find the person who has committed a crime, and sometimes the police makes mistakes. Sometimes officers are ³ _____ to find the criminal who has committed a terrible crime and sometimes they act too quickly because they are worried the public will be ⁴ _____ if they don't solve the crime. Individual officers can sometimes act in ⁵ _____ ways too, and believe someone is guilty just because they don't like them. The way to do good police work is always to follow all the clues in a ⁶ _____ way, even if they seem small and ⁷ _____. The results that this leads to may sometimes be ⁸ _____, but hopefully, they will be ⁹ _____.

1 (a) responsible   b irresponsible
   c legible   d illegible
2 a honest   b dishonest
   c regular   d irregular
3 a usual   b unusual
   c patient   d impatient
4 a logical   b illogical
   c pleased   d displeased
5 a fair   b unfair
   c important   d unimportant
6 a possible   b impossible
   c logical   d illogical
7 a important   b unimportant
   c pleased   d displeased
8 a intelligent   b unintelligent
   c expected   d unexpected
9 a correct   b incorrect
   c patient   d impatient

SELF-ASSESSMENT

Vocabulary

1 Match the words below to the definitions.

> fine   jail   judge   ~~shoplifter~~   theft   vandal

0 someone who steals things from stores: _shoplifter_
1 money that someone has to pay as a punishment: _____
2 a place where criminals are sent as a punishment: _____
3 someone who damages buildings or things in public places: _____
4 the crime of stealing: _____
5 person who decides the punishment a criminal should receive: _____

☐ /5

2 Circle the correct option.

0 They (climbed) / pulled out of the window when the fire got out of control.
1 The two men were accused of *stealing* / *robbing* a bank.
2 We have to find out who *committed* / *made* this crime.
3 She *chased* / *tripped* the pickpocket.
4 Someone *sent* / *broke* into our house.
5 Hurry up – we need to *fall* / *escape*!

☐ /5

3 Complete the sentences.

> arrests   clue   fingerprints   ~~solve~~   suspect   witness

0 I'm sure we can _solve_ this crime.
1 The police took his _____ and matched them on the database.
2 The police _____ criminals.
3 Only one _____ saw the crime.
4 The police thought that the watch was an important _____.
5 The police has caught the _____.

☐ /5

Grammar

4 Complete the sentences with the correct passive form of the verbs in parentheses.

0 CCTV cameras _are used_ (use) in many cities.
1 He _____ (arrest) yesterday for the theft.
2 The stolen money _____ (find) two days after the robbery in the back of a car.
3 Crimes _____ (solve) using science.
4 The popular detective series _____ (make) into a movie last year.
5 Several crimes _____ (commit) every day.

☐ /5

5 Find and correct the mistakes in the sentences.

0 We need to get our TV repair.
   We need to get our TV repaired.
1 I had my bike stealing.
   _____
2 Should we get delivered a pizza?
   _____
3 He's having a new suit make.
   _____
4 My mom is having her hair cutting.
   _____
5 She gets her cat checks by the vet.
   _____

Speaking language practice

6 Complete the dialogues with the words below.

> don't know   fine   OK   suppose   sure   try   worry

A
A: Tara and I are going to a dance workshop next weekend. Do you want to come?
B: I ⁰ _don't know_. I'm not very good at dancing.
A: It'll be ¹_____ Why don't you ²_____?
B: Yes, you're right. ³_____, I'll try.

B
A: I'm really nervous because I have to sing a song in the next school concert.
B: Don't ⁴_____! You have got a great voice.
A: Thanks. Well, I ⁵_____ I can do it!

☐ /5

Vocabulary	☐ /15
Grammar	☐ /10
Communication	☐ /5
Your total score	☐ /30

Unit 7

8 THINK OUTSIDE THE BOX

1 Look at the pictures and write the school subjects.

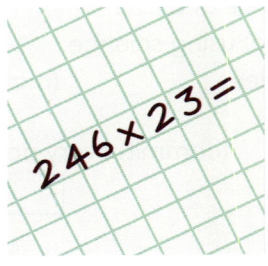

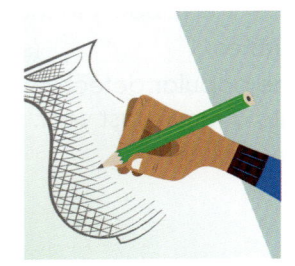

1 _math_
2 _____
3 _____
4 _____
5 _____
6 _____

2 Write the correct school subject for each definition.

1 You read books and plays in this subject.
   l _iterature_
2 You learn about the world and different countries in this subject.
   g _____
3 This subject teaches you how to look after your body so you aren't sick.
   h _____
4 In this subject you discuss important ideas, like the meaning of life.
   p _____
5 This subject helps you communicate with people from different countries.
   E _____
6 You learn about different chemicals in this subject.
   c _____

3 Read the comments and write the school subjects.

1 I think it's important to learn this, so that you know how to deal with money.
   personal finance
2 I really enjoy learning about the law in my country, and how to vote. _____
3 I'm working hard at this subject because I will need it when I go to Spain next summer.
   _____
4 I love sports so, of course, this is my favorite subject! _____
5 This is a difficult science subject, but I study it because one day I want to be an astronaut! _____
6 This is an important subject for me, because I want to be a politician in the future. _____

4 Circle the correct answers.

1 I love _____ about how people live in different countries.
   a studying
   (b) learning
   c memorizing
2 Don't forget: you need to hand in your _____ on Friday.
   a project
   b performance
   c practical test
3 I can't go out tonight. I need to _____ these dates for my history test.
   a learn
   b study
   c memorize
4 The examiner will ask you questions in the English _____ test.
   a practical
   b performance
   c speaking
5 Are you going to _____ Spanish next year or will you choose a different language?
   a study
   b perform
   c memorize

Unit 8

5 Complete the words in the sentences.
1 I find it difficult to l **e a r** n irregular verbs.
2 I usually s_ _ _ _y for about an hour every evening.
3 It's difficult to m_ _m_ _ _ _ _e a whole poem!
4 We have a p_ _c_ _c_ l t_ _ _t in home economics – we have to cook a meal!
5 For our music test we have to give a p_ _f_ _m_ _ _e on our instrument.

6 Circle the correct words to complete the text.

At Redfield High we believe in a modern approach to education. Of course, students here [1]_____ traditional subjects, such as math and history, but they also [2]_____ more practical skills, such as [3]_____, which we think are important for life. As well as the main subjects, there are lots of extra classes, such as yoga and [4]_____ design. We only have [5]_____ tests once a year and we don't expect students to spend a lot of time [6]_____ for them. We believe that old-fashioned methods of learning, such as [7]_____ lots of facts, aren't important in the modern world. The internet is there to check facts, so people don't need general [8]_____ in the same way that they did fifty years ago. We believe it's more important to teach our students critical [9]_____ skills so they can form their own opinions. We want our students to be [10]_____ and use their imagination in everything they do. We also believe that [11]_____ is a really important skill, so we encourage our students to work with each other in groups. We are lucky to have a lot of [12]_____ young musicians here, and all our music groups give a [13]_____ to the whole school at the end of each term.

1 a memorize (b) study
  c perform   d learn
2 a learn   b study
  c memorize d make
3 a chemistry b physics
  c cooking   d philosophy
4 a photography b fashion
  c film   d art
5 a writing   b writer
  c write   d written
6 a learning b memorizing
  c performing d studying
7 a memorizing b practicing
  c getting   d writing
8 a facts   b learning
  c knowledge d understanding
9 a understanding b thinking
  c learning   d knowledge
10 a intelligent b lazy
   c creative   d gifted
11 a performance b teamwork
   c study   d problem solving
12 a lazy   b practiced
   c talented d practical
13 a project b performance
   c teamwork d practical test

7 Circle the correct option.
1 (Why)/ What is Ted upset?
2 How / When do your tests start?
3 Who / What are you going to invite to your party?
4 What / Where does the performance take place?
5 Where / How did you get home?

8 Read the sentences. Complete the question to fit each answer.
1 Ellie and Jo **told me about the party**.
  a A: Who told you about the party?
    B: Ellie and Jo.
  b A: What *did Ellie and Jo tell you about*?
    B: The party.
2 Sam gave me this card.
  a A: What _____?
    B: This card.
  b A: Who _____?
    B: Sam.
3 Anna called me last night.
  a A: Who _____?
    B: Anna.
  b A: Who _____
    _____?
    B: Me.
4 Tom helped me with my homework.
  a A: What _____
    _____?
    B: My homework.
  b A: Who _____
    _____?
    B: Tom.
5 I saw Alex and Tim at the party.
  a A: Who _____
    _____?
    B: Tim and Alex.
  b A: Where _____
    _____?
    B: At the party.

Unit 8

8 THINK OUTSIDE THE BOX

9 Complete the dialogue. Write questions using the words in parentheses.

Rob: Hi, Dad. ¹*What are you doing* (what / you / do)?
Dad: I'm looking at some old pictures from school.
Rob: ² _____ (it / be / OK) if I have a look?
Dad: Yes, it's fine.
Rob: ³ _____ (who / take / these pictures)?
Dad: I can't remember who took them.
Rob: Wow! It looks very different from my school.
⁴ _____ (what / subjects / you / study)?
Dad: Oh, we studied all the usual subjects.
Rob: ⁵ _____ (you / enjoy / school)?
Dad: Not really. We didn't do many fun activities.
Rob: ⁶ _____ (what / your teachers / be / like)?
Dad: They were very strict!
Rob: ⁷ _____ (who / that / be)?
Dad: My best friend, Tom. We got along really well.
Rob: He looks cool. ⁸ _____
(you / stay / friends) with him since you left school?
Dad: No, I haven't. He moved to Canada and I haven't heard from him in years.

10 Read the answers. Complete the questions.

1. A: *Is it raining* now?
   B: No, it isn't raining now.
2. A: Where _____ ?
   B: Rosie goes to school in Sydney, Australia.
3. A: When _____ ?
   B: The movie finished at eight o'clock.
4. A: Who _____ ?
   B: Mrs. Cavendish teaches them French.
5. A: Who _____ ?
   B: She called Carl.

11 **WORD FRIENDS** Complete the sentences with *make* or *take*.

1. We decided to *make* some improvements to the course, so it's much better now.
2. Don't worry if you ____ a mistake in math.
3. I'm sure you'll ____ progress in English if you keep working hard.
4. It's a good idea to ____ notes during history classes.
5. I don't understand this sentence – it doesn't ____ sense!
6. We have to ____ a test in the summer.
7. There are some things we're not happy with at school, so we'd like to ____ a few changes.
8. Come and ____ a look at this picture – it's really funny!

12 Read the article on page 165. Match headings a–d to paragraphs 1–4.

a What are the advantages of homeschooling?
b Facts and figures about homeschooling
c Do homeschoolers get good results?
d Are there any disadvantages?

13 Read the article again. Mark the sentences true (T) or false (F).

1. [F] Homeschooling is possible in every country.
2. [ ] A study in the UK showed that homeschoolers are more successful than students at school.
3. [ ] Fran likes being in control of her studies.
4. [ ] Adam thinks he gets more attention now that he is homeschooled.
5. [ ] Homeschoolers are usually lonely because they don't have a large group of friends.

14 Complete the sentences with the correct form of the highlighted phrases from the text.

1. You should *make a real effort* to learn English vocabulary.
2. Winning this money will _____ in our lives.
3. Sara's very independent and doesn't enjoy _____ from other people.
4. It's difficult to _____ between the movies, because they're so different.

Unit 8

Learning at home

1 ____b____

Would you prefer to stay at home to study? In many countries, children have to attend school. In the United States, they have a legal right to an education, but it doesn't have to take place in a school. Parents can choose to teach their children at home. Around 1.5 million students are currently homeschooled in the United States and the number is growing.

2 _____

It's difficult to **make comparisons** between the achievements of homeschooled students and those of students at school. However, studies in the United States have shown that students educated at home often achieve better results in national tests than those in school. In the UK, homeschooled students regularly get places at top colleges.

3 _____

Most homeschoolers speak very positively of their experiences. Fran, fifteen, enjoys having the freedom to spend more time on subjects she likes. "At school, there's a set program of study that all students have to follow. I don't have to **take instructions** from teachers. I can follow my own interests more and explore subjects in more depth." Adam, fourteen, also sees benefits to homeschooling. "Teachers in schools have thirty students to think about. I have a tutor just for me. I love the fact that I can ask lots of questions, and he can really help me to understand things. That **makes a big difference** to me."

4 _____

People often assume that the biggest problem for homeschoolers is loneliness. In fact, this isn't the case. Most parents of homeschoolers **make a real effort** to create a network of friends for their children, and they often end up having quite interesting social lives. However, psychologists warn that students who are homeschooled may have difficulties later in life. Dr. Rob Alexander says, "School isn't just about education – it's about learning to fit in. At school, students learn teamwork, and they learn how to deal with a wide range of different personalities. You can't get that at home."

---

15 Complete the sentences with the verbs below. There are two extra verbs.

> would have found   hadn't rained
> had eaten   would have eaten   hadn't moved
> would have passed   would have gone
> ~~hadn't changed~~

1. If I _hadn't changed_ the TV channel, I wouldn't have missed my favorite show.
2. If it _____, we would have gone to the beach.
3. If we _____ to a small apartment, we would have gotten a dog.
4. If my mom had arrived home earlier, she _____ dinner with us.
5. Jack _____ the information he needed if he had looked online.
6. Emily and Liam _____ the biology test if they had studied harder.

16 Complete the sentences below with had/hadn't or would/wouldn't have.

1. If you __had__ called him, what would you have said?
2. If the dog _____ been on a leash, it wouldn't have run into the road.
3. Sally _____ told you the truth if you had asked.
4. Danny would have come to school today if he _____ broken his leg.
5. If the band had sold more tickets, they _____ canceled the show.
6. They wouldn't have called the police if their neighbor _____ turned down his music.
7. Mr. Taylor _____ sent Mike and Elliot to the principal's office if they hadn't been rude to him.

8 THINK OUTSIDE THE BOX

17 Rewrite the sentences using the Third Conditional.

1. It rained. The pool party was canceled.
   If *it hadn't rained, the pool party wouldn't have been canceled*.
2. Luke didn't study. He failed his test.
   If _____
3. The cat climbed a tall tree. It got stuck.
   If _____
4. Dad didn't read the recipe. He used the wrong ingredients.
   If _____
5. I didn't bring my cell phone. I can't show you the video.
   If _____

18 Complete the sentences with the correct form of the phrasal verbs below.

| calm down   fill out   get on   hand in   hand out   look over   look up   ~~mess around~~ |

1. Archie shouldn't *mess around* in class all the time – he needs to work harder.
2. The teacher wants us to _____ our projects on Friday, but I haven't started mine yet!
3. Remember to leave time at the end of the test to _____ all your answers.
4. _____! There's nothing to be upset or angry about.
5. I keep my dictionary with me so I can _____ words that I don't know.
6. It's time to stop playing video games and _____ with your homework!
7. You have to _____ a form to join the gym.
8. Tanya, please _____ these books – one to every pair of students.

19 Complete the questions with the words below.

| are   ~~been~~   do   is   was   would |

1. How have you *been*?
2. What _____ you guys doing tonight?
3. _____ you like it here?
4. How _____ your trip?
5. _____ this your first time in New Zealand?
6. _____ you like to join us?

20 Circle the correct responses.

1. Is this your first time in London?
   a Yes, I did.
   b I didn't go to London.
   c Yes, it is.
2. Would you like to come out with us?
   a I'd love to.
   b No, I don't, thanks.
   c Yes, I love it.
3. What are you doing on the weekend?
   a I didn't enjoy it.
   b I'm fine, thanks.
   c I'm going to a party.
4. Do you like it here in New York?
   a Thanks, that would be great.
   b Yes, it's amazing.
   c I'd love to.
5. How was your trip?
   a It was fine.
   b Sure thing.
   c Not really.

21 Match sentences 1–6 from an email reply to functions a–f.

1. [b] It was good to hear from you.
2. [ ] Call me if you can't see us!
3. [ ] You wanted to know about my town.
4. [ ] There are lots of interesting old buildings.
5. [ ] We're going to have a great time!
6. [ ] See you soon!

a ending your email
b ~~starting your email~~
c before you finish
d making arrangements
e giving useful information
f making it clear why you're writing

166 Unit 8

SELF-ASSESSMENT

Vocabulary

1 Match the words to the definitions.

> computer science   literature   math
> performance   practical test   project

0 a school subject in which you learn about numbers: _math_
1 a test in which you do/create something: _____
2 a school subject in which you learn about computers: _____
3 when you do something on a stage for an audience: _____
4 a school subject in which you learn about novels: _____
5 schoolwork in which you study and write about a topic: _____

/5

2 Circle the correct option.

0 What's the best way to (study) / memorize for tests?
1 You must *memorize* / *study* this number so that you can remember it.
2 We're *studying* / *learning* about plants in biology at the moment.
3 You won't do well if you're *lazy* / *creative*.
4 *Make* / *Take* a look at this picture.
5 Please *fill out* / *calm down* this form.

/5

3 Complete the sentences.

> critical   general   mess   mistakes
> ~~problem~~   teamwork

0 Max is really good at _problem_ solving, so I'll ask him what we should do.
1 Simon doesn't like working on his own – he prefers _____.
2 My _____ knowledge isn't very good.
3 We did some activities to develop our _____ thinking skills.
4 I made a lot of _____ on my English test, so I don't think I'll pass.
5 You won't do well at school if you _____ around in class.

/5

Grammar

4 Complete the questions.

0 _Do your friends go_ (your friends/go) shopping?
1 _____ (you/finish) that book yet?
2 _____ (why/Carrie/be) upset today?
3 _____ (who/call) the police last night?
4 _____ (who/you/see) yesterday?
5 _____ (you/have) lunch before class?

/5

5 Circle the correct option.

1 I ⁰(would have) / *had* gone to the mall if I ¹*wouldn't have* / *hadn't* had to visit my uncle.
2 If we ²*would have* / *had* seen the person who stole our bikes, we ³*would have* / *had* told the police.
3 Mom ⁴*would have* / *had* bought the video game if it ⁵*wouldn't have* / *hadn't* been expensive.

/5

Speaking language practice

6 Complete the dialogues with the phrases below.

> do you like   is this your first   how have
> how was   would you like   what are

A
A: Hi, Laura. Great to see you after so long!
   ⁰ _How have_ you been?
B: Fine.
A: Your house's nice. ¹_____ it here?
B: Yes, I love it!

B
A: Hi, nice to see you. ²_____ your trip?
B: Not bad. Not too tiring.
A: Good. ³_____ time in Miami?
B: Yes, it is. I'm looking forward to seeing it.
A: ⁴_____ you doing tonight?
B: I'm meeting some friends at the mall.
   ⁵_____ to join us?
A: Thanks. I'd love to.

/5

Vocabulary /15
Grammar /10
Communication /5
Your total score /30

Unit 8 167

SELF-ASSESSMENT ANSWER KEY

Unit 1
Activity 1
1 selfie stick 2 share 3 download 4 awful 5 perfect
Activity 2
1 useful 2 ugly 3 made 4 recess 5 evening
Activity 3
1 don't often watch 2 lives 3 don't like 4 isn't raining 5 doesn't want
Activity 4
1 don't 2 Is Jamie listening, is 3 is 4 Do you think 5 do
Activity 5
1 to pay 2 to listen 3 to stay up 4 waiting 5 to go
Activity 6
1 idea 2 could 3 sure 4 Why 5 not

Unit 2
Activity 1
1 cream 2 nuts 3 cheese 4 honey 5 flour
Activity 2
1 contestant 2 win 3 make 4 do 5 delicious
Activity 3
1 Have you ever tried 2 have just finished 3 have never seen 4 Has it stopped raining yet 5 I've already read
Activity 4
1 b 2 a 3 c 4 a 5 a
Activity 5
1 didn't go 2 wrote, hasn't replied 3 have never had, tried
Activity 6
1 Could I have 2 Of course 3 Would you like 4 Thank you 5 Excuse me

Unit 3
Activity 1
1 mild 2 freezing 3 degrees 4 flood 5 earthquake
Activity 2
1 path 2 make 3 discovered 4 really 5 totally
Activity 3
1 didn't see 2 went 3 took 4 didn't want 5 Did, have
Activity 4
1 had hurt 2 hadn't met 3 Had the weather been 4 Had the children cleaned 5 hadn't rained
Activity 5
1 screamed 2 had watched 3 returned 4 didn't finish 5 opened
Activity 6
1 I didn't realise 2 I didn't mean to 3 I really wanted 4 I thought you were 5 be more careful

Unit 4
Activity 1
1 diving 2 snowboarding 3 yoga 4 ice-skating 5 climbing
Activity 2
1 uniform 2 fans 3 score 4 player 5 take
Activity 3
1 'll win 2 's going to score 3 'm going to take up 4 'm meeting 5 'll pay
Activity 4
1 take up 2 don't practice 3 won't get 4 won't win 5 run 6 rains 7 'll play
Activity 5
1 D 2 D 3 S
Activity 6
1 Not much 2 What about 3 don't know 4 have any plans 5 First

Unit 5
Activity 1
1 ticket 2 trip 3 cruise 4 break 5 camp
Activity 2
1 double 2 sunglasses 3 guidebook 4 journey 5 travel
Activity 3
1 i 2 a 3 b 4 c 5 h
Activity 4
1 irresponsible 2 impatient 3 dissatisfied 4 illogical 5 incorrect
Activity 5
1 What I asked 2 first part 3 I said that 4 say that again 5 just saying

Unit 6
Activity 1
1 f 2 c 3 e 4 a 5 d 6 i 7 h 8 g
Activity 2
1 put 2 sense 3 in 4 go 5 has 6 co-workers 7 making
Activity 3
1 would get 2 would go 3 was/were 4 would travel
Activity 4
1 where 2 who 3 which 4 that 5 where
Activity 5
1 a laugh 2 Who's that boy 3 do you mean 4 tall one 5 at the back 6 She's wearing

Unit 7
Activity 1
1 fine 3 jail 4 vandal 5 theft 6 judge
Activity 2
1 robbing 2 committed 3 chased 4 broke 4 escape
Activity 3
1 fingerprints 2 arrests 3 witness 4 clue 5 suspect
Activity 4
1 was arrested 2 was found 3 are solved 4 was made 5 are commited
Activity 5
1 I had my bike stolen. 2 Should we get a pizza delivered? 3 He's having a new suit made. 4 My mom is having her hair cut. 5 She gets her cat checked by the vet.
Activity 6
1 fine 2 try 3 OK 4 worry 5 suppose

Unit 8
Activity 1
1 practical test 2 computer science 3 performance 4 literature 5 project
Activity 2
1 memorize 2 learning 3 lazy 4 Take 5 fill out
Activity 3
1 teamwork 2 general 3 critical 4 mistakes 5 mess
Activity 4
1 Have you finished 2 Why is Carrie 3 Who called 4 Who did you see 5 Had you had
Activity 5
1 hadn't 2 had, would have 3 would have, hadn't
Activity 6
1 Do you like 2 How was 3 Is this your first 4 What are 5 Would you like

GRAMMAR TIME ANSWER KEY

Unit 1.2
Activity 1
2 are wearing 3 are dancing 4 making 5 doesn't like 6 prefers 7 go 8 show
Activity 2
Students' own answers.

Unit 1.4
Activity 1
2 to buy 3 watching 4 playing 5 to stay 6 helping
Activity 2
2 to write 3 writing 4 studying 5 to earn 6 to pay 7 to bring 8 planting

Unit 2.2
Activity 1
2 has already washed 3 Have the kids had lunch yet, haven't 4 Have you done the shopping yet, have just returned 5 have never eaten 6 haven't finished
Activity 2
Have you ever watched a horror movie?
Have you ever made a cake?
Have you ever cooked a family dinner?

Unit 2.4
Activity 1
2 for 3 for 4 since
Activity 2
2 She won her skis in a skiing competition last year.
3 She made her sweater herself last winter.
4 She has met a famous actor in a park.
5 She has studied French for three years.
6 Her parents have taught her how to cook two years ago.

Unit 3.2
Activity 1
2 had never seen 3 had rained 4 had taken 5 hadn't spent 6 had had
Activity 2
2 Had you been abroad?
3 Had your parents visited the school?
4 Had you met the teachers?
5 What school subjects had you studied?
6 Had you traveled by plane?
Activity 3
Students' own answers.

Unit 3.4
Activity 1
1 called
2 I hadn't studied, didn't get
3 had never played, got
4 Had Mom given, asked
5 didn't want, had eaten

Unit 4.2
Activity 1
2 I'm having 3 start 4 isn't going to finish 5 are coming 6 I'll make
Activity 2
2 going 3 having 4 meeting 5 will 6 going

Unit 4.4
Activity 1
2 'll/will show, comes 3 will lose, don't change 4 isn't, will arrive 5 won't start, is 6 'll/will take up, gets
Activity 2
2 a 3 b

Unit 5.2
Activity 1
2 Should we check out
3 don't have to take your
4 ought to buy new sunglasses
5 Must not smoke
6 Must Sue take

Unit 5.4
Activity 1
2 can't 3 might 4 must 5 can't 6 could
Activity 2
2 must 3 could 4 could 5 must/might/may

Unit 6.2
Activity 1
2 wouldn't feel so bad if his friends didn't laugh at him.
3 would your family do if your aunt didn't help you?
4 would you do if you didn't get along well with your mom?
5 I were you, I wouldn't fight with your sister all the time.
Activity 2
2 would give, didn't have 3 would buy, was/were 4 wouldn't get, did 5 wouldn't complain, wasn't/weren't

Unit 6.4
Activity 1
2 who 3 which 4 where
Activity 2
2 She told me a lot of things which/that I had no idea about. 3 My great-grandmother lived in a village near Edinburgh, which is the capital of Scotland. 4 The lady told me about a house where my great-grandmother lived. 5 She had Shetland ponies which/that she often rode.

Unit 7.2
Activity 1
2 aren't used just for fun 3 wasn't seen in Central Park on Sunday 4 the robbers chased by the police 5 fingerprints found on food as well 6 was stolen
Activity 2
2 wasn't completed 3 were published 4 was published 5 is sold 6 wasn't written 7 is based

Unit 7.4
Activity 1
2 had your bike repaired 3 have your pictures printed 4 have your hair colored
Activity 2
2 them repaired 3 my hair cut 4 it styled 5 my nails painted 6 some pictures taken

Unit 8.2
Activity 1
2 How many tests did you take?
3 What were you doing at 5 p.m. yesterday?
4 Have you ever cheated in a test?
Activity 2
2 Who is going to take a French exam tomorrow? When is Jessica going to take her French exam? 3 Who wants to study in Belgium? Where does Mark want to study? 4 What happened in the science lab? Where did the accident happen? 5 What bit the biology teacher? Who did a giant spider bite? 6 Who was absent because of the strike? Why were the teachers absent?

Unit 8.4
Activity 1
2 wouldn't have found, hadn't gone 3 would have won, had played 4 hadn't copied, wouldn't have been called 5 Would the train have arrived, hadn't snowed

NOTES

NOTES

NOTES

NOTES

NOTES

NOTES

NOTES